SPIRIT OF RESISTANCE

SPIRIT OF RESISTANCE

The Life of SOE Agent
Harry Peuleve, DSO MC

NIGEL PERRIN

Pen & Sword
MILITARY

First published in Great Britain in 2008 by
PEN & SWORD MILITARY
An imprint of
Pen & Sword Books Ltd
47 Church Street
Barnsley
South Yorkshire
S70 2AS

Copyright © Nigel Perrin, 2008

ISBN 978-1-84415-855-3

A CIP catalogue record for this book is available from the British Library

Typeset by Concept, Huddersfield, West Yorkshire
Printed and bound in England by Biddles Ltd

Pen & Sword Books Ltd incorporates the Imprints of Pen & Sword Aviation, Pen & Sword Maritime, Pen & Sword Military, Wharncliffe Local History, Pen & Sword Select, Pen & Sword Military Classics, Leo Cooper, Remember When, Seaforth Publishing and Frontline Publishing

For a complete list of Pen & Sword titles please contact
PEN & SWORD BOOKS LIMITED
47 Church Street, Barnsley, South Yorkshire, S70 2AS, England
E-mail: enquiries@pen-and-sword.co.uk
Website: www.pen-and-sword.co.uk

Contents

Foreword

Even in that galaxy of heroes and heroines, muddlers and villains that made up the Special Operations Executive, Harry Peulevé stood out, for courage and tenacity. Not many men, having broken a leg on a parachute jump into occupied territory, came out a cripple over the Pyrenees and promptly asked to go back again. No one else managed an escape from Buchenwald, ending up a few months later in the American lines with two SS prisoners in tow.

There have been a lot of weak books about the exploits, and the failures, of SOE. It is a relief to read a different one. Nigel Perrin has been through all the papers that have now turned up at Kew, as well as getting hold of various surviving members of Harry's family and reading the books that are worth pursuing on the subject, while keeping clear of the junk that still abounds. He dispels a good many myths and displays the truth about a genuine hero; for whom, after what he had been through in war, peacetime life turned tame.

Neither in Great Britain nor in France, from both of which his ancestors came, both of which he served in war, nor in Denmark where he has left a family, nor anywhere where free men and women gather, should Harry Peulevé be forgotten. His life, described below, provides a splendid example of what a single soul can do, if he has stout friends to help him and a sound cause for which to fight.

M.R.D. Foot

Preface and Acknowledgements

My interest in Harry Peulevé grew from curiosity about a block of flats on Portman Square in central London, just behind Selfridges at the southern end of Baker Street, which I regularly walked past on my way home. Although I already had a vague idea of this building's connection with wartime secret agents, it was only when I eventually embarked on some background research that I began to discover what role Orchard Court had really played. From makeshift offices in one of its second-floor apartments, a shadowy government organization called the Special Operations Executive had selected, trained and despatched more than 400 men and women to organize resistance in occupied France. They came from all walks of life, civilian and military, volunteering to parachute behind enemy lines and build underground networks capable of sabotaging Germany's war effort from within. All were told of the great risks involved and the terrible consequences they faced if captured, yet few refused the challenge. Many of them were destined never to see Orchard Court again.

The heroic actions of these undercover agents quickly caught the public imagination after the war, sparking off a number of films, biographies and fictional spin-offs, though as I continued my research I became more intrigued by those whose stories had not been so widely recognized. Amongst them was one that particularly attracted my attention: an ex-BBC cameraman who had undertaken two missions, during which he overcame crippling injuries to arm and train thousands of guerrilla fighters; later captured, he endured appalling torture, deportation, evaded execution by a hair's breadth in Buchenwald concentration camp and eventually reached the American lines after spending six months masquerading as a French prisoner. Ranked by his commanding officer as one of the best half-dozen of his agents, I was surprised that his extraordinary career hadn't been represented more fully.

Initially I wondered if there could be a good reason for his relative obscurity and had reservations about how much material might still be available, but after contacting Peulevé's family in Denmark and gaining access to his unfinished memoirs, it was obvious that much of his story had been left untold. I also discovered that many who knew him were disappointed that no biography had been written following his death in 1963. To a great extent this became the reason for writing a book, to do my best to preserve the memory of an uncommonly determined and greatly admired man.

In putting this project together I must firstly acknowledge the great debt I owe to the Peulevé family, who supported me from the beginning: Madeleine and Marie-Louise Peulevé were of inestimable help in providing family documents and answering countless questions; Jo Woollacott gave me access to many other papers and photographs; and Margaret and Anna Byskov offered translations and made it possible for me to research the locations of Harry's exploits in the Corrèze, Dordogne and Cote d'Azur. I am deeply grateful to all of them for their generosity, hospitality and trust. I must also mention Tony Rushton, who was always willing to offer his assistance and was killed in a car accident just a few months before the book's completion.

Trying to find interview sources more than forty years after Harry's death was inevitably a difficult business, and many of those who appear in the story were too ill to help or have died since. However, I was privileged to be able to talk with several ex-agents, most notably Stéphane Hessel, Peter Lake, Cyril Watney and Jean Melon. I also received reminiscences and help from a number of surviving members of the French Resistance, and particularly have to thank Charles Thouloumond of the Corrèze ANACR, Alfred Pisi of the Cannes ANACR, Roger Ranoux, Raymond Lacombe, André Odru and René Coustellier.

A number of archives and museums provided essential information, and I am grateful for the assistance of Dr Roderick Bailey, Ann Brooks and the staff of the Imperial War Museum; Howard Davies and the staff of the National Archives, Kew; Samuel Gibiat and the Archives Départementales de Corrèze, Tulle; Dr Rémi Fourche and the Musée Henri Queuille, Neuvic, Corrèze; Patricia Reymond and the Musée Edmond-Michelet, Brive-la-Gaillarde; the

Archives Municipales, Brive-la-Gaillarde; the BBC Archives; Westminster City Archives; Jean-Louis Panicacci and the Musée de la Résistance Azuréenne, Nice; Marie Gatard and the Amicale Anciens des Services Spéciaux de la Défense Nationale, Paris; Brian Baxter at the REME museum at Arborfield, Berkshire; Yvonne Taverny and the Grande Chancellerie de la Légion d'Honneur, Paris; the Bundesarchiv, Berlin; the Archivo Histórico Comarcal del Alto Ampurdán, Figueres; the Ministerio del Interior, Spain; and Sabine Stein and Sandra Starke of the Buchenwald Archives, Weimar.

For details on radar I have to thank one of Harry's former radio pupils, Eric Atkinson, as well as Alan Brock; Louis Meulstee supplied technical information on wireless sets. Rhiannon Looseley generously gave her time to help me with translation and research, as did Jasper Snyder and Siân Miles. Judith Hiller supplied excerpts from her husband's diary and offered additional useful information. Francis Suttill helped me with details on his father and the events surrounding the Prosper collapse. Julie Dubec and her family were able to provide me with eyewitness accounts and very kindly invited me to visit their house where Harry operated. For research on Schönebeck I have to thank Leo Finegold, and especially Thoralf Winkler and Maurice Falissard for providing invaluable sources. Bruno Kartheuser gifted me one of his excellent works on Walter Schmald, while Guy Penaud offered his considerable knowledge of resistance in south-western France. I am also deeply grateful to M.R.D. Foot for his help in answering my questions, offering many useful revisions and writing the foreword. Of course, any errors in the text are mine, not his.

Thanks also to Marcus Binney; Suzanne Melon; Peggy Watney; David Harrison; Marcel Jaurant-Singer; Noreen Riols; Eileen Nearne; Sarah Helm; Phoebe Atkins; Pamela Windham Stewart; Stuart Wright; Angela Kelly; Tania Szabó; Kay Lake; Mike Cartwright; Roger Luxton; Michael Ferrada; Colin Peulevé; Sean Taplin; Richard Pearson; Lynda Martin and Asociación San Jorge, Seville; Nadège Bidart; Denise Freygefond; Suzette Litschgy Burgmann; J.P. Lescure; the late Gaston Collin; John Chillag; Randy Trahan, Kevin W. Murphy and Jim Dupre; Philip Vickers; Robert Marshall; Robert Favier; Thierry Watrin; Jean Overton Fuller; Kevin Reynolds; Alan Shillaker; and Bob Body. My sincere apologies to anyone I've not included. Lastly I have to thank Henry Wilson at Pen & Sword, editor Bobby Gainher, my agent Robin Wade and my family, without whose support this book could not have been completed.

I wish to thank the following for permission to reproduce copyright material: Little, Brown for the extract from *Christine* by Madeleine Masson; David Higham Associates for the extract from *War Diaries 1939–1945: Field Marshal Lord Alanbrooke* by Alex Danchev and Daniel Trotman; The History Press for the extract from *Between Silk & Cyanide* by Leo Marks; Farrar, Straus and Giroux for excerpts from *The Theory and Practice of Hell* by Eugen Kogon, Copyright © 1950 by Farrar, Straus & Giroux, Inc.

Author's Note

I have tried as far as possible to let Peulevé tell his own story, corroborating his memoirs with information from recently released SOE files at the National Archives, along with numerous other documentary sources, interviews and conversations with his family. Untangling actual events from the tales of derring-do that surround Peulevé's reputation proved to be a real challenge: references to his missions in France have often relied on half-truths that have established themselves over the years, and some incidents recorded elsewhere have consequently been omitted.

While I have attempted to present Harry's involvement with SOE as fully as possible, it was beyond the scope of this book to offer more than a brief overview of the organization's broader activities in France; similarly, I have concentrated only on presenting the relevant details concerning the French Resistance in the Corrèze, Dordogne, Cote d'Azur and other areas where Harry operated. Those looking for more wide-ranging accounts on these subjects should refer to the bibliography and particularly to Foot's *SOE in France*, which even after forty years remains an indispensable source.

The names of SOE circuits are given in capitals throughout the text; agents' code names have been italicized.

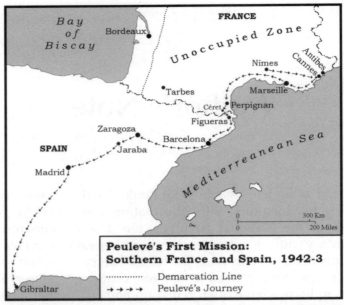

Peulevé's First Mission:
Southern France and Spain, 1942-3

.... Demarcation Line
→ → → → Peulevé's Journey

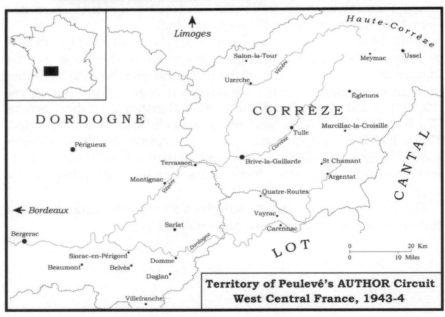

Territory of Peulevé's AUTHOR Circuit
West Central France, 1943-4

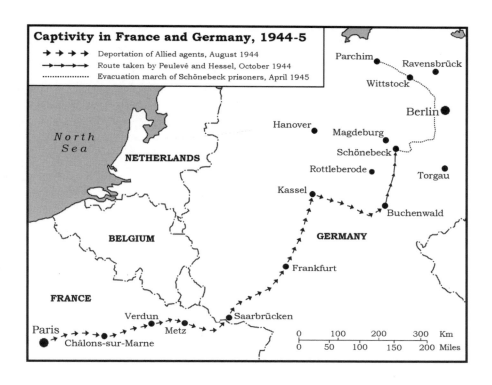

Captivity in France and Germany, 1944-5

➔ ➔ ➔ ➔ Deportation of Allied agents, August 1944
➤➔➤➔➤ Route taken by Peulevé and Hessel, October 1944
·················· Evacuation march of Schönebeck prisoners, April 1945

Parchim
Ravensbrück
Wittstock
Berlin

North Sea

NETHERLANDS

Hanover
Magdeburg
Schönebeck
Rottleberode
Torgau
Kassel
Buchenwald

BELGIUM

GERMANY

Frankfurt

FRANCE

Verdun
Saarbrücken
Paris
Metz
Châlons-sur-Marne

0   100   200   300   Km
0   50   100   150   200 Miles

Chapter 1

Origins

The Peulevé family tree has its roots in Normandy, but the beginnings of its English branch can be traced back to Leonard Auguste Peulevé, born in Beaumont-sur-Oise, north of Paris on 20 April 1856. Brought up in the market town of Lisieux, he ran away at the age of fourteen after a family disagreement and arrived in Paris just before the invading Prussians began laying siege to the city's walls. Witnessing the terrible deprivations endured by its inhabitants as they starved through the winter, he managed to escape before the rise of the Communards and made his way to England, where he found work as a rivet cutter for the Birmingham Metal and Munitions Company.[1] After deciding to settle in the area and learn his trade he met a local chemist's daughter, Lizzie Sperry, at a roller-skating hall. Although initially afraid of the Frenchman's imposing character, she agreed to see him again; her father was a much more unwelcome presence in her life at the time, and Leonard provided the possibility of a way of leaving the family home. They were married in 1880 and had four children: Augustus Albert was born later that year, followed by Leonard Otho in 1882, Jean Louis in 1883 and Dorothy Lisette in 1892.

Augustus and Dorothy showed musical talents, while Jean joined a local manufacturing firm. Leonard, possessing a more gentle and artistic nature, wished to become a cabinetmaker, but his father wasn't impressed by such aspirations and sent him to be educated at a college in France, from which he returned unable to speak English. After several jobs in private libraries he joined Carter's, the seed merchants, becoming a manager at one of their Paris branches whilst also running his own landscape gardening business. During a holiday in England, Leonard met schoolteacher Eva Dallison, the daughter of the vicar of Aston, whose fiancé had recently broken off their engagement. Although frail in appearance Eva possessed a strong-willed and impetuous nature, and announced to her sisters that she would have Leonard instead. They were married at St James' church in High Wych, Hertfordshire, on 22 March 1913, and settled in Saint-Prix, a northern suburb of Paris.

At the end of the year Eva became pregnant, but soon rumours of a possible German invasion began to spread and Carter's consequently decided to suspend Leonard's shop in July. Banks and other essential services also began to close soon after and the city's paralysis was followed by the inevitable: France declared war on 3 August and Eva went into labour the same day. A local doctor was called, and after a long and difficult labour their first child, Annette Eva Peulevé, was born.

Like many stranded tourists they were desperate to get back to England and managed to escape the chaos just in time, taking the last ship from Le Havre; arriving penniless at Waterloo station, Leonard had to borrow money from a porter in order to get them to a friend's house in south London. A few days later he joined up and was soon posted to the front with the Royal Army Service Corps, whilst Eva rented a house in Littlehampton. By the spring of the following year she was expecting her second child and on 29 January 1916 Henri Leonard Thomas Peulevé was born in the East Preston district of Hastings. Throughout his life he would be 'Harry' to his friends, though his family always knew him as 'Henri' or 'Henry'.

As Leonard was easily able to travel from his posting to their home in Saint-Prix he suggested that Eva return to France with the children. Leaving England in July, the family were reunited and lived there in relative safety until the early months of 1918, when German aerial bombardments made it too dangerous to remain. Eva and the children moved temporarily to Brittany, though they were able to join Leonard again when he was posted to Orange in August, staying at a hotel run by the Mazarde family. The warmth of the Provençal climate and the hospitality of their hosts made the war a distant distraction, and for the children it was an especially happy time; the Mazardes enjoyed spoiling them and made a habit of dangling fruit and bons-bons outside their window from the room above. When the November armistice came the hotel celebrated by offering free champagne to the locals, which to Eva's dismay resulted in Harry's introduction to alcohol, making him behave very strangely, much to the delight of onlookers.

Although life had been pleasant in Orange the family was repatriated in November, and following demobilization Leonard had

2

to find work again. Unable to return to their home in Paris, they went to stay with Eva's sister Katharine, who lived in Birmingham and fortunately had more than enough space to accommodate them comfortably. Katharine had a more Victorian outlook than Eva and was not impressed by the childrens' basic grasp of English, which was tinged with an American accent due to their contact with the soldiers in France. However they were offered some respite when a family friend invited them to stay at her house in Colwyn Bay during the summer, where they were joined by Eva's parents, her sisters Margaret and Beatrice, and Beatrice's son, James.

Moving closer to London to find work the family took a flat in Richmond, though the employment prospects proved no better and they were reduced to living on handouts from the Officers' Benevolent Association. Thankfully things improved the following year when Leonard was accepted for the position of Algerian pro-consul, and they took the boat for Algiers in April 1920. Posted initially to Oran, Annette went to a local convent school where the nuns delighted in looking after 'Ri-Ri', as Harry became known. In October, Leonard was promoted to Vice-Consul, and they moved to a bungalow in a rural area near the port of Bougie, where the only water supply was from a rooftop tank, electricity was non-existent and a local donkey regularly wandered through the house, eating the candles as it passed from room to room. A Spanish maid was employed, but her love of horses soon caused problems with the neighbouring farmer, as she would repeatedly free his stock by secretly cutting the tethers on their legs.

For Harry and Annette these sun-filled days were often spent playing in the foothills of the Atlas Mountains or on the beach with the local children, both being fascinated by the girls' silver-fringed veils and vividly coloured clothes. However, their home in Bougie was becoming more and more difficult for Leonard to sustain as the commission he earned from British ships began to dry up, the coal shortages at home reducing the number of steamers entering the port. By December 1922, there was no choice but to return to England, and they made their way back to a miserable English autumn and Aunt Katharine's house.

Leonard went into partnership running a show-garden business near Wellesbourne, while Eva found work as a supply teacher, lodging with Leonard's parents at Stratford-upon-Avon. She was finally able secure a permanent position as headmistress of a village school at nearby Moreton Morrell in April 1925, coinciding with

Harry's move up to Stratford's King Edward VI grammar school (also known as Shakespeare's school). Harry and Annette's cousin James came to stay during the school holidays and together they spent many hours damming up the village ford, much to the annoyance of nearby residents, or spying on the gypsies who camped nearby, though they were careful to keep their excursions a secret from their mother. The local vicar's son would often bring his crystal wireless set for them to listen to, and they became captivated by Grandfather Leonard's stories of his days selling rats amongst the *apaches* in Paris, though only Annette and Harry could understand him when he forgot himself and lapsed into French.

It seemed that the family had at last found some stability, but it was not to last. Leonard's business suddenly ran into trouble after a fire destroyed the premises, resulting in the partnership being dissolved. This affected him enough to provoke an episode of neurasthenia (a commonly used term of that time to describe 'shell-shock') during which he disappeared only to be found in a French hospital some days later. Eva decided that a change of scenery would help and in the summer of 1926 she took the job of head-mistress at St Thomas' school in Winchelsea on the Sussex coast, which included the use of a stone-built house on Hiham Gardens, opposite the New Inn. Harry was accepted at nearby Rye Grammar School and joined the church choir, but the children's frequent change of schools made them feel like outcasts, and the poor state of their uniforms caused by Eva's lack of housekeeping skills was often the subject of taunts from other pupils. Annette noted how protective her brother was on her first day at the school, carefully shepherding her all the way to the headmaster's office.

Having recovered from his illness and in search of a new vocation, Leonard volunteered to design and lay out the small garden of Winchelsea's Court Hall, a medieval building that was opened to the public shortly after his work was completed. Towards the end of 1927 he also received an unexpected job offer from the Polytechnic Touring Association (an early travel agent, later to become half of Lunn Poly), which was in need of a courier for a new tourist centre in Dinard on the Brittany coast. Like the resorts of the Côte d'Azur, Dinard attracted many affluent British and American expatriates, and Leonard would have no problem in developing relationships with the hoteliers eager for new business. His organizational abilities were an ideal match for this kind of position, and though it meant spending long periods away from the family, they were able to stay at a small pension during the holidays.

Though both parents were now working again, Eva's single-mindedness had made relations with some of the governors increasingly difficult, and after a final clash she was forced to take a new post at a school in the nearby village of Fairlight in June 1928, moving to a cottage near the cliffs. Harry joined St Leonards Collegiate School, while Annette went to a convent school in Hastings, and on their long journeys home they would pool their meagre pocket money to buy sweets, though their mother had forbidden them to buy ice cream – she was convinced that the shopkeeper kept his stock under the bed at night, and that they would risk typhoid if they ate it. On rainy days they would sometimes get a lift in the coastguard's sidecar and in return he would often borrow the Peulevés' retriever, Dandy – in the event of trouble at sea, the dog proved to be very useful in searching for bodies washed up on the rocks.

Eva's restless nature continued to lead her in search of a better life elsewhere, and in an effort to bring the family together she made up her mind to open a finishing school in Dinard, teaching languages to the daughters of wealthy families. Although apparently unaware of the credentials needed to establish a school of this kind she resigned from her job, cashed in her pension and made arrangements to leave England in September 1929. On arrival she soon set up in a large house named 'Les Frimas', which was to serve as the school as well as a family home; Harry was to board at his school at St Leonards, whilst Annette lodged with a school friend. Though she was happy with her new home, her brother's stay was short even for a Peulevé, but his motives were understandable enough – he ran away when he found that the headmaster had a habit of visiting the dormitories at night. The next day the coastguard telephoned Leonard to come and pick up his son, marking the end of Harry's schooldays in England.

He was not placed in a French class, though he did receive occasional private tuition; however, the lack of stability during his early life had put paid to any hope of an academic career and he spent much of his time with the expatriate community in the town, becoming involved with a drama production for a charity performance. The producer was an affluent retired man in his late forties named Arthur Larking, who had previously worked in the theatre and now spent his time either in Dinard, London or Bandol on the

French Riviera. Attracted by the charismatic teenager's abilities on the stage, he soon became something of an adoptive godfather to Harry and a close friend of the family.

Through his courier job Leonard had built up a large number of contacts within the local holiday trade, some of which helped to supplement his income from the company. When he was asked to relocate to Normandy he foolishly informed his employer about the perks he had received from the hoteliers and was promptly dismissed. The loss of income came at a bad time as Eva's school project was failing to attract the expected clientele, and they began to advertise their property as a guest house in order to make ends meet. A hefty tax bill towards the end of the year finally ended the Peulevés' stay at Les Frimas and they moved to a more modest bungalow, with Eva resorting to giving English lessons at home, whilst Leonard took on a job running a local agency for a South African tennis coach. The Christmas of 1930 was a frugal affair, by February their various debts had made staying in Dinard untenable and the family's belongings, including the children's school certificates, were pawned in return for a ferry ticket home. Arthur Larking saw them off with a gift for each of them, though Annette was inconsolable, having had to spend the last of her money to have Whiskey, her pet terrier, put down. Returning to an England in the grip of the Depression, their future seemed more uncertain than ever.

They stayed at first with Eva's sister Margaret in Richmond, moving soon afterwards to a rented house in Grove Avenue, Twickenham. Eva went back to supply teaching, though Leonard could only find temporary work here and there; Harry also began a part-time position at a local wireless shop, partly influenced by his cousin James who was living with them whilst training to become an electrical engineer. During the summer Harry, Annette and James skated together at the Richmond Ice Rink, swam at Teddington Lock and regularly sneaked into the expensive seats of the local Luxor cinema, though Harry knew that he would soon have to think about the more serious matter of finding a trade and leaving the family home. Having gained some knowledge from his time working in the shop, and with aspirations to become involved in the theatrical world, he decided to enrol at the London Radio College in Earl's Court, based just around the corner from the tube station on Penywern Road, and moved into a nearby boarding house in mid-1931.

After obtaining his certificate in Electronic Technology the following year, he received an invitation from Arthur Larking to spend the summer at Bandol, which he eagerly accepted. Larking enjoyed the opportunity of introducing the young man to life on the Côte d'Azur, and they spent a lot of time together on the beach, sailing or in the company of Arthur's wide circle of friends. It served to reinforce his already strong affections for a country that had been so prominent in his life, and it was during this time that he became completely comfortable with its language. Amongst the expatriates that Harry was introduced to was a girl named Phyllis, the daughter of one of Arthur's friends in Menton; Phyllis' background was wealthier than Harry's, but her mother was happy for him to escort her and a holiday romance soon developed between them.

At the end of the season Harry returned to England to find a job with his newly acquired qualification and was employed as a junior engineer by Pye's Radio Research Lab based in Cambridge. It was a useful start, but he quickly gained enough knowledge to secure a research post with the Baird Television company in 1935, working at their labs in Crystal Palace. Baird, who had been experimenting with television systems since the early 1920s, had convinced the BBC to broadcast a regular service using his primitive 30-line system, the objective being to produce a 'high-definition' television service that could broadcast to the London area. Although Harry was now involved in developing this cutting-edge technology, his salary was still meagre, and he often had to call on Arthur Larking at his flat in St George's Square for assistance, Arthur being known as something of an 'easy touch' in times of need.

By 1936, the BBC was planning to launch its new television station at Alexandra Palace and Harry applied for a job with them in October. He was officially accepted by the BBC on the 19th, but a fire swept through Baird's Crystal Palace site shortly before he was to leave at the beginning of December and the premises were largely destroyed. Harry felt deeply for the company, though his timely exit was a coincidence for which he was to receive much teasing.

Annette moved to London to pursue her ambition of a career in dressmaking, and her brother, tired of his bedsit in Notting Hill Gate, suggested that they share accommodation, taking a part-furnished top-floor flat at 126 Alderney Street in Pimlico. They got on well together and Harry often had calls from his many friends, including two chorus girls from the Windmill Theatre. He had also kept in touch with Phyllis from his time in Bandol and saw her when she visited London for the Coronation season in the summer of 1937. Phyllis' mother was working hard to find a wealthier suitor for her daughter and had arranged for her to tour South America for six months; meanwhile, Harry was overjoyed when Phyllis secretly pledged to become engaged to him upon her return.

His new job at the BBC meant working a rota of two long days, from seven in the morning until eleven at night, with the following day off. When Harry began, Alexandra Palace employed rival broadcasting systems from Baird and Marconi EMI: Studio 'A' was used by Marconi and Studio 'B' by Baird, with each system transmitting on alternate weeks. The two hours of programmes each day included news reports, plays and magazine programmes like *Picture Page*, and were watched by around 1,200 viewers in homes across greater London, although many more flocked to the department stores to see sporting events or public occasions. Initially employed as a maintenance engineer, Harry later transferred to the position of cameraman and was one of the first to work with the new 'Emitron' mobile cameras, a bulky contraption which required one technician simply to push it around the studio. By February 1937, only the Marconi system was in use, but delivering live broadcasts still remained a chaotic business, with dozens of actors and crew members rushing from one set to another to keep the schedule running. This required everyone in the studio to work very closely together and generated a unique sense of camaraderie; Harry quickly became part of this community at Alexandra Palace, and made friends with many of those who starred in its productions.

In 1938 the two women who owned the Alderney Street flat gave up their Spanish residence and returned to London, forcing their tenants to find accommodation elsewhere. This minor problem was not enough to dampen Harry's spirits – he was enjoying his work at the BBC and looking forward to the return of his fiancée-to-be, who had continued to write to him from South America. However, the long-awaited reunion did not turn out as planned when Phyllis told him that she could not make good her promise of engagement and that their relationship could not continue.

The shock of this rejection had a profound psychological effect on Harry. Taking a train to Brighton, he wandered the streets for several hours before approaching a policeman, asking him for an aspirin. When questioned at the station, the only information he could remember was Phyllis' telephone number, having no idea about where he lived or why he had travelled from London. Harry's parents were eventually contacted and drove down to collect him, but were shocked to find that he didn't recognize them at all, and for the next two weeks he behaved as if his memory had been completely erased. He made a sudden recovery and was able to return to work without any problem, though his family were careful not to divulge the details of his illness to his employer. This reaction, known as hysterical or fugue amnesia, obviously suggested the intensity of feeling that Harry had towards this young woman, though it appears that he didn't suffer any further physical or emotional effects from the incident.

After more than two years at Alexandra Palace, Harry had established himself in his field and seemed to be on the way to building a successful career in television. However, by the summer of 1939, the future looked anything but certain. Continued British and French attempts to appease Germany had failed to prevent the occupation of Czechoslovakia by Hitler's Third Reich, and now any attack on Poland's territory would force Britain and France to honour their pledges to defend her.

By August war seemed inevitable, and by the time Chamberlain had declared his ultimatum following Germany's invasion of Poland on 1 September, Harry had already left the BBC to enlist with the Royal Artillery Territorials at Leigh-on-Sea. The following day he called his sister, telling her that he had heard on the BBC grapevine that London was expected to be bombed heavily, and she should get out as soon as she could, persuading her to stay with her parents now living in Norfolk. On 3 September war was finally declared, Alexandra Palace was closed down and Harry Peulevé prepared to join the ranks of the 82nd Essex Anti-Aircraft Regiment.

Chapter 2

Frustrations

Peulevé was surprised by the brevity of his basic training, noting: 'If it had not been for the fact that I had been in the Cadet Corps at school, I would not even have known how to march in time, for all the training the army gave me.'[1] After this cursory introduction to soldiering, he was expected to join the 193rd Battery at the Leigh-on-Sea Regimental HQ at the beginning of October, serving as a gunner. However, his technical background at the BBC had already been noted, resulting in a swift transfer to the Royal Army Ordnance Corps (RAOC) and a posting to the Royal Military College of Science at Lydd on the Kent coast for training. There was a pressing need for professional technicians like Peulevé, and his electronics expertise made him an ideal candidate for instruction on the new and highly-secret technology known as GL (Gun-Laying) radar.

At the outbreak of war an effective aerial early warning system was already in place. Known as Chain Home, it comprised a network of radar installations across south-east England that could identify incoming enemy aircraft by the radio-wave 'echoes' they produced. As a means of increasing the accuracy of anti-aircraft fire against these targets, coastal defence batteries additionally employed GL radar sets, which reported range, elevation, position and other data, and assimilated this information with other variables such as wind speed and gun temperature via a crude mechanical computer known as a Predictor. This type of radar application was still in its infancy – the Mark I variant current at this time required a crew of five to operate its separate receiver and transmitter, housed in separate cabins mounted on trailers. Once thoroughly acquainted with the equipment, it would be Peulevé's job to maintain these sets and support the work of the gunlayers, who relied on it to direct their fire. Finishing the course at the end of January 1940, he was elevated to the rank of armament Staff Sergeant and attached to a field workshop at Arras, as part of the British Expeditionary Force (BEF).

Chamberlain's government had agreed in February 1939 to send a modest military presence to France, but the strength of the Expeditionary Force grew substantially after the outbreak of war, with 158,000 troops and 25,000 vehicles being transported by the end of September. However, years of neglect by a succession of governments had left the British Army completely unprepared for such a role – relying predominantly on infantry with little armoured support, the BEF was outmoded and suffered from poor training, shortages of equipment and few experienced officers. Major General (later Field Marshal) Montgomery, who was in command of the 3rd Infantry Division at the time, later concluded that it had been 'totally unfit to fight a first class war on the continent of Europe'.[2]

The command of the BEF was given to General Lord Gort, who was subordinate to the Commander-in-Chief of both British and French armies, General Maurice Gamelin. A First World War veteran in his late sixties, Gamelin became known as an evasive and equivocal leader, but was resolute in his determination to avoid another Verdun, which had been responsible for the slaughter of more than 150,000 French soldiers in 1916 and was a potent national symbol of loss. He had accordingly placed his faith in a policy of isolating Germany's economy through a naval blockade, which would give the French time to build up its army in order to launch an offensive some time later, perhaps in 1941 or 1942. This defensive, reactive outlook was shared by Britain, and their general sense of reluctance to take the initiative quickly spawned the term 'phoney war' or *drôle de guerre*.

It was expected that if Germany mounted an invasion it would come from the north, through Belgium and Holland. Gamelin believed that Germany's reliance on its armoured units made an attack through the Ardennes impossible, claiming that the River Meuse was 'the best anti-tank obstacle in Europe',[3] whilst to the south lay the Maginot Line, an impressive system of fortifications running from the Swiss frontier up to Longwy on the border with Luxembourg. Agreeing with this analysis, the Supreme War Council agreed to a strategy known as Plan D, or the Dyle Plan, whereby British and French forces would respond to a German advance by taking up defensive positions along the River Dyle, east of Brussels.

Through the worst winter for years, British troops started strengthening their positions along the Belgian border, and in order to help build additional installations the BEF formed the Auxiliary Military Pioneer Corps. Consisting of 30,000 men, it was composed of labourers rather than soldiers, ill-equipped and mostly without training. By the spring the BEF had swelled to nearly 400,000 men, comprising ten divisions, although only a quarter of this number were battle-ready troops.

Peulevé's first impressions of the sprawling BEF General Head-quarters at Arras were very different to what he had imagined. For a soldier supposedly at war he found that life here was relatively simple and easy-going – his only responsibility was to make daily inspections of the gunlaying equipment at four anti-aircraft bat-teries, whilst the evenings were spent in the local *estaminets*. Rumours of German spies dressed as nuns were common, but evid-ence of the war was more apparent in the newspapers than in the heart of British GHQ. However, this sedentary existence did not sit well with Peulevé, who felt increasingly frustrated by the com-placency that surrounded him. These feelings became all the more acute when the Germans started to send reconnaissance aircraft over Arras, as the gunlaying technology he had been trained to use proved virtually useless, the fire from the AA guns falling well short of their targets.

On 9 April, Germany occupied Denmark and began an offensive on Norway. Plans had already been made by the Allies to mine the waters off Narvik to deter any attack, but disagreements between British and French governments ensured that by the time a decision had been reached, German forces were already on their way. Allied troops were sent during the following weeks to prevent the invaders consolidating their positions, but a combination of ineffectual planning, muddled leadership and German air supremacy would be responsible for their failure to defeat the occupiers.

Increased numbers of enemy aircraft were seen over Arras on the evening of 9 May, though once again the anti-aircraft defences made little impact on their targets. A few hours later the German attack on Belgium and Holland finally began, and Plan D was executed; on the same day the beleaguered Chamberlain was eventually forced to resign, with Churchill, previously First Lord of the Admiralty, taking his place. The British and French left their positions at the border and moved up to the River Dyle as planned, but the main thrust of the German attack came through the Ardennes, the weak point between the Dyle defences and the Maginot Line, which was only lightly defended by the French.

Despite Gamelin's confidence about the impenetrability of the Meuse, Generals Rommel and Guderian crossed it at Houx and Sedan on 13 May, and rapidly made their way into French territory, effectively cutting the Allied armies in half. The German Army had long awaited the opportunity to redress the defeat of 1918 and, like the men of his Panzer division, Erwin Rommel had to keep reminding himself that 'we had broken through the Maginot Line and were driving deep into enemy territory. It was not just a beautiful dream. It was reality.'[4] By 15 May, Holland had fallen, and the British and French lines in the north were being forced back towards France. Stunned by the speed of the German breakthrough and paralysed by poor logistical planning, France's cumbersome armoured divisions failed to counter-attack effectively, whilst the more mobile Panzers continued advancing on a 50-mile front towards the French coast.

Some weeks earlier Peulevé had seen Lord Ironside, Chief of the Imperial General Staff, make a speech at a football match where he declared the Expeditionary Force to be equipped to deal with any attack, but this unfolding disaster clearly indicated a different reality. Soon streams of Belgian and Dutch refugees started to flow through the roads surrounding Arras, the first few travelling in cars, carrying mattresses on their roofs as meagre protection from the fighters strafing them, being followed by the miserable train of those on foot, their possessions in handcarts; Lieutenant General Alan Brooke, Commander of the BEF's II Corps, described this exodus as 'the most pathetic sight, with lame women suffering from sore feet, small children worn out with travelling but hugging their dolls, and all the old and maimed struggling along'.[5] Watching helplessly as this dismal procession continued south, Peulevé became increasingly tormented by his inability to do anything to relieve this tragedy, feeling 'frustration at not having been trained, frustration at not being in a position to do much about the situation, and anger at the circumstances which brought it about'.[6] However, these collective scenes of misery merely signalled the beginning of his own personal ordeal, the consequences of which would haunt him for the rest of his life.

Orders were given to fit open sights to the AA guns, so that they could be used to defend against the German tanks that were now closing in on Arras. The BEF's General Headquarters attempted to meet the crisis but its communications were poor, suffering from confusion between departments in the outlying villages. Increasing levels of chaos ensued as transmission of orders and information failed to keep pace with events, and by 22 May, Lieutenant General Sir Henry Pownall, Chief of the General Staff, described it as 'a hopeless position and too absurd because we haven't yet encountered the real German Army; this is only their (armoured) cavalry that is sending us reeling'.[7] Though the defence of Arras would continue, the order was given for the RAOC workshop to join the evacuation and Peulevé, 'horrified and depressed',[8] watched the way in which the men in his Company, including officers, started to fall over themselves to obey the command.

Any hope that their vehicles would leave in convoy soon evaporated, as they became separated amongst the hordes of people filing along the roads. Taking one of the trucks Peulevé started driving south towards Amiens and then toward the only base he knew of, at Le Havre, picking up stragglers from all services along the way who had either been walking or hitching rides on the carts of the refugees. Initial feelings of desertion soon began to play on his mind: 'I had to face it. We were running away as fast as our cowardly little minds could urge us on.'[9] Yet it was even more traumatic to witness the indignities of others who were overcome by the situation. On his way Peulevé was stopped by a corporal of the Royal Engineers, whose officer was lying prone in the middle of the road. Clearly distracted, tears were streaming down his face as he frantically fired rifle shots into the wood ahead, yelling 'I'll get the bastards!' Unable to communicate with him, Peulevé had no alternative but to knock him out with the butt of his rifle, carrying him to his car and leaving him under the corporal's care.

By the time they arrived at Le Havre it was clear that the panic had spread and the great swarms of soldiers already at the port left them with little hope of being evacuated. Thinking there might be a better chance further south, Peulevé headed towards Nantes, crossing the Seine at Rouen, where he encountered a company from the Pioneer Corps lining the road on either side. These men were mostly veterans from the previous war, proudly wearing their 1914–18 ribbons, and seemed determined to make a stand even though they were armed with nothing more than rifles. As Peulevé drove through this line they began to hurl derisory comments at those in the truck, denouncing the younger generation for running away whilst the real soldiers stuck to their job. There was nothing Peulevé could have done to help, as the fourteen men in the vehicle only had four rifles between them, yet the sickening sense of guilt after running this gauntlet was enough to make him rip the stripes from his arm in self-disgust.

Some time later they stopped at a vineyard and were met by the owner who offered them a few bottles of his wine. Peulevé asked if he had any news on whether the French Government had collapsed yet, but the man was surprised that he could even contemplate defeat, declaring, 'Never ... never will we become Germans.' Asking where they were going, Peulevé told him they were returning to England. In complete disbelief, the man was only able to mutter, 'Good God, are you going to leave us to fight alone?'

Their chances of being picked up seemed much better when they eventually got to Nantes, though Peulevé and his men were still forced to shiver through the next twenty-four hours, up to their necks in the water, before they found space aboard an available vessel. Arriving at Liverpool they were then taken to Leicester and assembled in a public park, with sentries posted at the gates. Unable to understand what was going on, a man next to him asked a passing milkman to sell him a couple of bottles. His reply was unexpected: 'Go back to France, you bastards, and get it from the NAAFI.' After a couple of days of milling around they were given leave, though whilst waiting for his train at Leicester station Peulevé was accosted by a man wearing a Land Defence Volunteers armband, who growled, 'I suppose you've come back from France. Well, I was in the first lot and we didn't run away like your shower did.' The humiliation was complete.

These experiences had a profound effect on Peulevé's attitude to the war and his place in it. Though he had successfully evacuated his men, he felt that he had not been able to do anything to defend the country he loved, and this lasting sense of shame would govern many of his motives through the rest of the war:

> I went home and thought the whole thing over. We were now in a state of siege. The only way I could wipe out the degradation and humiliation that I felt would be by getting back into a fighting unit where I could prove I was not a coward.[10]

He began trying every channel he could think of to get himself transferred to a more active role, but his knowledge of electronics was too important to the Army. Restoring his stripes, he was returned to the Royal Military College of Science, being posted to Bury Technical College in Lancashire where he was to spend his time instructing trainee wireless operators on the principles of radio technology. In January 1941, AA Command offered him a commission, and though he was not passed through an Officer Cadet Training Unit (OCTU) due to time constraints, Peulevé was officially made a Second Lieutenant in April; transferred to 3rd AA Corps School as an Instructor, he was quickly promoted to Captain on the basis of his now extensive knowledge of radar. During September he was posted to a Wireless Company with 1st AA Division, mainly giving lectures on specialist topics, before returning to London in November to carry out radar maintenance work at Golders Green and Hendon.

After the intense and deeply affecting experiences of the previous year, this job seemed far removed from active service – it would have been easy for him to remain with AA Command and see out the war relatively quietly. However, the memories of what he had encountered in France and particularly the frustration that he felt over his own conduct provoked him to bombard the War Office with more requests to be transferred. Though Peulevé's motivations were largely personal, others like him also found this inertia unbearable; Harry Rée, who would later pursue a similar vocation, commented on this impetus:

> You see, after the fall of France most of us in the army in this country had damn all to do. We were pushed off to Exeter or Wales or Scotland, nice safe places where there was very little to do, while wives and families were often in London or Coventry or Plymouth, all places which were being bombed – they were at risk, while we weren't. I think a lot of men resented this.[11]

In early 1942 Peulevé happened to hear about a commando raid on the French coast, where technicians had been employed to bring back details on a secret German radar station. This was Operation Biting, in which Major John Frost of the 2nd Parachute Battalion led more than a hundred paratroopers, several engineers and a radar expert on a mission to steal components from a 'Würzburg', an early-warning radar set sited on the cliffs at Bruneval, near Le Havre. Frost's force parachuted into the area, ripped the relevant components from the Würzburg installation under fire and made their way to the shore, where Royal Navy landing craft successfully picked them up. Thinking that there must be a need for technicians in roles like this, and especially for those with a second language, Peulevé tried telephoning the War Office again one evening while on duty. With no idea of who to ask for, he was passed around the switchboard until someone was found to take his details, being told that he would be contacted if anything suitable came up.

Some days later he received a request to report to room 055a at the War Office, off Horse Guards Parade. On arrival he was directed by a secretary to a small barely furnished room where he was greeted by a tall, elegant man who introduced himself as Major Gielgud. In his late forties, Lewis Gielgud had far more in common with the arts than the military; the elder brother of actor John Gielgud, he shared his passion for the theatre and had written several plays and novels whilst travelling the world as Under Secretary General for the Red Cross. Conducting their initial conversation in French, Gielgud was immediately impressed by his candidate – although only five feet nine, Peulevé's broad shoulders suggested considerable strength, but it was his force of personality that was most striking. Through piercing grey-green eyes he possessed a remarkable ability to charm and persuade, offset by a natural modesty that made him all the more engaging. Combined with the fluency of his French and his technical expertise, Gielgud felt confident that he could offer him a more engaging alternative to AA Command.

Gielgud agreed that Peulevé's involvement in raids like Bruneval might be possible, but suggested that his French might be put to better use. He proposed that he attend a special three-week course, during which time his abilities would be evaluated; if he seemed to be the kind of material they were looking for, he would be given more details about the work involved. It was also implied that, even if he failed the course, there might still be another opportunity to do more for the war effort than just drawing circuits on a blackboard. The Major made it clear from the outset that this course was in no way compulsory, he could refuse on the spot and his superiors would be none the wiser. But there was to be no turning back in Peulevé's mind and several days later he received a letter asking him to report to 6 Orchard Court, a residential block on the eastern side of Portman Square. Though he didn't know it, he was being directed to the offices of the French Section of the Special Operations Executive.

Chapter 3

The Racket

The Special Operations Executive (SOE) grew from an amalgam of three departments formed in 1938. Section D of the Secret Intelligence Service (SIS, or MI6) had been created with the intention of developing subversion and sabotage within countries threatened by Nazi Germany; directed by an ambitious, debonair officer of the Royal Engineers, Major Lawrence Grand, it identified sabotage targets, planned research into any possible means of subversion and sought to build up networks of contacts within neutral countries for supporting such activities. Another department, known as General Staff (Research), was set up by the War Office to look into the possibilities and potential for irregular paramilitary warfare. Renamed MIR in April 1939, it was led by the more pragmatic Major John ('Jo') Holland, a fellow RE officer who was to develop the guidelines for, and the means to undertake guerrilla actions, drawing on his experiences of insurgent tactics employed by the IRA and T.E. Lawrence's Arab forces. Lastly, the Foreign Office had also instigated 'EH', or Electra House (named after the building where it was based), which was to control propaganda activities. Even more obscure and vaguely defined, it was to provide the means of carrying out 'black' propaganda (that is, not being seen to emanate from the British Government) and was placed in the hands of Sir Campbell Stuart, a newspaper man who had gained experience in this field during the First World War.

These separate elements lacked clear lines of demarcation, with Section D and MIR particularly suffering from overlapping objectives. A central body was badly needed and in a memorandum drafted by Neville Chamberlain in July 1940, it was declared that 'a new organisation shall be established forthwith to co-ordinate all action, by way of subversion and sabotage, against the enemy overseas.'[1] Under the remit of the Minister of Economic Warfare,

Hugh Dalton, the three previously separate concerns were thus amalgamated into the Special Operations Executive, and reorganized into two departments, SO1 and SO2. SO1 was EH's domain, in charge of propaganda, whilst SO2, combining MI R and Section D, was responsible for subversion. However, SO1 eventually broke away in 1941 becoming known as the Political Warfare Executive (PWE), and so SO2 henceforth became known as SOE.

Moving from cramped offices at St Ermin's Hotel in Victoria to a block in Baker Street in October 1940, SOE immediately began acquiring more and more residences in the Marylebone area to accommodate itself, using the intentionally vague title of the 'Inter-Services Research Bureau' (ISRB) to obscure the real nature of its work. Its headquarters at No. 64 soon ran out of space and expanded into the top floor of Michael House at 82 (previously Marks and Spencer's head office) and Norgeby House at 83; shortly afterwards, Montagu Mansions, Chiltern Court (above Baker Street Underground station) and a host of nearby blocks and houses were dedicated to SOE's work. This rapid growth quickly required substantial administrative support to handle finance, procurement, research, internal security and many other departments, and at its peak SOE would be responsible for more than 12,000 staff, including overseas stations.

SOE's first Executive Director (a position referred to as 'CD') was Frank Nelson, who had previously been a Conservative MP and undertaken intelligence work for SIS in Switzerland. His daunting task was to construct an organization with no precedent, and to this end he installed two formidable ex-employees from Section D and MI R: George Taylor, an Australian businessman 'of enormous energy and high intelligence'[2] and previously Section D's head of Balkan operations, became his chief of staff; and the equally capable 'Tommy' Davies from MI R, who would become known as one of SOE's 'hard men', was to cover training, supplies and general administration. SOE had been envisaged by Dalton as a civilian rather than military body and consequently a number of its key figures came through the old-boy networks of city institutions such as Courtaulds, Hambros Bank and Slaughter & May, though one important exception was Brigadier Colin Gubbins, who was brought in in November 1940 as Director of Operations and Training (or 'M'), taking over some of Taylor's and Davies' responsibilities.

A Scots Highlander in his mid-forties, Gubbins was an intense, energetic officer whose orthodox military appearance disguised formidable powers of observation and insight. Although a decorated veteran of the First World War, it was his experiences serving in revolutionary Russia and Ireland that sparked his keen interest in the use of irregular tactics. In April 1939, he joined Holland at MI R to further develop the principles of guerrilla warfare, publishing highly secret pamphlets including *The Art of Guerilla Warfare* and *The Partisan Leader's Handbook* before making a trip to advise the Polish General Staff on organizing resistance. Gubbins returned to Warsaw as chief of staff to the British Military Mission in August, narrowly avoiding the advancing Soviet and German forces by escaping through the Balkans, and went on to lead several 'Independent Companies' – which later evolved into the Commandos – in occupied Norway during May 1940. An inspirational leader, his force of character would be instrumental in shaping SOE, later becoming CD in 1943.

Like MI R before it, SOE divided its work into country sections, which for reasons of security were to operate separately from each other. As far as French operations were concerned, there were four distinct divisions at this time: 'DF' ran escape lines within France; 'EU/P' organized Polish groups in north-eastern France around Lille; 'RF' Section aided Gaullist resistance using French nationals; and 'F' Section was responsible for infiltrating predominantly British agents, who were bilingual and had some previous experience of living in France. F Section's brief was specifically to encourage, guide, train and equip resistance groups, which could be then employed to commit acts of sabotage on strategic targets (factories, railways, communications and so on) and support and exploit other subversive activities.

The head of F Section (simply known as 'F') was Major Maurice Buckmaster, who had taken on the position in October 1941. Educated at Eton, he was unable to take up an exhibition at Oxford due to his father's bankruptcy, instead taking up a succession of jobs and travelling extensively across France, gaining an intimate knowledge of its geography and people. In 1932 he began managing the Paris office of the Ford Motor Company and spent three years heading its European operations before the outbreak of war, when at the age of thirty-seven he became one of the Intelligence Corps' most senior subalterns; posted to France with the BEF, he saw action at Dunkirk in 1940 and took part in de Gaulle's ill-fated Dakar expedition before receiving an invitation to join SOE.

Over 6 feet tall, with thinning, fair hair and strikingly blue eyes, Buckmaster made an immediate impression but was from a very different mould to Gubbins. Described by another Baker Street employee as having a 'gentle, slightly self-deprecatory manner',[3] he seemed unlikely to rise any further in the organization – SOE's Controller for Western Europe, Robin Brook, made the observation that 'He knows his job within the Section intimately, but never quite gets outside it',[4] and Gubbins agreed, summarizing him as a 'Staff Officer rather than a Commander'.[5] However, while some found fault with his more personable approach there was no doubt over his devotion to the job, and especially to his agents. Leo Marks, head of the coding department, also witnessed the same qualities but considered them to be strengths rather than weaknesses: 'I'd noticed that no matter how late I phoned ... he was always waiting in his office, and his first concern was for the safety of the agent. Not all country section directors shared that attitude. To some of them, agents in the field were heads to be counted, a tally they could show CD. But Maurice Buckmaster was a family man.'[6]

Though it had been demonstrated that agents could be infiltrated into France in the latter half of 1940, it was only during the following year that F Section really introduced itself at all. Its first agent to be dropped by parachute was George Bégué, who landed near Valençay, north of Chateauroux, on 5/6 May; over the next seven months another thirty-six would follow him. A number of these, including Ben Cowburn, Virginia Hall and Philippe de Vomécourt would prove to be some of its great assets, though the results of F Section's efforts as a whole by the end of 1941 were minor, and reflected a fledgling organization in urgent need of more operational experience.

Whilst individual indiscretions inevitably resulted in the capture of many agents, inadequate communications with London (only two of their wireless sets in France were working in September 1941), and limited numbers of RAF supply aircraft at SOE's disposal, made mounting sabotage attacks very difficult. Moreover, mission objectives were often 'supremely indefinite',[7] and agents' results were dictated by what their circumstances would permit. At a time when resistance groups only represented a tiny fraction of the population, insurgence was difficult to instigate and denunciations from French civilians posed a significant threat to agents and French *résistants* alike. Despite its success in destroying a handful of targets and forging links with the leaders of embryonic dissident movements,

F Section had not fulfilled early expectations and had yet to build up networks capable of carrying out coordinated acts of resistance. There was disappointment that more had not been achieved, but this was unchartered territory. As Buckmaster succinctly put it, 'It was no use trying to do things by the book. There was no book.'[8]

In these early days SOE was generally viewed with distrust, being commonly referred to as 'The Racket' even by those working in Baker Street. Its air of novelty led most senior officers in the regular armed forces to view it as a group of dangerous amateurs, and the Chiefs of Staff (to whom SOE played a subordinate role) were reluctant to allocate it valuable resources such as arms, air or naval support, at least until it could prove its worth. Likewise, the long-established SIS considered that clandestine work should be left to professionals, and that their intelligence networks were likely to be endangered by the short-term nature of SOE's objectives in their territories. Whereas SIS preferred to work quietly in the background, SOE's intentions to encourage sabotage and subversive activity would inevitably cause disruption and make life more difficult for all British agents across occupied Europe. Though SOE would gradually gain supporters amongst the Chiefs of Staff, relations with SIS would continue to remain competitive, if not hostile, for the rest of the war.

Due to the unusual nature of F Section's work there was no single method of recruitment, and it employed soldiers and civilians alike. Connections with Section D and MIR staff provided many of the first agents; some like Peulevé were identified as a result of enquiries to the War Office; others would be recommended through its own liaisons with the three Service ministries and departments of governments-in-exile; refugees and other immigrants coming into the country would be noted as French speakers and investigated further; some were introduced on personal recommendations, or were identified from the Ministry of Labour or other government sources. Whilst the bulk of the intake were British, many French-Canadians were also recruited along with South Africans, Mauritians and others from the French colonies.

Arriving at 6 Orchard Court for the first time in mid-March, Peulevé found himself joining nine other prospective agents who had been allocated to training group 27N. Just a short walk from SOE's headquarters in Baker Street, this luxurious second-floor flat was used by F Section to plan operations and brief agents on their missions (its staff were actually based on the second floor of

Norgeby House, but dealt with agents at a secondary location for security reasons). Keeping agents separate from each other as they passed in and out was essential to maintaining their anonymity, but this demanded some dexterity on the part of Buckmaster's bilingual doorman, Park, a model of discretion who would often be required to politely detain one agent in the ornate black-tiled bathroom while another was hurried out down the stairs.

At this time Major Buckmaster's small team included: his deputy Nicholas Bodington, who had worked for Reuters before joining in December 1940; Gerry Morel, an agent recently reassigned as an operations officer, identifying targets and mission objectives; Jacques Vaillant de Guélis and André Simon, two former BEF liaison officers now employed as conducting staff; R.A. Bourne-Patterson, a Scottish accountant in charge of finance and planning, and John Coleman, a quartermaster handling the Section's stores and equipment. F's staff also included a Romanian-born woman in her mid-thirties named Vera Atkins (originally Rosenberg), a civilian who spent most of her time 'floating between them'.[9]

Joining in April 1941 after a personal recommendation from old friend and F Section's first head Leslie Humphreys, her sharp intellect, faultless memory and tireless attention to detail made her the perfect administrator – looking after all aspects of agents' welfare, she doled out their wages or 'weekly dollops',[10] managed all aspects of their field preparation, arranged their accommodation, checked reports on refugees to identify possible recruits, dealt with incoming wireless messages and wrote Buckmaster's daily operational résumés, dubbed 'Comic Cuts'.[11] Known for being single-minded, cool and inscrutable, she nevertheless gained a unique rapport with many of the agents who relied on her, and her restrained maternal influence soon came to define the persona of F Section, permeating every aspect of life at Orchard Court.

Though her role was to 'float' between departments, this was to some extent an essential requirement of all those involved in the day-to-day running of F Section, as time constraints and the limited size of the organization meant that there was a constant need to prepare agents before they left for France. Staff would regularly work six or seven days a week, and eighteen-hour days were more a rule than an exception.

Civilian recruits and those from the ranks were each issued with the uniform of a Second Lieutenant, although officers like Peulevé retained their own; for reasons of security Peulevé's RAOC status would be kept, though the issue of rank was considered of relatively minor importance within SOE. Like the others he would also take on a training name to ensure anonymity, being known as 'Hilaire Poole' (training names were picked to use the same initials as their real ones, though only first names were usually employed within the group). Having been kitted out, they were driven down to Wanborough Manor, a sixteenth-century country house north of the Hog's Back between Guildford and Farnham, which SOE referred to as STS 5 (Special Training School). A number of requisitioned estates such as Wanborough had been converted for SOE's use, providing each country section with a site where preliminary training could take place away from the public gaze.

On the way down Peulevé could see that his group was a mixed bunch, with some of the civilians looking distinctly uncomfortable in their new uniforms. However, a few of them, notably Claude de Baissac (now renamed *Clement*), Francis Suttill (*Fernand*) and Roger Landes (*Robert*) were to become some of F Section's most prominent figures, and all would play a part in shaping Peulevé's own destiny. With them also went their conducting officer, André Simon, who was to act partly as a mentor, and partly as a means to evaluate the recruits' progress.

The three-week course on the estate at Wanborough was designed to introduce its civilian students to the basics of military training and discipline, and provide a method of weeding out those SOE did not think suitable for its kind of work. The school's commandant was Major Roger de Wesselow, an enthusiastic, affable, Coldstream Guards officer who would assess their abilities as they progressed through a demanding programme of physical exercise, weapon training, unarmed combat, handling explosives, map reading, field-craft, basic signalling and problem-solving scenarios. The intention was to cover 'a little bit of everything',[12] teaching a variety of basic skills which could then be developed in further courses.

No indication was ever given as to the reasons for this training, though most deduced that some sort of commando role was likely. Nor was SOE ever mentioned, as a certain percentage would inevitably return to the civilian world or their unit before the end of the course (Buckmaster expected on average to finish with eight in a group). A student was always aware that he could leave at any time, and was under no obligation to remain at the manor.

There was something of a pre-war atmosphere to Wanborough in the evenings, since its inhabitants could enjoy many luxuries that were now impossible to find in the outside world; yet certain restrictions were imposed. French was spoken compulsorily, and Peulevé and his group were prohibited from making telephone calls, though they were allowed to send and receive censored letters from home via a PO Box in Wimpole Street. Students were also never quite free from being scrutinized by de Wesselow and his team, who were just as interested in an individual's behaviour at the bar as on the assault course, and groups were regularly taken for a long evening at a local pub to identify those who might find it difficult to keep their mouths shut. Every attempt was made to record the smallest details of their students' personalities and habits, however seemingly trivial, as even table manners or mumblings in their sleep could give away an English background. The overall objective of the school had to be to identify those with the right mixture of prudence, self-awareness, intelligence and practical ability, without which an agent might not survive, or indeed jeopardize the lives of others.

When considering those who volunteered for such hazardous work there is a tendency to assume that there must be some psychological denominator that identified them, though Buckmaster later stated that there was 'no common definition' of an F Section recruit. Profession served as no indicator; among those selected from civilian backgrounds were shop workers, salesmen, schoolteachers, dentists, journalists, miners, even theatrical performers. Neither was there any similarity in temperaments, some having been conscientious objectors while others bore a violent hatred for all Germans. Gielgud's successor as SOE recruiting officer, Selwyn Jepson, had this to say about the kinds of people he interviewed:

> Of course when talking to them and digging deeper ... I often came on a personality's desire to prove itself – to discover if it could function effectively in situations of greater demand on its capacities than it normally met. In short, 'to overcome'. And where was a better opportunity than this work I was suggesting? There were also the adventurous ones; simpler, more extrovert people who didn't doubt their capabilities in this direction and would enjoy exercising them to a fuller degree than hitherto. Sometimes I suspected the death-wish syndrome in this type; from these I slipped away without committing myself. To gratify it would surely have endangered other agents.

Then there were those seeking escape or relief from domestic pressure. An unhappy marriage, loss of a loved one that might be assuaged by devotion to a cause; perhaps when the loss had been through the war simply to carry on where the dead had to stop.

Above and beyond these personal motives one has to remember the basic fact that of all stimuli war is the strongest, enough to deny self in a common need to defeat the enemy.[13]

Lieutenant Colonel James Hutchison, head of the Gaullist RF Section during 1942–3, noted that some of his agents became addicted to the dangers inherent in clandestine work, and could be easily tempted into taking unnecessary risks. However the simplest and most insightful observation about the character of these volunteers came from one who joined them, suggesting that their only common bond was that they were all 'individualists',[14] possessing a kind of independence of spirit that set them apart from the rest.

By the end of their three weeks at Wanborough Manor two of the group had been considered unsuitable and removed from the course, while Peulevé and the others were introduced to a new conducting officer, Lieutenant Robert Searle (Simon was to leave on a mission to France later that month), and sent for the next stage of their training at STS 23, based at Meoble Lodge, south of Loch Morar in the Western Highlands of Scotland. SOE had inherited it, along with a number of houses across the Arisaig and Morar districts from its predecessor MI R, and had been keen to use them for running the 'Group A', or paramilitary courses, which essentially taught the same kinds of skills as at Wanborough but in greater scope and detail.

With only a single main road running through the area – known as 'The Road To The Isles' – maintaining security was relatively easy, although the locals were required to show passes when travelling in and out. The nearby West Highland railway line was particularly useful for training purposes as well as transport, but above all it was the wild and lonely terrain, with its bare mountains, icy lochs and deep gorges that made it an ideal place for testing the physical capabilities of its recruits.

Even today Meoble Lodge can only be reached by boat or by an arduous hike of several miles, and its spartan accommodation soon gave 27N an idea of what was to come over the next few weeks. Aside from the early morning runs and other physical challenges, recruits were taught how to prepare and place explosive charges, being sent on 'schemes' or mock missions to blow up a vehicle, bridge or railway line using targets scattered across the training area. In addition a great variety of exercises, such as how to survive in a harsh environment and live off the land, drive a train, jump from a moving vehicle, break into a house or stalk an enemy across country were all designed to equip them with skills that could aid them in occupied territory.

Weapon training was carried out using a variety of British and foreign small arms including those used by the enemy, though particular attention was given to the recently introduced Sten sub-machine gun, which was to become as much a symbol for resistance movements as the Kalashnikov AK-47 is today, and for similar reasons. Above all the Sten was very much a no-frills weapon – being largely constructed from pressed metal parts it was cheap to produce, with several million being manufactured between 1941 and the end of the war. Its rugged design meant that contact with water or mud did not prevent it from firing, and it could also be dismantled into three parts, making it easy to conceal. Equally important was the fact that it took 9mm ammunition, which was widely available in Europe and used by German troops for their equivalent weapon, the MP40. Despite being effective only at short ranges and prone to jamming and accidental discharge, its simplicity and availability made it ideal for arming large numbers of underground fighters, and was favoured by SOE as the weapon of choice for guerrilla warfare.

Two instructors who would be instrumental in shaping SOE's training methods were Captain Eric Sykes and Captain William Fairbairn, a placid-looking duo sometimes referred to as the 'Heavenly Twins'. Their appearance was misleading – both had been members of the Shanghai Municipal Police before the war, and drew on their shared experience to construct new approaches in hand-to-hand fighting, combining karate and other martial arts with more unorthodox methods used in the Chinese underworld. In addition to unarmed combat, they were also keen proponents of 'instinctive' shooting, which taught students the importance of speed when dealing with an enemy at close quarters. Traditional pistol aiming techniques gave an opponent a good chance of firing first, therefore the preferred method was to fire two sufficiently accurate shots as rapidly as possible – as long as they found the head or torso, the target would be dead. These courses were also supplemented by 'silent killing' classes, which employed the use of garottes and knives for dealing with sentries and similar situations; Fairbairn and Sykes designed a knife specifically for these purposes, which went into production in 1941 and became widely used by SOE personnel as well as Commando units.

Whatever the subject, the overall emphasis at STS 23 was always on practical application and the use of direct methods devoid of unnecessary complexity. A note to the instructors made this clear: 'Time available to students is limited. It is essential, therefore, to confine the teaching to what is simple, easily learned and deadly.'[15] Another typical directive on close combat techniques stated:

> The Queensbury rules enumerate, under the heading of 'fouls', some good targets which the boxer is trained not to defend. This, however, is WAR, not sport. Your aim is to kill your opponent as quickly as possible. A prisoner is generally a handicap and a source of danger, particularly if you are without weapons. So forget Queensbury rules; forget the term 'foul methods' ... 'Foul methods', so-called, help you to kill quickly.[16]

The instructors and commandant at STS 23 found Peulevé puzzling. Although he had no problem getting on with the other students, he appeared to doubt his own potential and was uncomfortable with the constant observation that the group was subjected to. One instructor remarked that he was 'An odd type of person who does not seem particularly interested in anything. He attacks most things in a half-hearted manner peculair [sic] to himself, which makes him appear less intelligent than the others. Personally I think he is capable of doing well, but needs some sort of impetus to start him going.'[17] The Commandant agreed, judging that 'He is probably more capable than he realises. Afraid of not being able to do things, he is inclined always to leave himself a loop-hole.'[18] This apparent lack of confidence also left them questioning his psychological suitability for clandestine work, speculating that 'Whether or not his nerve would stand prolonged strain is open to doubt.'[19]

There is no report relating to Peulevé's parachute course, but he was almost certainly next sent to STS 51 at Ringway airfield near Manchester; owing to constraints on time, it's likely that he was only there for three or four days, though five to seven was the standard, pending weather conditions. The course would begin using static apparatus on the ground to simulate the experience of leaving an aircraft, progressing to jumping from a balloon or aircraft at 700 feet the following day. After two or three additional descents from a Whitley bomber over nearby Tatton Park during daylight, the dreaded final exercise would be made at night, giving students some idea of the conditions they would face when actually dropping over France. Peulevé only received the most cursory grounding in the basics, but this was by no means uncommon for SOE trainees, and he gained his 'wings' before moving on to the Group B stages of his training.

Based on the judgements made by the schools and conducting officers at the Group A schools, each student would specialize in one of several possible roles and would be sent to a relevant school to prepare them. In Peulevé's case the decision had already been made, as his interview with Gielgud had identified his obvious qualifications for the job of W/T (wireless telegraphy) operator. Wireless operators were trained at STS 52, at Thame Park near Oxford, and Peulevé arrived there in early June along with three others from his group: Roger Landes, an architecture student who had spent most of his life in Paris before moving to England and qualifying as a W/T operator with the Royal Corps of Signals; Louis Lee Graham, another promising student already identified by his instructors as having the qualities of a 'thoroughbred racehorse type – intelligent, quick and sure of himself';[20] and a rather less athletic, but equally determined Jewish businessman from north London, Marcus Bloom.

W/T operators were always a highly valuable asset for SOE – without them a network had no link to London and was virtually paralyzed. They were also the most vulnerable of agents and their average life expectancy in the field was no more than a few weeks. STS 52 did its best to prepare them, teaching the technical and theoretical aspects of wireless, how to send and receive coded Morse messages, the importance of security (when, where and how to transmit) as well as the use of a variety of ciphers. It was a longer course of five weeks, into which a great deal had to be crammed.

At this time SOE was only just becoming independent in its radio communications, having previously relied on SIS to provide wireless sets and to relay all traffic to and from its agents. This freedom to operate alone was welcome, though SOE quickly had to come up with improvements on the clandestine equipment that SIS issued. Peulevé was firstly acquainted with the Mark XV, a pre-war set that weighed 45lb and had to be carried in two suitcases, before being trained on SOE's A Mark I and newly introduced Type 3 Mark I (or 'B1') designs, which were still very heavy but small enough to fit into a single case. These sets only needed a low power transmitter to send a simple Morse signal, as the short-wave frequencies used were capable of bouncing off the earth's atmosphere, greatly increasing their range; however, they did require the use of a 20-metre wire aerial, which was awkward enough to extend fully, let alone conceal from an inquisitive neighbour. They were also dependent on a small quartz crystal, housed in a small two-pin plug and inserted into the top of the set – cut to a specific thickness, this crystal determined the particular frequency on which the agent's transmissions would be sent. Agents might carry several of these fragile components, two or three of them being used for separate day and night schedules, with one reserved for sending emergency messages on a wavelength continually monitored by the home station.

Along with producing wireless sets, SOE would also devise its own ciphers, though in the summer of 1942 agents were still being taught to use 'Playfair' and various double-transposition systems already employed by SIS. Developed in the mid-nineteenth century by British inventor Sir Charles Wheatstone, the Playfair system is a substitution cipher that uses a five-by-five square grid, into which a keyword is placed (in Peulevé's case the word used was PARCHMENT). The grid is filled with the remaining unused letters in alphabetical order, with one box including two letters to fit; the message to be sent is then broken into pairs of letters, which are substituted using a simple set of rules.

SOE also relied heavily on poem codes, based on a popular nursery rhyme, song or sonnet selected by the coding section and memorized by the agent. Each message would begin with an indicator group of five letters, signalling which five words from the text had been used to create the key – with this knowledge the recipient could then easily decrypt it. Although relatively simple to use, this method had an obvious weakness: if a transmission was intercepted and the Germans could crack enough of the code to discover the rhyme or text being used, they could then apply it to reveal the entire message.

Neither of these systems was very secure, but alternatives like double-transposition ciphers presented other problems for an agent, as they were very time-consuming and laborious to use. It was not until the following year that a much safer alternative became available – known as the Letter One-Time Pad (LOP), it had the great advantage of using a unique key for each message transmitted. Wireless operators were issued with microfilmed rows of keys, and a table for enciphering and deciphering messages, printed on a handkerchief-sized flammable silk – after each key was used it could be cut away and destroyed, while the silk could be burned in the event of imminent capture. Without the table and specific key for each message the system remained unbreakable, as the agent had memorized nothing.

The actual work of a W/T operator in an occupied country depended on a timetable for sending and receiving messages, known as a signal plan. In 1942 the signal plan would give the wireless operator pre-set schedules (or 'skeds') giving the times when they would be expected to make contact with the home station. Having prepared the set, inserted the crystal and tuned it to the assigned frequency, the operator would initially send a call sign, which would be acknowledged by the home station before he sent his enciphered message. Once completed, he would then receive a transmission from London replying to his previous messages (receiving and transmitting would later be done at different times, to avoid long prolonged communication). W/T operators had to work quickly as they were at their most exposed when on the air, and risked being caught by German D/F (direction-finding) vans, which were capable of intercepting unidentified radio signals and pinpointing the source of their location in a matter of minutes. As a precaution agents in towns and cities often preferred to use car batteries or even bicycle generators to power their sets, as it was also a common ploy of the German D/F teams to identify a radio post by cutting off the electricity in a district, street by street, until the monitored frequency on their receivers went dead. These cat-and-mouse games demanded substantial resources on the part of the *Sicherheitsdienst* (SD, the German counter-intelligence services), but the capture of a W/T operator and his set could disable a network for months or even destroy it completely.

The station that received this traffic in 1942 was based at Grendon Hall in Buckinghamshire (another was added a year later at Poundon Hall, just a few miles away). Staffed by young women of the First Aid Nursing Yeomanry (FANY), it systematically recorded and deciphered incoming messages before relaying them by teleprinter to London, but many of the transmissions that reached Buckmaster's desk were anything but straightforward to interpret. Agents were supposed to include two checks in their messages,

31

one 'true' and one 'bluff': the bluff check could be given away if captured, while the absence of the true check would indicate that an agent was under enemy control. However, the Signals staff at Grendon would often find that checks were completely absent, as operators working under pressure often considered them superfluous or too time-consuming to bother with, making it difficult to identify whether an agent was in the hands of the Gestapo or just in a hurry.

Additionally a poor radio signal caused by German jamming, or errors made whilst transmitting meant that many messages received were difficult or impossible to make sense of. These 'indecipherables' would cause many headaches for SOE's coding section in Baker Street, which had little choice but to work around the clock to crack them. Failure to do so would mean that the W/T operator would have to come up on the air again to resend the message the next night, greatly increasing his chances of being caught.

For the teaching staff at Thame Park, Peulevé presented a difficult problem. Having previously worked on cutting-edge radar technology, his technical knowledge now well exceeded that of his instructors, who perceived his apparent disinterest in their classes as a sign of arrogance. For someone as eager as Peulevé, spending time being trained on topics he could have lectured on was pointless and frustrating, and led to increasing tensions as the course progressed. This antagonism was witnessed by the Commandant, who reported that Peulevé 'appears to have a bad inferiority complex and is very touchy. Gives the impression of lacking enthusiasm and of being conceited', stoically concluding that he would 'endeavour to make the best of difficult material'.[21] Though feeling that he was only wasting time, Peulevé recognized that he would at least have to show some effort to stay on the course, and satisfied the instructors that he was capable of sending and receiving Morse messages at around twenty words per minute, adequate if unremarkable.

Following wireless training, the final Group B courses were held at Beaulieu in Hampshire, known as the 'finishing school', where agents were prepared as much as possible for clandestine life in an occupied country. A number of houses on the estate at Beaulieu were requisitioned for SOE's activities from 1941, teaching students from all country sections. The courses covered a wide range of topics, including how to create and manage networks, the use of cut-outs (couriers who only maintain contact with one or two people to avoid compromising a whole network), arranging safe houses, what kinds of people to recruit and how to recruit them, the structures of German security services, identification of German uniforms and ranks, organizations sympathetic to the Nazis, types and uses of disguises, coding and ciphers, and a number of other subjects. As with Group A schools, the course would assess its students' capabilities in the final week using schemes.

Peulevé was sent to Hartford House (STS 32a), one of the smallest houses at Beaulieu, accommodating only two or three students at a time, where instruction concentrated on personal security considerations relevant to W/T operators, along with lots of daily practice sending and receiving radio transmissions. It is not clear exactly how long Peulevé spent here, but it seems that he was sent to Beaulieu primarily to take part in as many schemes as possible and gain the maximum experience of life as an agent before being sent to France at the end of the month. He faced a much more intensive schedule than most students faced, and the demands of having to complete his training in such a short space of time would prove to be a thorough test of his abilities.

The W/T schemes that operated across the country were intended as far as possible to simulate the pressures of living and operating in occupied Europe, using MI 5 and the local police as a substitute for German security services. Peulevé's schemes were to take place in the south Manchester area and began with his travelling to a safe house near Northwich to make contact with the name given by the instructor. He was then assessed on how he presented his cover story, handled meetings, contacted his circuit organizer in public, passed messages, used letter boxes (pre-arranged locations for leaving messages) as well as his efficiency in sending and receiving wireless messages. It was also common to assess how students might react to the ordeal of being arrested and questioned; this gave the course instructors an opportunity, albeit without the real threat of torture or execution, to see how the agent might face interrogation by Gestapo or Vichy Police, and what capacity they might have for handling pressure and thinking on their feet.

Any number of mistakes were possible during these schemes, though the most frequent were poor security and repeated errors in coding or transmission. In a number of cases agents who failed a scheme for a sufficiently serious reason never saw any active duty, regardless of the months they had spent training. Instead they would be transferred to the 'ISRB Workshops' at Inverlair in Scotland (also known as 'The Cooler'), where they would be relegated to relatively menial duties until the knowledge they had gained could no longer endanger any further operations.

Peulevé's performance during the schemes at Beaulieu proved that the lack of confidence he had shown in Scotland had disappeared, and his report was much more complimentary than those of previous schools: 'We found the student to be exceptionally keen, hardworking and quick to learn from his mistakes. H has an alert practical mind. His questions and conversations show that he has fully realised the problem of personal security that will confront him in his work, and is anxious to acquire now any knowledge which may prove useful later.'[22] In just four months F Section had successfully transformed Peulevé from being a lecturer on the periphery of the war into a fully-fledged secret agent, a valuable resource that Baker Street now aimed to deploy as quickly as possible.

After leaving Beaulieu, Peulevé had a few days to see Annette and his parents, who had moved to Thetford in Norfolk, though of course he could not mention anything of his impending departure for France. Telling them instead that he was being posted overseas, he managed to remain vague on the details despite his mother's persistent questions. With a very real possibility that he might never see them again, he took a train at the end of the week to report to Buckmaster at Orchard Court.

Chapter 4

Scientist

Though Peulevé had only just completed his training, the planning for his first mission to France had already started some weeks earlier. Claude de Baissac, who had trained alongside Francis Suttill on the organizers' course, had been chosen to start a new circuit in the Bordeaux area named SCIENTIST (the names of professions were commonly used for christening F Section's networks). Bordeaux was strategically important for two main reasons: it was an accessible port for blockade-runners, supplying Germany's economy with oil, rubber and other vital raw materials from the Far East, and was also used as a base for German U-boats, patrolling the Atlantic for Allied convoys. SCIENTIST's job would be to make an assessment of Resistance groups in the area, and to recruit and train teams capable of carrying out sabotage on enemy naval installations and other key targets.

At the age of thirty-five, de Baissac was Peulevé's senior by some years. Born to aristocratic landowning parents in Mauritius, he was educated in Paris and joined a mining company in Madagascar in 1931, but later returned to France to work in advertising. After the armistice in 1940 he left to make his way over the Pyrenees, being imprisoned in a Spanish jail for seven months before reaching Gibraltar and eventually boarding a ship bound for Glasgow. Strong-willed and single-minded, Buckmaster described him as 'the most difficult of my officers without any exception ... occasionally brilliant, brutally lazy and always charming',[1] though he never questioned his ability to produce results; de Wesselow's report from Wanborough also noted his 'Excessive, though not obnoxious self-confidence, leading to an impetuous approach ... Extremely French and volatile. Plenty of courage and guts.'[2] As Roger Landes was expected to become the W/T operator for the new PROSPER circuit in Paris, de Baissac chose Peulevé for his mission, having been

35

impressed by him during their training at Wanborough and Meoble. They were to leave at the end of July, weather permitting.

France had changed considerably since Peulevé's evacuation in May 1940. Germany's swift victory, delivered just six weeks after the start of the offensive, offered Hitler revenge for the humiliation of 1918 and a shining example of Nazi superiority. Under the terms of the armistice the country was split into two main areas: the northern 'occupied zone', which included the bulk of France's industry and food production was administered by the Germans, while the poorer, more agricultural 'free' or 'unoccupied zone' remained under the French Government now seated at Vichy, led by the elderly Maréchal Henri Philippe Pétain, a widely respected veteran of the First World War. After a meeting with Hitler at Montoire in October, commemorated by a photograph of the two men shaking hands, Pétain declared in a radio broadcast that 'It is in a spirit of honour and to preserve the unity of France ... that I today embark on the path of collaboration.' This collaboration was intended by Pétain to strengthen the idea of French autonomy and equality under occupation; yet it was a façade, and Vichy's policies would be increasingly forced to comply with Germany's wishes.

Defined by the slogan of *Travail, Famille, Patrie* (Work, Family, Fatherland), a National Revolution was planned to sweep away the liberal, secular values that had led to the country's collapse. Combining nostalgic fantasies of peasant rural life, customs and folklore, the importance of family and Catholic moral values, Vichy offered a vision of the future founded upon a mythical past. Pétain became a figurehead for this new era of innocence and enjoyed considerable support as 'the shield' of France, upholding its dignity in the face of defeat. However, as Germany began to transport its resources back home the consequences of shortages and soaring prices soon made a mockery of the government's propaganda. The detention of one-and-a-half million French prisoners of war meant that many households were missing the wages of fathers and husbands, and soon making do became a way of life, coining the term 'Système de Débrouillage' or 'Système D'. Increased demand for goods also drew in black marketeers and speculators, who sprang up 'like mushrooms after rain'[3] and became commonplace across France.

To deflect some of these ills Pétain looked to familiar scapegoats. The privations of honest citizens could be attributed to the Jews, Freemasons, communists, foreigners, gypsies and other minority groups who were branded as enemies of France, and soon policies were implemented to target them. By September 1940, forty-five internment camps had been set up, and before the end of the year Jews were banned from holding senior positions in public offices, the media and education. Following Germany's declaration of war on Russia in June 1941, Vichy also placed particular accent on the threat of Bolshevism. Courts, known as 'sections spéciales' were set up to deal specifically with communist-related crimes, and the *Légion des Volontaires Français Contre le Bolchévisme* appealed for volunteers to fight with Hitler's troops against Russia, though it only drew a few thousand recruits.

A year after its inception, Pétain recognized that belief in his *rénovation française* was slipping away. In a speech during August 1941 he warned that 'Disquiet is taking hold of peoples' minds, doubt is seizing their spirits. The authority of my government is questioned; its orders often poorly executed.' Despite introducing more repressive measures acts of terrorism continued to spread, including a number of communist-led assassinations of German officers in the autumn, which resulted in the first French civilian hostages being shot in reprisals. By March 1942 the deportation of six thousand Jewish men to concentration camps had gone ahead with no intervention from Vichy, and the appointment of Pierre Laval as head of government the following month only served to underline Hitler's increasing influence on Pétain's leadership: Laval, advocating a policy of close collaboration, publicly declared that he wished to see a Nazi victory in Russia to defeat the threat of Bolshevism. He also announced the *relève* (relief), a plan to send French workers to aid the German economy in return for the release of French POWs, at a ratio of three workers for every soldier released. Although the return of prisoners was welcomed, Germany's increasing demands for French labour over the following months would become a key factor in increasing public hostility towards his administration.

Britain had accepted Pétain's former minister Charles de Gaulle as the voice of 'Free France' since his arrival in London in June 1940, and though his popularity at home was initially weak it was clear that growing disaffection for Vichy was strengthening the Resistance. By 1942 three main groups had emerged in the occupied zone: the right-wing OCM (*Organisation Civile et Militaire*, largely composed of military men and civil servants); the *Front National* (communist); and *Libération-Nord*, which attracted socialists and trade-union members. In the unoccupied zone there was also *Combat*, which appealed to a conservative audience; *Libération-Sud* (separate from *Libération-Nord*, but with similar views); and *Franc-Tireur*, which was more independent, being composed of ex-Radicals, lapsed communists and Catholics. The *Front National* was also significant in the south, and its paramilitary wing, the *Francs-Tireur et Partisans* (or FTP, not to be confused with *Franc-Tireur*) was formed in February 1942, drawing many of its leaders from the International Brigades who had fought in the Spanish Civil War.

At the beginning of the year de Gaulle had sent an emissary, Jean Moulin, to attempt to integrate and unify this confusing array of groups under his flag. Moulin's travels across the *zone sud* were for the most part successful, and the prospect of a united secret army, bolstered by increasing public sympathy for the Resistance, was gaining momentum by the summer. However, support for Pétain as the legitimate leader of France was far from extinguished, and F Section agents operating in the unoccupied zone remained very much in enemy territory.

Peulevé and de Baissac were to parachute into southern France near the city of Nîmes, but their journey to Bordeaux would be a circuitous one. After landing they were to make their way to a safe house in Cannes, where Peulevé was to stay while de Baissac travelled on to Tarbes, near the Spanish frontier. Delivering a package containing 50,000 francs to a local Resistance leader named Hêches, he would then be guided over the demarcation line and into the occupied zone to meet his organizer, Robert Leroy (*Louis*), an SOE agent who had been in Bordeaux since June. *Louis* would brief de Baissac on the local situation before Peulevé was fetched to transmit de Baissac's first report to London.

Whilst other agents could find themselves waiting around for months before leaving for a mission, Peulevé had only a matter of days to prepare. Much of this time was spent at Orchard Court studying and memorizing details of the false identity he was to use. Although his spoken French did not carry an English accent, his cover story would be that he came from mixed parentage and had lived in England for a time, but that he had returned to do his military service in 1938, serving with the 110th Infantry Regiment at Calais; elements of his own real-life background were also incorporated to increase the plausibility of his story, such as his knowledge of Dinard and the Côte d'Azur. Every detail had to be known intimately, and F Section's operations staff would relentlessly

38

examine him on the details of his occupation, family and personal history until he knew them inside out. Even then, this cover might have to be revised to adapt to a sudden change of circumstance in the field. An agent never had the luxury of taking any aspect of his security for granted.

An identity card along with other relevant forged documents was supplied to back up his story, though the continual changing of the formats of these papers by the authorities caused many headaches for the counterfeiting section and it was impossible to be sure that those he was issued with would pass inspection once in France. Authentic clothing was also an important aspect of disguise and SOE employed tailors to provide garments with a French cut, using French fabrics where possible, and had to attend to the smallest details such as buttons, zips and labels to ensure that nothing was of British origin. Likewise suitcases, money and all personal articles would have to be artificially aged or worn in beforehand to appear genuine. Every component of cover had to support the whole appearance of an agent: mannerisms, accent, hairstyle, even the kind of fillings in an agent's teeth were all potential giveaways, and had to be checked thoroughly before he could be considered ready for departure.

Peulevé and de Baissac pored over maps of the areas they were to parachute into and later operate in, and studied relevant reports compiled from agents' debriefings, which detailed all manner of aspects of living in a particular area such as local regulations, the political tendencies of the population, the number of police controls, the activities of existing local resistance and so on. The final revised instructions for their mission were given the day before departure, confirming their objectives, relevant addresses and passwords to be used when meeting contacts, instructions on letter boxes, the amount of money they were to take and the codes to be employed for sending messages to London. Though he was to use 'Henri Michel Chevalier' as his cover name, Peulevé also had several field names that would be used by fellow agents or by London when referring to him, including *Hilaire, Paul, Edmond* and *Jean*. For the purposes of wireless communication a separate call sign, *Mackintosh*, was to be used as an additional security measure. De Baissac would be known by the code name *David*.

Infiltration by air was only undertaken during the 'moon period', the few days either side of a full moon when pilots and reception committees could take advantage of the increased visibility. Having nearly come to the end of July's window for parachute operations there was now very little time to make their departure and on 30 July both men left Orchard Court, being driven out of London and up the A1 to Gaynes Hall, a secluded country house near St Neots used as a holding station for agents waiting to leave. The FANY staff who ran it did their best to make their stay as comfortable as possible, though apprehension was unavoidable when the daily roster of agents scheduled to leave was chalked up on the blackboard – several days of bad weather, or other agents being considered a higher priority could mean returning to London and having to wait another month before trying again.

Thankfully de Baissac and Peulevé had no such hold-ups to endure, and the following morning they saw their flight confirmed on the board. Having done all they reasonably could to prepare, they could now only wait for dusk. In the sleepy surroundings of the estate Peulevé took advantage of the facilities:

> That afternoon I had taken a siesta in one of the rooms of the Station and heard the plonk-plonk of a tennis ball – a sound which personified the quiet, country-house atmosphere of peace-time Britain in summertime: I dozed off thinking that this would be the last sound I should hear of the country which I loved so much and which, so far, I had served so badly. At last I had been trained to perfection and was prepared to meet the enemy on his own terms.[4]

After two years of humiliation and self-reproach over what had happened in France, he knew that he was now only hours away from returning to make a real contribution to the war.

As was customary both men were given a good dinner by the Commanding Officer before taking a car to RAF Tempsford, a few miles south. Accompanied by Buckmaster and conducting officer Jacques de Guélis, de Baissac and Peulevé were driven through the nearby village, over the railway crossing and the short distance up to the airfield's entrance. Since March 1942, Tempsford had been home to 138 and 161 Squadrons, both of which were dedicated to carrying out 'Special Duty' missions, transporting agents, arms and supplies all over occupied Europe. SOE was considered an unnecessary and extravagant drain on the RAF's limited resources and had only a dozen Halifaxes, two Wellingtons and ten virtually obsolete Whitley bombers at its disposal for parachute operations, though 161 Squadron would also ferry agents to and from secret French landing fields using half a dozen smaller Lysander and Hudson aircraft.

The passengers were purposely kept away from the hangars and Nissen huts of the main airfield for security reasons, being taken instead to a cluster of buildings on the far side of the perimeter known as Gibraltar Farm. Here a thorough last-minute search of the agents was made for any signs of any British markings, currency, ticket stubs or anything else that could give them away. Once the inspection was over, Peulevé was issued with his forged identity card and other documents, ankle bandages, a Luger pistol and a flask of rum, along with his suitcases, one containing his heavy W/T set and the other clothes and personal items. One last article had to be considered, though not all agents felt the need to take them: in case of capture, 'L' (for lethal) tablets offered a quick alternative to torture and the risk of giving away the details of their circuit. Peulevé opted to pocket his before donning his overalls and parachute, finally making his way out towards the waiting Halifax.

Briefly shaking hands with their young but experienced Czech pilot, Captain Leo Anderle, and his crew, they were stowed along with their luggage into the dark, uncomfortable fuselage. Some minutes after the lumbering aircraft began rolling down the runway and Peulevé caught his 'last glimpse of the neat and tranquil countryside slipping away'[5] through the observation window as they climbed into the fading light. Turning south, it was dark by the time they reached the Channel and crossed it without incident, but on approaching the French coast they were greeted by a few barrages of anti-aircraft fire, which immediately stirred Peulevé from the effects of the Station dinner. He suddenly thought once more of how they were to 'drop like sacks of potatoes'[6] into occupied territory, and the unreality of his situation began to unsettle him. However, the flak soon died down, and he and de Baissac managed to doze as the Halifax continued its way unhampered towards Nîmes.

Successfully identifying a landing field at night posed considerable problems even for the highly-skilled crews of the Special Duty squadrons, who had to rely on a combination of dead reckoning and the use of landmarks, rivers and the lights from towns and cities to lead them to their target. The reception committee was expected to receive them in an area near the small town of Caissargues, just west of Nîmes airport, yet as the aircraft circled the pilots could see nothing on the ground.[7] Having no doubt that they were over the

41

right location, they were left with the choice of either dropping 'blind' (without a reception) or turning back. As the Halifax had limited fuel a decision had to be made quickly, and both men agreed to take their chances and jump. Removing a circular section in the fuselage floor, the despatcher clipped the strap from Peulevé's parachute to the static line before he moved into position, sitting facing the tail of the aircraft with his legs dangling below. The drill learnt at Ringway flooded his mind briefly before he was given the green light and jumped, closely followed by de Baissac.

Engulfed by the aircraft's slipstream, Peulevé saw his parachute begin to open but immediately felt something hit him in the eye. As blood began to stream down his face, he looked up to check his canopy but could already feel that something was wrong. He was obviously dropping far too quickly, but as the ground rushed to meet him there was little he could do: 'In a flash I thought "This is it ... this is the end of everything." In that split second I thought that I would now never have the opportunity to prove myself in the face of the enemy.'[8]

De Baissac's exit had been almost as disastrous. After leaving the aircraft his harness had become twisted and though he managed to readjust it after a few seconds his parachute still hadn't fully opened. He hit the ground hard, but was fortunate in suffering nothing more than what seemed to be a sprained ankle. After removing his harness, he spotted Peulevé's body some distance away, being dragged across the field by his parachute.

Peulevé had survived the drop, but only just. He had deduced that the spade, routinely issued for burying parachutes, must have fallen out of his overalls and had been responsible for striking him in the eye. More seriously, the 'resounding crack'[9] that he'd heard on landing had been his right leg shattering on impact, which now appeared to have 'bits of bone sticking out all over the place'.[10] Just as he began to wonder where his partner was, Peulevé was suddenly hauled backwards as his parachute caught the wind and lifted him out of the dirt, but managed to reach his knife and cut away his harness before he reached the edge of the field. Unable to see any trace of de Baissac, he assumed that he'd probably been killed by the drop; hastily binding his leg as best he could using his knife as a splint, Peulevé began inching his body along the ground until he fainted.

Safely parachuting agents into enemy territory at an altitude of 500 feet was a difficult task even for an accomplished bomber crew.

With relatively little instrumentation and in the presence of cloud and strong winds mistakes were inevitable, and it seems that on this night both men probably jumped at less than half that height. De Baissac later heard that five days prior to their drop another agent had been killed near Clermont-Ferrand in the same circumstances, and in a message to Buckmaster, SOE's Air Liaison Section noted that this was just one of 'several deplorable incidents'[11] that had occurred during the month.

After tracking down his fellow agent it didn't take long for de Baissac to assess the situation. Without the help of a reception committee he was left with few options, especially as he expected his ankle to start swelling soon. All he could do was throw the W/T set into an overgrown ditch and leave Peulevé where he was with his share of the money and all of their provisions. He also asked him to wait until the next morning before trying to summon help from one of the nearby farms, giving de Baissac several hours to put some distance between them. Leaving his wireless operator to fend for himself, *David* started to limp off in the direction of Nîmes.

It may seem somewhat callous to leave a seriously injured man alone in this predicament, yet such scenarios had been covered in their training. There was no point in both of them being found and very possibly arrested, so it was simply a matter of expediency. However, Peulevé was not left totally alone for the night, as a large bird had perched on a branch a few feet above his head, though he didn't consider this a welcome guardian angel and spent the night throwing stones to dissuade it from attacking his leg.

When morning finally came he was able to spot a farmhouse a few hundred metres away showing some signs of activity. He began the slow and agonizing process of dragging himself towards it and eventually got near enough to attract the attention of a middle-aged woman working outside. Her first words were, 'What the bloody hell are you doing here?'[12] Peulevé, not wanting to disclose that he was British, declared himself to be a Gaullist agent who had parachuted the previous night. Evidently unimpressed, she replied, 'You are bloody lucky, because most of the neighbours round here are collaborators.'[13] Valentine Benoit called for her elderly mother and together they clumsily attempted to lift Peulevé into a wheelbarrow, but he was in excruciating pain whenever they moved him. Realizing this was an impossible task, they called on a sympathetic neighbour named Camille who provided a stretcher to carry him into the house. The chances of finding a taxi willing to take him to a hospital in Cannes were negligible, but Camille offered to drive him to the Clinique des Franciscaines in Nîmes, a nursing home run by Franciscan nuns on rue Jean Bouin.

Peulevé was immediately admitted, using the cover story that he was on holiday and had been sitting in a tree picking figs when he fell. It wasn't the most likely of scenarios, especially considering that figs were out of season, but it appeared that no one was particularly suspicious. Three days later the surgeon was ready to set his leg, which posed another problem as there was a risk of his speaking English when coming round from the anaesthetic. As they wheeled him back out of the theatre after the operation he did his best to keep silent, though he couldn't be sure if the nurses might now know something of his real identity.

Installed on a ward in the clinic, Peulevé had to try and maintain his story for long enough to allow his leg to heal, but he knew this was a tall order – it would be several weeks before he could even stand, and might be months before he could walk. A nurse asked for his ration card, which all French people were expected to carry, but London had only issued him with a *feuille semestrielle*, a card that entitled him to apply for one. For someone to be travelling without a food ration card would seem highly suspect, so Peulevé simply said that he had forgotten it. His only hope of getting hold of one was to write to an address that de Baissac had been issued with, that of a man named Georges Audouard who belonged to a circuit of croupiers working at the Municipal Casino in Cannes. Fortunately Audouard responded a few days later, employing his son to courier over enough food tickets to see him through August.[14]

He was grateful for visits from the Benoits and their friends, who brought what they could in the way of presents and provisions, though it soon became clear that they would have to be more discreet as they were constantly under threat of denunciation from their pro-Vichy neighbours. To add to their concerns an RAF supply drop accidentally fell right into the centre of Nîmes later that month; although the police were alerted and found two men awaiting the drop nearby no arrest was made, despite their bizarre excuse that they had been unable to sleep and decided to play boules instead (fortunately many of the local *gendarmerie* were Corsicans, who were ready to turn a blind eye to the work of the Resistance). Soon afterwards a neighbour declared to the Benoits that he had seen a parachutist come down with this second drop and that he would shoot him if he saw him again. Although these events made Peulevé feel uneasy, he could nothing about his situation until his leg healed. At least the doctors and nuns of the clinic were not asking too many questions, even if they were beginning to suspect that he might be a fugitive.

August drifted into September. Peulevé had more trouble obtaining ration cards from the Audouards, and even when they finally appeared they were either out of date or incomplete. All of this continued to cause problems with the clinic, but he managed to convince them that the poor postal service was to blame. Aside from having to offer excuses regularly to cover himself, passing time on the ward was also beginning to try Peulevé's patience sorely – having spent so long preparing for the chance to fight back, he was now more useless than ever.

However, in the middle of the month more news arrived via Audouard's son, who told Peulevé that it had been arranged for him to assist the CARTE organization, run in conjunction with an Englishman named *Raoul*, and that he was to stay at their house in Cannes. Despite his condition, there was no doubt in Peulevé's mind that he had to go; not only was he tired of being pent up with nothing to do, but the longer he stayed at the clinic the more risky his situation would become. Against the advice of his surgeon, Dr Simonet, who stressed that his leg would need at least another month to heal before trying to walk, he agreed to take the train to Cannes, pointing out that he would at least be accompanied on his journey.

On arrival they took a taxi to the Audouards' villa in Avenue Windsor, a secluded street situated on the eastern side of town off the rue d'Antibes. As they passed the boutiques and beauty salons that Peulevé remembered from his youth on the Côte d'Azur, it seemed that little had changed, though it was evident that the local population had grown considerably. Since the summer of 1940 many Jews, communists and other threatened minorities had fled from Paris and the occupied north for the relative safety of Vichy territory, with a sizeable proportion of this exodus heading for the Riviera. While the constant flow of people in and out of the towns of south-eastern France boosted the local economy, it also encouraged a thriving black market to accommodate the needs of affluent newcomers, with a corresponding increase in the numbers of local informers and profiteers. This, along with the significant support for the Vichy Government in the region, the vigilance of the police and security services, the anti-semitism (600 Jews had been just been rounded up in Nice and sent to a transit camp at Drancy near Paris) and the volatile nature of the local Resistance groups made it an especially perilous location for someone in Peulevé's predicament.

Though he had previously sheltered other British agents and Allied airmen on the run, Audouard was surprised when Peulevé mentioned that de Baissac had given him his address, as he had no idea that London had been recommending him as a port of call. The family was extremely hospitable, but Peulevé soon found that the situation there posed almost as many security problems as he had faced in Nîmes: one radio operator was already transmitting from the villa, while two other *résistants* were staying in another room, sleeping on the floor (a member of a separate group in Cannes could not believe that the police hadn't yet raided the house, likening it to a beehive).[15] He was soon to learn that this casual lack of precaution was endemic, and that CARTE, the region's main resistance network, was even more vulnerable than he could have imagined.

Chapter 5

Carte

SOE's involvement with CARTE had begun the previous year, when an F Section organizer named Francis Basin (*Olive*) arrived to begin the URCHIN circuit in September, establishing himself at Antibes, just a few miles east of Cannes. He soon made contact with a local doctor, Elie Lévy (*Philippe*), whose villa at 31 Boulevard du Maréchal Foch was already being used as a meeting place for a motley assortment of Resistance leaders, ranging from communists to senior members of *Combat and Libération*. With Lévy's help Basin set about creating the foundations of his network, and by February 1942 URCHIN had seventeen six-man teams ready to carry out propaganda activities and sabotage between Marseille and Monte Carlo. However, it was to be one of Lévy's neighbours, a forty-year-old artist named André Girard, who would attract most attention from SOE's officers in London.

Several agents had already encountered Girard, but F Section's real interest was triggered when Basin met him in December 1941. Using the name *Carte* as his personal *nom de guerre*, Girard had built up an extensive array of senior military contacts in the early days of Vichy, and though primarily operating along the Côte d'Azur he claimed to have important connections across the rest of the *zone non-occupé* as well (some of his sources had already impressed a number of American diplomats with intelligence they had gathered).[1] If Girard's CARTE network had the range of influence suggested it could prove an invaluable resource for SOE's work in south-eastern France, and a useful platform for supporting other Allied operations further down the line. Moreover, Girard's stubborn refusal to align himself with de Gaulle, Pétain or anybody else made him far more appealing, as an independent force would be much easier to manage politically.

In January 1942, Lieutenant Peter Churchill, the *Raoul* mentioned to Peulevé, an athletic former ice-hockey international and son of a consular official (like Peulevé's father, Churchill had also briefly served as Algerian pro-consul at Oran), was sent by Buckmaster to meet *Carte* and assess the situation, being infiltrated by submarine at Miramar near Cannes. Girard was able to convince Churchill that he was worthy of SOE's support, and in April a talented, sensitive, former schoolteacher from Hull named Isidore Newman (*Julien*) was brought ashore at Antibes to act as W/T operator, relaying communications for both CARTE and URCHIN through to London. Girard had big ideas for his network and he soon had Newman sending increasingly unrealistic demands to back his plans for expansion – in one transmission sent in June, F Section was requested to supply 600 W/T sets by felucca, a narrow Mediterranean sailing vessel used to transport agents and supplies from Gibraltar.

In an effort to gather more intelligence on CARTE, Buckmaster decided to send his deputy Major Bodington to evaluate the situation in July, but unfortunately Basin was arrested in Nice shortly after his arrival and Bodington only attended a few brief meetings with Girard before swiftly returning to London, leaving behind his wireless operator Harry Despaigne (*Ulysse*) to hold the fort. Churchill was then parachuted back on 27 August as the organizer of a new circuit, SPINDLE, and appointed as SOE's principal representative to CARTE.

Though there was little evidence to support Girard's claims about his underground movement, SOE had become entranced by the idea of its potential. An initial evaluation tentatively suggested that 'it would seem that we are onto something of value',[2] but Bodington's mission report went much further, describing CARTE as 'well informed and strong' and vouched for Girard's ability to run an efficient operation, declaring that 'Not one penny will be spent which is unaccounted for, not one delivery of material will become "lost"'.[3] In order to secure British support Girard had shrewdly given them exactly what they had wanted to hear, asserting that he was able to draw on a secret army of 300,000 men and could instigate an interim military dictatorship in collaboration with the armistice army (the German-regulated French army under Vichy), capable of wresting power from the Vichy Government before an Allied invasion. It would, however, require enormous resources to become operational: an estimate of 3,750 tonnes of *matériel* would be needed to arm and equip Girard's clandestine fighters, including

50,000 Sten guns, two million grenades and a hundred tonnes of high explosive.

Despite some lingering suspicions over CARTE's lack of security and the apparent squabbling within his organization, F Section committed itself to supporting Girard and managed to obtain an endorsement from the Chiefs of Staff, who sanctioned the start of limited supply operations. In addition a short-wave radio station, *Radio Patrie*, set up by the Political Warfare Executive (PWE, the propaganda component of SOE until 1941) had begun transmitting in early September, employing the skills of pre-war broadcaster Maurice Diamant-Berger (better known in France as 'André Gillois') and journalist Jean Gandrey-Rety, both associates of Girard who had accompanied Bodington on his return to London in August.

Radio Patrie aimed to help train and organize new members of CARTE who were to operate in three-man 'cells' across southern France. However, its transmissions soon attracted criticism from de Gaulle's officers in London, who, apart from their indignation at not being consulted about the station, pointed out the great opportunities it offered to the enemy for infiltrating its own agents. Despite these obvious security problems, SOE was being swept along with the promise of great things from Girard, also agreeing to the idea of an internal radio network across the Riviera and even a wireless link to communicate with a smaller CARTE sub-network based in Paris.

For reasons of security Peulevé had not been briefed on the situation in any detail and knew nothing of Girard or his liaison officer Churchill, though he soon found out how unreliable the organization really was. Contacting *Raoul* to find a doctor to take the plaster off his leg, he was told that Girard had made arrangements for him to visit an eminent surgeon sympathetic to their cause. Peulevé duly took a taxi to the clinic, but on arrival he was told that the doctor would not be available until the afternoon. After waiting five hours the doctor finally appeared, but immediately became very suspicious when Peulevé mentioned the name of Colonel Vautrin as he had been instructed (Vautrin was a regional representative for French Military Intelligence and had helped Girard to avoid arrest on several occasions). Faced with awkward questions about how the injury occurred, Peulevé had no choice but to make a hurried exit and take a cab back to the Audouards' villa, leaving him 800 francs lighter.

Incensed by this foul-up, he informed Churchill of his escapade, who then cycled to Antibes to extract an explanation. Although he knew that an aloof character like Girard was unlikely to offer an apology, Churchill was nevertheless astonished by the way his protestations were brushed aside, Girard casually admitting that he had forgotten about the appointment and that another one could be arranged easily enough.

Peulevé only stayed for a few more days with the Audouards before making the first of many moves from one safe house to another, initially to an address of one of Girard's men in Antibes. He was well aware of the risks involved in giving shelter to a British agent, but was equally surprised by how reluctant many of his hosts were to offer more than the minimum of help, especially as his injury made travelling extremely difficult. Besides these problems Girard also wanted to get Peulevé working in tandem with Newman as quickly as possible and by 27 September, London had received a request for an additional signal plan, Peulevé having destroyed his original one after landing. With his leg being slow to heal he was unable to offer a great deal of help, but Newman was grateful for any assistance he could get, being completely snowed under with the enormous workload generated by the network. He had repeatedly requested that telegrams be shortened, complaining to Buckmaster that *Carte* 'leaves me no initiative concerning any necessary abbreviations',[4] but Girard was a man who preferred to give orders rather than take them and had flatly refused to make any changes.

This matter soon came to a head when Churchill was forced to take sides and gave his support to Girard, with Newman being ordered to work into the early hours of the morning to shift the outgoing messages. Following this decision Churchill also began accusing Newman of slandering Girard, discouraging Peulevé and generally being a 'dangerous influence and detrimental to the discipline of the organisation',[5] sending the mystified *Julien* from Antibes to Marseille for no apparent reason other than to stop him working. Buckmaster was then suddenly informed that Newman would be put aboard November's monthly felucca back to Gibraltar, and that Churchill planned to replace him with a very different character, a combative, foul-mouthed Russo-Egyptian agent named Adolphe Rabinovitch (*Arnaud*) who had recently arrived in Cannes. Harry Despaigne (Bodington's W/T operator who had stayed behind in August) decided to make his own way out of the situation – unimpressed by Churchill's lack of direction and appalled by the poor security he encountered during his daily meetings with Girard, he eventually refused to work for them and returned to England via Spain (meeting his future wife along the way).

SOE had convinced itself that Girard's lack of military training was no obstacle to his success, but his need to play the *'grand seigneur'*[6] definitely was. His lack of discretion and insistence on personally directing operations was a particular problem for Churchill, who had almost completely failed to establish any influence on CARTE's affairs. Though Churchill had been shocked by the way reception committees awaited felucca operations 'like a Bank Holiday crowd on Derby Day',[7] Girard had largely ignored his advice to tighten security, and *Raoul*'s alienation of Newman, Despaigne and several other fellow SOE agents by complying with Girard's wishes only served to weaken his position, though he continued to inform London that relations on the Riviera were 'never better'.[8]

Considering Girard to be a liability, Peulevé began forging closer links with one of his more efficient lieutenants, Romano, who was based in Cannes and supplied boats, safe houses and other services for CARTE. Romano's communist group was largely responsible for the donkey work of the organization, though Girard's recent unreasonable behaviour over delaying promised payments for supplies of petrol and food was straining their relationship. Romano was able to help Peulevé with finding somewhere to stay, but broke off relations with Girard and then Churchill soon afterwards; Peulevé tried to act as mediator to patch things up between them, but Churchill said that London had given instructions to keep his distance from this communist sub-circuit.

Moving back to Cannes, Peulevé stayed briefly with the Audouard family again, where he met Fergus Chalmers-Wright, another of his training colleagues who had just arrived by felucca and was now working for PWE. A few days later Peulevé was told to take a taxi to a small flat near Mougins, sited further up behind the town, where he was to stay in the care of a young Belgian. Still unable to walk and without a food ration card, he was forced to rely on his assistant visiting a black market restaurant three times a day, ferrying food back to him in a mess tin.

Under orders from Girard and Churchill, Peulevé had reluctantly continued to send wireless messages to London, but it didn't take long before the neighbours became suspicious of the Belgian's errands and surmised that someone was being hidden in the flat. Girard was made aware of the possibility of a police raid but refused to have Peulevé relocated, claiming there was nowhere else for him to go; on receiving this news Peulevé protested to Churchill, but, as with Newman, he took Girard's side and insisted that he continue with his transmissions. The combined effects of being cooped up for long periods, the lack of improvement in his leg and an increasing pile of telegrams were now beginning to push Peulevé to the edge, and he finally refused to work. Considering him insubordinate, Girard replied with an ultimatum, threatening to withdraw all support if he didn't cooperate. In an effort to boost Peulevé's spirits Churchill went to visit him at the flat:

> Hilaire's leg is not healing. He looks puckered up and grey and strictly corned off ... I bring a bottle of whisky for him and a strange Joe with a pleasant mush who fetches in the groceries. But Hilaire will not practice the piccolo [wireless] and who can honestly blame him at that. I can weep when I consider this harpist [wireless operator]. He is a hospital case I fall down on. Anyway this guy has no wish to quit and I will be a Chinaman's daughter if I really know what he does wish to do apart from gazing out of the window with a dumb, grey, creased-off look on his handsome pan. Also I fancy he hates my guts and does not consider me very much better than a dead loss, which is about what I feel.[9]

It's little surprise that Peulevé had lost all confidence in *Raoul* considering the lack of support he had received, and he was determined to ignore Girard's threats, asking the Belgian to find him an alternative safe house and doctor. Things went from bad to worse when his new abode quickly drew the attention of the police and he was forced to take refuge at the house of one of Romano's men, where he was introduced to one of his younger recruits, an enthusiastic twenty year old named Jacques Poirier. Having grown up in the Neuilly district of Paris, Poirier attended the Lycée Pasteur before his family moved to Cannes just before the outbreak of war; at the end of 1941 a neighbour noted the teenager's obvious interest in joining the Resistance and discreetly arranged a meeting with Romano, who in turn began using him to deliver messages and underground newspapers across town. Now an experienced errand boy eager for promotion, he lied to Romano about the fluency of his English and was given the job of personal aide to the injured British agent. Following a second visit to a doctor's clinic Peulevé was in desperate need of some time away from the tensions in Cannes, and Poirier obliged by suggesting he stay at his family's house at Beaulieu-sur-Mer, just east of Nice. Gratefully accepting the offer, he immediately left with his new assistant.

Although the Poiriers made their guest very welcome Peulevé knew that he would soon have to leave, and this time for good. Aside from the security risks already posed by CARTE, the Allied landings on the beaches of Algiers in early November had provoked the Germans to occupy southern France, with Italian forces taking control of Corsica and eight departments east of the Rhône. The French authorities had already tolerated a certain amount of under-cover intelligence activity by the Gestapo on the Riviera, but the official introduction of Nazi headquarters at Cannes and Nice would substantially increase the threat of capture for agents and *résistants* alike.

Peulevé's options for escape were limited. Several of Romano's men had already made an unsuccessful attempt to steal one of several motor torpedo boats moored in Cannes harbour, and the only other obvious route was the felucca to Gibraltar, though the condition of his leg made a November sea crossing impossible. Escaping by air was also considered, Poirier's father having served as a military pilot before the war: an ambitious plan was hatched to fly Peulevé and the whole Poirier family to Algiers using a seaplane moored near Marseille, but several German aircraft flew in to sur-round it on the day they planned to leave. The only other means of airborne evacuation would involve travelling north to somewhere within range of an RAF Lysander, a small reconnaissance aircraft used for pick-up operations. Aside from the difficulties in arranging a flight, it would also involve the risk of crossing several hundred miles of occupied territory.

The remaining route out of France was over the Pyrenees into neutral Spain, making contact with the British consulate in Barcelona or using one of the clandestine 'body lines', escape net-works which passed agents and Allied airmen down to Gibraltar (Peulevé had already been issued in London with a map of an escape line through Andorra, secreted in the back of a matchbox). This would be an arduous journey for someone barely able to walk, but he didn't have the time to wait for another opportunity. He also considered taking Poirier and contacted London to recommend bringing him to England for training as a SOE agent. When Buck-master agreed to the idea, Peulevé immediately set about making plans for their departure.

He briefly returned to Cannes, but soon ran into trouble when the police summoned him over a faked ration card that he'd been using. Having been given the name of a contact in Marseille with connections to take them over the border, Peulevé now wanted to leave without delay; he attempted to contact Churchill first, but he had already left to arrange an aircraft reception near Aix-en-Provence which was to take him, Girard and several army generals to London. Having received no information from *Raoul* as to Peulevé's whereabouts or the reason for his irregular contact, F Section was becoming anxious and had begun nightly transmissions from 24 November to try and reach him; however, Peulevé would not be coming up again. Leaving his radio behind, he took the next train for Marseille with Poirier.

Their exit was timely as CARTE would soon be extinct, the seeds of its demise having been sown earlier that month. With meticulous care Girard had constructed detailed files on all of its members, using questionnaires which covered more than sixty criteria, including names, addresses, professions, relevant skills, political affiliations and so on. He kept these files about his study at Antibes and even though they were regularly distributed, no precaution was ever taken to encode them. In November, one of Girard's assistants, André Marsac (*End*), carried 200 of these files in a briefcase on his way to Paris; dozing off in his compartment on the long journey from Marseille, he awoke to find that the briefcase had gone, pilfered by a German agent. This important haul not only exposed many of those linked with CARTE in the south but also compromised the network's contacts in Paris, which would have dire ramifications for a number of F Section's networks during the coming year.

By December Henri Frager (*Louba*), who had served as CARTE's chief of staff and representative in London, recognized that Girard's power was waning after the German occupation of the south, and split the organization, hoping to direct more effective actions under his own command. In an effort to defuse the situation F Section called Girard, Churchill and Frager back to London for talks in March 1943, but soon Baker Street's staff began to realize how misplaced their faith in *Carte* might now have been, reporting that he had 'physically and mentally gone to seed'[10] following months of strain and the sudden news of his family's arrest in April. While Churchill and Frager both returned to France to continue their work,

Girard was later moved to the United States where he remained for the rest of the war.

Relieved to be out of Cannes at last, Peulevé and Poirier had an uneventful journey until they reached Toulon, where great plumes of smoke could be seen rising above the harbour – rather than let their vessels fall into the hands of the approaching Nazis, the French Navy had decided to scuttle its fleet on the morning of 27 November, just as German tanks were rolling into town. Arriving at Marseille, they made their way to the house of Abbé Winter, an ex-cavalry officer who lived on the outskirts of the city. He was a striking figure, with his flowing white beard, soutane and 'three rows of decorations earned from previous wars',[11] whose religious orders did not prevent him from keeping a cache of old rifles under the bed, or even hiding a dismantled anti-tank gun under the altar of his church. Nevertheless, Peulevé was aware that their presence was an added liability to the Abbé's security and was keen to move on as quickly as possible.

After being given the name of a smuggler in Perpignan, they took another train to meet him, but were unprepared for the substantial German presence in the area. They found their contact easily and he agreed to take them over the Pyrenees and on to Barcelona, but the fee would be 100,000 francs each, double what they had expected to pay. Though still carrying some of the SOE funds he had arrived in France with, Peulevé did not have enough cash to meet this new price, so the smuggler suggested that they seek help from a Jewish family who were also using his services and staying at a small hotel nearby.

With few options left, Peulevé decided to take the risk of introducing himself to them as a British officer, explaining his situation and offering to confirm that his government would honour their loan by broadcasting a specific message on the BBC's French Service in due course (Peulevé could only promise to send a message from Barcelona, having no W/T set with him). Whether it was his force of personality that won them over or simply generosity on the family's part, they agreed to give him the money. The smuggler was given a down payment later that afternoon and planned to accompany them to the border town of Céret the following day.

Having stayed at the same hotel, both Peulevé and Poirier were disheartened the next morning to see that the family that had loaned them the money was to leave with them, even though they had requested to travel alone. As they approached Céret they were stopped and subjected to a spot check by two Vichy policemen, one of whom spotted a discrepancy with Peulevé's *carte d'identité*, noting that it had been issued in Marseille but that he'd mentioned living in Cannes. Expecting the worst, he was amazed when the gendarme merely commented, 'Well, you won't need one now, anyway, will you?'[12] Poirier was treated more harshly, although after being grilled for some minutes he was also allowed to continue.

Beckoning to the driver to stop some way outside the town, their guide and his companion told Peulevé's party to follow them off the bus. They wasted no time in starting towards the border, but after an hour the guide told them to rest while he and his friend went on ahead to check for any patrols. Peulevé and Poirier were thankful for some time to relax, but after half an hour it slowly began to dawn on them that they had been deserted. With no possibility of completing the journey unaided, they reluctantly walked down to the main road and took a bus with the family back to Perpignan. Having exhausted his funds Peulevé's only option was to return to Marseille to seek an explanation from Abbé Winter, but as they waited for the next train at Perpignan station Peulevé suddenly recognized the two smugglers on the next platform. Though unarmed he and Poirier managed to sneak up and corner them – confronted by their angry customers the Frenchmen meekly agreed to take the afternoon bus back to Céret to complete the journey they had started.

The quickest route into Spain would be through the valleys, skirting the villages of Maureillas and Les Cluses to reach the frontier town of Le Perthus. However, the presence of Gestapo and immigration controls in this area greatly increased the chances of being picked up. The preferred alternative for most smugglers was to journey south over the mountains to Las Illas and follow the narrow path known as 'Le Sentier des Trabucayres' (The Highwayman's Path), long used by bandits to cross the border at Col de Lli, a 500-metre-high pass near the hamlet of La Vajol. This hike of around 20 kilometres would not be especially difficult for Poirier, but it was an almost superhuman undertaking for a man in Peulevé's condition, and would require every ounce of his stamina and determination to stand any chance of making it.

It was dark by the time they left Céret on the evening of 21 December, but the full moon helped to illuminate their way as they joined the rocky, winding trail that led up towards the Albères mountains. With few landmarks to navigate by, the steep, densely-forested terrain became increasingly disorienting and even their guides found it difficult to keep to the right path; as the cold and the relentless pace of his companions began to take their toll, Peulevé's reliance on walking sticks made progress agonizingly painful and he had to frequently call on Poirier's help to keep up. These signs of weakness only seemed to spur their guides to race on ahead and, after reaching the pass at the border, they were told to wait for another smuggler who would lead them the rest of the way, but as the two Frenchmen quickly vanished into the night it was obvious that this was yet another scam. Guessing that they were now over the worst, Peulevé and Poirier made the decision to risk carrying on alone and after an hour's trek they began to make out the sprawling plains of Empordà emerging in the first light of dawn, marking the beginning of their slow descent into Spanish territory.

Having travelled non-stop for eleven hours since leaving Céret, Peulevé was now completely exhausted. Poirier thought it unwise to rest in case they aroused any suspicion amongst the locals, but his partner insisted that he had to find somewhere to recuperate and they entered the tiny village of Cantallops, just east of La Jonquera. Walking down the narrow main street they noticed a bus headed for Barcelona, but on boarding they were horrified to meet with the inquisitive gazes of several Guardia Civil. They immediately got off and began retracing their steps, but it was too late, there was nowhere to run and within seconds the police had caught up with them, levelling their rifles and ordering them to halt.

Unable to offer their papers for inspection (due to the danger of French nationals being returned to the Germans at the border, they had torn them up some hours before), Poirier claimed to be a Quebec-born French Canadian who had taken part in the Dieppe raid earlier that year, while Peulevé posed as Captain Hilaire Poole, an escaped British POW. The Spanish officer politely explained that they would be escorted to the British authorities in Barcelona, but that they should check in to a nearby hotel for the night. Relieved by this reaction, they invited him to dinner that evening to show their gratitude; however, during the night Poirier was surprised to find that two guards had been posted outside their door. Despite their misgivings about the situation, they reasoned that there was nothing they could do now, and were anyway too tired to attempt an escape through the window.

The next morning the Spanish officer and his men drove them towards Barcelona as agreed, though Peulevé was told that they must call at the town of Figueras on the way in order that they could

57

go through the formality of surrendering their Spanish currency to the local magistrate. After being given receipts for their money, the two men stopped at a bar where Peulevé bought drinks with the few pesetas he had been allowed to keep. They expected to have lunch at a nearby police station, but after a short journey through the centre of Figueras the car drove through the gates of what appeared to be a prison. A few moments later the courteous nature of their escorts suddenly evaporated as Peulevé and Poirier were hustled into an office where their details and fingerprints were quickly taken before they were shoved into a filthy cell with twenty others.

Having been led to believe that they would be spending Christmas in Barcelona, it was now clear that a very different fate awaited them, and their confusion and fear only intensified when they began to understand the kind of place they were in. The square prison perimeter had watchtowers installed at each corner, within which was a main building constructed with cells around the outer wall and a courtyard in the middle, used for exercising and eating. Their cell, designed to hold eight prisoners, had just a hole in the corner to serve as a latrine, and the lack of room meant that a number of men had to stand whilst the others slept. The only times when they appeared to be let out were during an hour's 'recreation' in the courtyard at ten o'clock every morning, and on Sundays, when they were obliged to attend Mass in the prison chapel. The food consisted of little more than cabbage stalks and water and most of the inmates lived in a state of perpetual hunger.

After a few hours they were taken out and lined up with other new internees, seen briefly in turn by the prison doctor, then shaved from head to foot and forced under a cold shower before being returned to their cell. The other inmates were mostly French refugees from a variety of different backgrounds, including a pilot, a few students, a factory worker, a radio commentator and a concert pianist. For them Figueras was a particularly grim place, being despised by the Republican political prisoners who held them responsible for France's failure to come to their aid during the Civil War. The jailers used this rift to their advantage, offering the Republicans a reduction in their substantial sentences if they agreed to supervise the French prisoners and do their work for them. These Spaniards would make life uncomfortable for many of Peulevé's cellmates, though he, being an Englishman, was fortunately not targeted.

Although the police officer had deliberately used a misleading story to bring Peulevé and Poirier into custody, the reason for their incarceration had been a simple one. Crossing the border without papers was an offence and the political situation of the time made it all the more likely for Allied personnel to be interned – Franco's Spain was heavily under the influence of Germany, which continually pressed for a tough line to be taken against enemy servicemen. The British Ambassador, Samuel Hoare, was well aware of the influence that the Gestapo had over the Spanish police and was constantly coming up against German encouragement of anti-British feelings within the government. His reply was to make every effort to keep relations with Spain as cordial as possible, though this inevitably meant that issues such as releasing British internees could not easily be forced, resulting in a long waiting game for those in the prisons and camps. One SOE agent stated that on average it took three months for the British embassy in Madrid to extricate one of its subjects.[13]

After their long trip into Spain, both men were now out of the war and stuck in limbo unless they could contact the British authorities. In Peulevé's case life had seemed to pose one problem after another since he'd left England and he was beginning to reach the end of his tether. However, during the fourth week one small opportunity finally presented itself when, on a routine interrogation in Governor Jefe's office, Poirier saw his interpreter giving him a communist salute. Returning the gesture, he was convinced that this must be a trap, perhaps related to the Governor's questioning in some way, but the interpreter later approached him in the courtyard during exercise, asking if he could do anything to help a fellow comrade. They managed to beg some paper and an envelope, and Peulevé wrote to the British embassy, asking the communist to post the letter for them. They could only pray that it would get through and spent their time anxiously waiting for news.

On the tenth day Peulevé and Poirier were at last summoned to the prison office where they were met by a British attaché. Peulevé's rage over their detention was apparent from the start, though Poirier managed to subdue him for long enough to explain their situation more calmly. The attaché promised to have them transferred to an officers' internment camp soon, but also made it clear that relations with the Spanish Government were difficult, and that they must bide their time whilst the embassy worked on their behalf.

Peulevé remained unimpressed, didn't expect any quick results from their diplomatic efforts, and was therefore astounded when on 2 February they were given back their personal belongings and led out to join a small group assembled in the courtyard; roped together, they were then marched through Figueras to a rail yard, where they were put aboard a freight van. After a long and uncomfortable journey they reached Barcelona in the late afternoon, where they waited for several hours before moving off again, travelling through the night without food or water. The following morning they arrived at Zaragoza, being ushered into the back of a truck and driven through the winding, mountainous roads that lead to Jaraba.

A small spa town about 70 miles south-west of Zaragoza, Jaraba had been a popular health resort during the nineteenth century, but was deserted by most of its residents when the Civil War came, making it an ideal site for a prison camp. Conditions here were much better than at Figueras: the inmates were accommodated in half a dozen hotels, usually two or three to a room, the food was reasonable and they were left almost unguarded, able to roam anywhere within the 500-metre perimeter around the town; beyond that, the surrounding mountains served as a natural barrier to discourage any escape attempt.

Peulevé found a couple of fellow agents amongst them, including a colourful character named Denis Rake (*Justin*), a 42-year-old W/T operator and one of F Section's earliest recruits. A former circus performer and music-hall singer who preferred not to carry a gun (he had managed to excuse himself from SOE's weapons training courses on the grounds that he was averse to loud bangs), Rake had originally landed on the Riviera in May 1942 destined for the HECKLER circuit in Lyon, but he was arrested a few weeks later when he attempted to cross into the occupied zone. His subsequent adventures, which included an affair with a German officer in Paris, eventually led him to Marseille, Perpignan and finally into Spanish territory, being held at Genova, Figueras and the notorious concentration camp at Miranda del Ebro, before his transfer to Jaraba. Peulevé was also introduced to a middle-aged PWE agent, Henri-Paul Le Chêne (*Victor*), who had organized PLANE, a minor French circuit around Clermont-Ferrand, and was now acting as the camp's British commanding officer. The sociable Rake was easy enough to get along with, but most found Le Chêne an unscrupulous character, Poirier describing him as 'a peculiar individual'[14] and Rake simply as 'a big liar'.[15]

Within a few days of Peulevé's arrival, Michael Cresswell, an attaché from the British consulate, visited the camp to keep them informed on progress. Cresswell was an important element of MI 9's presence in Spain (MI 9 aided Allied personnel in escape and evasion across occupied Europe), helping many to elude the Spanish authorities, though he emphasized to Peulevé that they would have to wait for things to improve politically before any definite plans for his release could be expected. As Spain was largely pro-German at this time Britain had continually tried to persuade the Franco government that the Axis powers would eventually be defeated, and that it was in Spain's interests to remain on good terms with the Allies. However, since much of the news of the war in the Spanish press came from German sources, progress was slow and Hoare found that 'with the Germans in virtual charge of Madrid, persistence became my stock in trade.'[16] While Cresswell pointed out that attempts to escape would be counter-productive, he was at least able to offer money to make their stay more comfortable, Peulevé receiving 600 pesetas.

Being interned at Jaraba was not an unpleasant experience when compared with the lot of Allied prisoners elsewhere. Rake's recollections suggest a lifestyle without any hardship: 'We spent a lot of time bathing in the hot springs. We fished quite a lot. We invited one another to our hotels for a meal. In the evenings we used to go to the local café and very often Spanish singers would come to entertain us.'[17] Time drifted by in this forgotten backwater – feeling so far removed from the war some inmates became careless and openly talked about their clandestine work in France. However, this aimlessness was at odds with Peulevé's plans and after spending six weeks in Jaraba the lack of any news was once again pushing his patience to breaking point. In late March, another visit from a British delegate restated the familiar orders of military attaché Brigadier Torr – little could be done at the moment and they would eventually be released when diplomatic relations improved – but Peulevé had had enough. Having already spent three months in Spanish custody, he retracted his promise not to attempt to escape and started saving his weekly allowance. He would now get out of Jaraba using his own methods.

A French journalist named Jacques Pecheral had already given him an idea of how he might be able to reach Madrid. The medical

61

officer of the camp would sometimes refer patients for treatment or assessment by the board at a hospital in Zaragoza, and though guards would accompany them to the waiting room they would not return until called for by the doctor, which offered ample time to escape. Pecheral had already planned to ask the MO to let him see a dentist and, inspired by his idea, Peulevé started limping around the camp, using his previous injury as a useful excuse for needing to see a surgeon. Having established good terms with the Spanish doctor, Peulevé had no problem in obtaining dispensation to join Pecheral on his hospital visit. They left on 11 April, the guards escorting them into Zaragoza and leaving Peulevé in a clinic as expected. Waiting for a few minutes in case they returned, he then quietly made his way out of the hospital and down the street. Hailing a taxi, Peulevé told the driver that he was a German pilot and that he should take him to Madrid.

Peulevé had not wished to leave Poirier behind, so it was arranged that if the escape was successful he would wait at a specified point on the Zaragoza-Madrid highway until three o'clock. Poirier managed to evade the guards and hiked across the mountains to the rendezvous, arriving before the agreed time, though as the minutes ticked by it became apparent that he was waiting in vain. It later turned out that they had only just missed each other – having arrived slightly earlier at the same spot Peulevé had waited for as long as he dared, but the taxi driver had started to become suspicious of the situation, leaving him no choice but to continue on without his friend. The only compensation was that Poirier managed to re-enter the camp without the guards being alerted to his wasted excursion.

Having kept up the flimsy pretence of being an airman trying to reach the German embassy, Peulevé was told by the driver that he could stop overnight with a family that lived nearby. His stay passed without incident and as they drove through the city the next morning Peulevé suddenly asked to be taken to the British embassy instead; the driver was confused but complied anyway, more interested in being reimbursed for his considerable journey. After explaining his story to Major Haslam and the embassy staff there were some signs of disapproval, as an escape was bound to cause problems with the Governor at Jaraba and make the Ambassador's life more difficult. Similar irritation had also been witnessed by Rake, who despite being released through official channels was berated by Hoare, who exclaimed, 'Really, I think sometimes you SOE people are more trouble than you're worth.'[18]

Now out of Spanish hands, there was still the problem of getting to the coast and back to England. Peulevé was provided with identity papers stating that he was a deaf mute in order to avoid language problems, and though there is little information regarding his sixteen-hour train journey from Madrid to Algeciras, he appears to have made his way into Gibraltar without a problem, taking a room at the Rock Hotel. (Peulevé unexpectedly found Pecheral staying there along with Rake, who had been released from Jaraba with Le Chêne at the end of March.) After a few days experiencing the novelty of freedom again he was issued with a British passport under the name of Harry Poole and put aboard one of fourteen troop carriers belonging to convoy MKF 13, a motley collection of converted luxury liners led by the SS *Franconia* that had just arrived from Algiers.

Shepherded by an equally mixed bag of sloops and other naval vessels, the first half of the trip proved to be uneventful, but as the convoy passed the north-west coast of Spain on 29 April, it was attacked by two German anti-shipping aircraft and subjected to three further raids later that evening, though none of the ships was seriously damaged. Peulevé landed on the Clyde on 2 May; exhausted but relieved to be home again, he was quickly handed over to SOE's staff. Once back in London he reported to Buckmaster at Orchard Court, who recalled his first words as, 'Sorry I made a mess of it ... When can I go back and try again?'[19]

Chapter 6

Violette

Whilst waiting to be debriefed Peulevé was moved to one of F Section's safe houses, a flat on Elvaston Place in South Kensington, where he was able to restore some of the considerable weight he had lost in Spain. During his interrogations at Orchard Court he gave detailed descriptions of his experiences and his opinions on the CARTE fiasco, but having left the Cote d'Azur six months previously his information was by then somewhat out of date. It would be some time before he could return to France; nonetheless, Buckmaster wanted to get Peulevé back to full strength as quickly as possible, and by 18 May had begun making plans for him to attend paramilitary and W/T refresher courses.

Following some leave he travelled up to the Highlands to begin the first of these at Arisaig (STS 21), about 10 miles west of Meoble, on 2 June. It lasted just two weeks, after which he returned to London to an unexpected reunion with Poirier, who had arrived in England at the end of May. Released from Jaraba shortly after Peulevé's escape, he'd flown from Gibraltar to Bristol, fortunately avoiding the previous flight which was shot down by a German fighter over Portugal, killing all of its occupants. Told to surrender his passport only to SOE personnel, he was greeted with suspicion by MI5 and quickly taken off to the Royal Patriotic School in Wandsworth, a detention centre for those entering into the country with a questionable background. It took several days for F Section to catch up with him, but he eventually arrived at Orchard Court where Buckmaster informed him that his training would be starting immediately. As a security precaution his French background was to be kept a secret and his new identity, 'Jack Peters', was added to the General List as a junior officer in the British Army.

Peulevé advised him not to bother with the hotel Vera Atkins had booked him into, recommending that he take a room at the Pastoria instead, on the south side of Leicester Square. A preferred choice over the accommodation offered by SOE, it was a favourite of Peulevé's and several other F Section agents; Rake was particularly fond of it for its menus, recalling that 'Throughout the war the food at Pastori's [the hotel owner] was miraculous. That is honestly the only word I can use to describe it, for how it was done I cannot conceive.'[1] Having caught up with each other's recent news, there was an opportunity for Peulevé to spend some time acquainting Poirier with his favourite nightspots in the West End, although the younger man had some trouble in keeping up, having only got drunk for the first time after his release in Madrid.

Some days before leaving for his W/T course Peulevé spent an evening with the widow of an RAF pilot at the Studio Club in Knightsbridge, where he was introduced to a vivacious, petite and very attractive dark-haired girl from south London. Close to her twenty-second birthday, Violette Szabó (née Bushell) had been born in Paris to an English father and French mother, and like Peulevé grew up spending time in London, the Midlands and northern France, though her family finally settled in Stockwell when she was eleven. Working as a shop assistant in Brixton after the outbreak of war, Violette's tomboyish and headstrong nature had compelled her to join one of the Services, but she was instead persuaded by a friend to work in the fields with the Land Army. Still with a mind to do something more vital she returned to London in July 1940, where she met a dashing French Foreign Legion officer, Etienne Szabó; they married in August, and a year later she was at last able to enlist with the Auxiliary Territorial Service (ATS), serving as a gunner on an AA battery. Violette was discharged in the spring of 1942 and gave birth to a daughter, Tania, in June, but just four months later she too became a widow, when Etienne was killed while serving in North Africa.

Peulevé's partner spoke very good French and he later forwarded her name to Orchard Court for consideration as a potential recruit, but she was deemed a security risk on the grounds of her Italian parentage. However, during her interview she mentioned that her friend Violette might be a more suitable candidate, and after being cleared by security on 1 July she was passed on to Selwyn Jepson, F Section's recruiting officer. Feeling a great need to fight back after the recent death of her husband, she volunteered herself immediately and was accepted by Jepson for training as a courier. By accident, Peulevé's recommendation had resulted in a completely different outcome than the one he had imagined and would have fateful consequences for both him and Violette.

F Section had begun using women agents in mid-1942. Though some in SOE had moral reservations about the question of recruiting females, there was also a problem of legality – women were not recognized as combatants by the Geneva Convention and were therefore completely unprotected if captured. Gubbins skirted around this problem by using the FANY (First Aid Nursing Yeomanry) as cover. SOE had employed FANYs since its inception as signallers, coders, drivers, telephonists, clerks and training section staff, and it was thought that agents attached to this organization could claim 'cap-badge' status if arrested behind enemy lines to avoid being treated as a spy. It also meant that SOE could disguise its activities from the British public, creating an innocuous front for women who were 'specially employed'.

Most were picked to become couriers, as they were considered less likely to attract the suspicion of German patrols as they delivered messages from village to village, but a few served as wireless operators and a couple even became organizers. They were trained in the same way as their male counterparts and would be liable to the same penalties if caught, yet they often showed equal, if not greater, courage when put under pressure. In the course of the war F Section sent thirty-nine women to France, approximately 8 per cent of the total number of agents infiltrated. Thirteen did not return.

After completing his short W/T course at Thame Park, Peulevé ran into Violette again, though this time she was wearing a FANY uniform. Whether he concluded that she had been recruited by F Section immediately, or later came across other evidence to confirm his suspicions, isn't clear, though she stuck to her cover story that she was working as a driver. As the month progressed they began to see more of each other, going out to their favourite nightclubs and restaurants, talking into the early hours; yet the closer they became, the more Peulevé became frustrated by the necessary deception required of them. They now belonged to the same secret organization but could not say a word to each other about who they really were, or the extraordinary dangers they would both soon be facing.

Having completed his refresher courses, Peulevé was considered ready to begin preparation for his second mission, this time as an organizer of a new circuit in the rural Corrèze department of west-central France. Its aim, as a 1943 directive from the Chiefs of Staff stated, was to make 'a special effort towards supplying the resistance groups ... with the means enabling them to play an active part when they are required to do so in support of Allied strategy'.[2] In effect this meant training and arming the Resistance to be ready to offer guerrilla support when the Second Front came, cutting lines of communications and hampering German attempts to mobilize their forces. Sabotage would be a vital aspect of this work and in order to gain specialist knowledge of the subject Peulevé began a three-week demolitions course in mid-July at STS 17, sited on the Brickendonbury Estate near Hertford.

Specifically designed to teach agents how to carry out industrial sabotage, the course was led by George Rheam, who before the war had worked for the Central Electricity Board. A tall, serious man, he followed the rules that other training schools had sought to instil in their pupils, namely to achieve an objective in the simplest and most effective way. The key lay in teaching agents to survey a target carefully and concentrate on its weak points, rather than attempting to blow an entire installation to bits – charges placed on the frames of machinery made from cast iron rather than steel obviated the need for large amounts of explosives, whilst a hammer blow to a single component of a locomotive, or bolts secreted into the gearing of a crane could result in damage requiring weeks or months to repair. Peulevé received a favourable report from this course, the instructor remarking that 'Although this student has not previously worked in industry he was quick at picking up the essentials and showed an intelligent appreciation of the special features,' later adding that he had the subject 'well under control'.[3]

F Section had come a long way since the summer of 1942 when Peulevé had left on his first mission, and was now operating twenty-four circuits across France; however, it had not yet dedicated any of its organizers to developing resistance in the Corrèze. In an attempt to extend the reach of his SCIENTIST circuit around Bordeaux, Peulevé's old partner Claude de Baissac had reconnoitred the region and found that its terrain was ideally suited to guerrilla activity, but local resistance groups were in desperate need of money and arms. Sending a report to London in July 1943, he advised that they would need close supervision and support if they were to become an effective force, recommending that another organizer and W/T operator be introduced to manage the situation more closely.

During talks following his recall to London the following month, Buckmaster agreed with de Baissac's assessment but wanted to take the Corrèze completely out of his hands – the growth of SCIENTIST, which now ran from the edge of Poitiers down the Atlantic seaboard towards the Spanish frontier, was beginning to pose serious dangers to its own security and could not be allowed to expand further. Peulevé's new circuit would therefore be starting from scratch, fulfilling an important role in linking the existing PIMENTO and WHEELWRIGHT circuits to its south, SCIENTIST in the west and STATIONER, covering the Haute-Vienne, Indre and Creuse departments to the north. Although de Baissac had been eager to retain personal command of the Corrèze, he approved the appointment of Peulevé as his successor and handed over the details of the contacts he'd already made.

Aside from F Section's expansion, French resistance had been affected by several important changes during 1943. The movement of German troops into the Vichy zone had largely disposed of any remaining illusion of French independence under Pétain, and the increasing German demand for labour after the introduction of the *relève* had led to the deeply unpopular STO (*Service du Travail Obligatoire*), the compulsory deportation of French workers introduced in February. Another equally loathed and feared creation was the *milice*, a ruthless paramilitary body formed from French volunteers and headed by Nazi sympathizer Joseph Darnand. Officially responsible for targeting elements in society deemed anti-social such as black marketeers and communists, it was equally likely to carry out raids against *résistants*, Jews, *réfractaires* (men who had gone into hiding to avoid the STO draft) and anyone else it considered potentially subversive. As these *miliciens* had a greater local knowledge than their German counterparts their presence inevitably made life more dangerous for SOE's agents, but news of indiscriminate attacks on civilians, compounded by the miseries of the occupation and the clear collaboration of Vichy's ministers also led to increasing support for the resistance.

At the beginning of the year *Combat*, *Franc-Tireur* and *Libération-Sud* had agreed to merge to form a new organization, the *Mouvements Unis de la Résistance* (MUR), which took its direction from de Gaulle. The MUR employed regional chiefs to delegate its orders amongst local groups and its military wing, the *Armée Secrète* (AS) became one of the major Resistance powers in France, only rivalled by the communist FTP. Through the spring these politically opposed forces began to establish the first 'maquis', small guerrilla groups that lived in the relative safety of the hills and forests, taking their name from the Corsican word for the thick scrub found along the Mediterranean coast. Although willing to fight, they were very poorly equipped and mostly without training or arms. The maquis were to be the focus of Peulevé's attentions in the Corrèze – by arranging supply drops and instructing them on how best to use weapons and explosives, they would be the means to carry out sabotage and *coups de main* (surprise attacks) on local enemy targets in the months before D-Day, and provide an underground army capable of holding up German units when an Allied invasion finally arrived.

Towards the end of August, Poirier returned to London, having just completed his training at Arisaig. He was accompanied by one of his fellow students, Cyril Watney, a twenty-year-old Signals officer whose family had known his before the war, whilst living at Beaulieu-sur-Mer on the Riviera. With no relatives in England, Poirier soon became an adopted member of the Watney family and often stayed with them at their home in south London. After being introduced to Peulevé, Watney was so impressed that he asked to be assigned as W/T operator on his forthcoming mission, even though he had yet to complete his training. Buckmaster unsurprisingly vetoed the idea, as Peulevé was one of the few organizers capable of doubling as a wireless operator and Watney could be put to better uses. However, he acknowledged his friend by choosing a similar surname, 'Pontlevé', for his cover, and would cross Peulevé's path again in France.

Violette had meanwhile left London to undergo a SOE student assessment course at Winterfold in Surrey while Peulevé was attending his sabotage training, but he was able to see her when she returned at the end of the month. Despite his joy at their reunion, their secret lives continued to require more excuses from each other and Peulevé found it increasingly difficult to keep up their charade, later commenting on how their 'pathetic pretence saddened me, especially as our relationship had become extremely intimate. I had to go back to France without being able to tell her, and she also had to go without being able to tell me.'[4]

There has been some debate over the years as to how far Peulevé's romantic involvement with Szabó actually went. That he had fallen in love is obvious from his own writings, though exactly what her feelings were towards him is more difficult to fathom, and it's impossible to be sure that she perceived their relationship in the same terms. Considering that she had lost her husband only a few months before their first meeting, she may not have wished to become involved with another man so soon; alternatively she might have harboured fears about the possibility of another loss in her life if she committed herself again. Nevertheless it's clear that, even when compared with other celebrated figures within SOE's ranks, these two people possessed unusually impressive personalities, being driven by the same overwhelming need to prove themselves, and that a strong bond had developed between them in the few weeks they had known each other.

As the time came for Peulevé to leave for France, he told Violette that he was to be posted to the Middle East. She 'consolingly replied that she would be still driving the General'[5] when he returned, though he knew that her training must be about to start. In order for his posting to appear genuine, Peulevé wrote a series of love letters and handed them to Vera Atkins at Orchard Court – these were to be mailed at regular intervals from Cairo and Beirut during the time he was away, though it's not known whether Szabó ever received them. He stuck to the same story when visiting his parents, now living at Saxby in Suffolk, though he secretly confided in his sister, telling her that if he were captured he would probably be put up against a wall and shot.

The decision to send Peulevé alone to the Corrèze would inevitably make his job more laborious, but it also meant that he had no one to worry about except himself. Poirier had been agreed as his assistant and would follow as soon as his training was completed, with additional agents being dropped once the foundations for the circuit were established. As on his first mission, he was to travel under the name of 'Henri Chevalier', and would be known by the new codename of *Jean*. The new circuit would be named AUTHOR.

Chapter 7

Grandclément

Peulevé's leg injury had now completely healed, but being parachuted into France again was out of the question. The alternative
was to travel by Lysander, a single-engined, high-wing monoplane
originally used for coastal reconnaissance and as a spotter for
artillery units. 'Lizzies' were slow and heavy but had the significant
advantages of being very strong and capable of landing on short
grass airstrips, making them ideal for SOE's clandestine operations.
They were adapted for special operations by adding a passenger
ladder to the side of the fuselage and a long-range fuel tank underneath, though limited cabin space behind the pilot's seat still meant
that only two agents (or three at a push) could be accommodated per
flight. Peulevé was to be flown to a field near Angers in north-
western France, from where he would make his way to Paris to meet
one of de Baissac's contacts, André Grandclément (*Bernard*). As
leader of the *Organisation Civile et Militaire* (OCM) movement for
Bordeaux and the south-west, Grandclément's substantial network
could then pass him into the Corrèze to meet with its Resistance
leaders.

September's full moon had already passed when Peulevé arrived
at Orchard Court to report for the final time. Accompanied by his
conducting officer, André Simon, he made his way into the small
courtyard below where he met two other F Section agents, a 32-year-
old, dark-haired, Swiss woman with striking features, Yolande
Beekman (*Yvonne*), and Harry Despaigne (*Ulysse*), who had been
involved with CARTE the previous year; they were also joined by a
gruff, serious-looking, Alsatian Lieutenant named Henri Derringer
(*Toinot*) and his French conducting officer, both from RF Section's
headquarters at Dorset Square. With the six of them squashed into
two waiting staff cars, they made their way out of London towards
Tangmere.

Just a few miles from Chichester, RAF Tangmere was used by 161 Squadron as a forward base for Lysander operations, enabling pilots to make the best of the aircraft's limited range. As was customary for agents travelling on this route, both cars stopped at the Spread Eagle hotel at Midhurst where Peulevé and his fellow agents spent an hour in the cellar bar, helping themselves to a few large whiskies before carrying on. Arriving at the station in the early evening, they were shepherded into an ivy-covered brick building opposite the base's main entrance; discreetly shielded by tall hedges and entered via a back door, the eighteenth-century Tangmere Cottage was used specifically to house the Squadron's pilots and agents being ferried to and from France. As on the eve of his first mission they were all treated to a lavish dinner, although the Commanding Officer's generosity with his best claret could not help but remind Peulevé of the disaster that had beset him and de Baissac after the same hospitality at Tempsford.

As they readied themselves to leave, the conducting officers checked every inch of the agents' clothing for any sign of English origin before issuing their kit, which in Peulevé's case included his cipher keys and silks, wireless crystals, nearly a million francs hidden in several large tins of digestive and kidney powders, a stiletto and a revolver, along with a flask of rum and a thermos of coffee for the journey. His 'L' tablets had been already sewn into the lapels of his suit in London, and a wireless set would be supplied later via Grandclément's network. Though he would only be carrying a single suitcase, Beekman and Despaigne were also issued with cases containing new 'B2' wireless sets, lighter than previous models but still bulky items in the cramped rear of a Lysander

The pilots for this flight were Wing Commander Bob Hodges and Flying Officer Jimmy Bathgate, and the operation, code-named 'Milliner', was to land at a designated field between the villages of Le Vieux Briollay and Villevêque, just a few miles north-east of Angers. Walking out to the two waiting aircraft, Beekman was to accompany Despaigne, with Peulevé and Derringer in the second. Bathgate did not inspire confidence in his passengers, telling Peulevé that he would be following Hodges' aircraft as he was not familiar with this particular landing ground (Bathgate was a relative newcomer, having only joined the Squadron the previous month after transfer from Transport Command). However it was a clear night, and once both aircraft were airborne they quickly passed Selsey Bill and were over the Channel. Flying low over the French coast to avoid radar detection, they hedge-hopped over the fields of Normandy, watching the flickering lights from blacked-out villages pass by in the darkness.

They encountered more cloud as they flew deeper into France, but Peulevé thought he recognized a more distinct silhouette through the rear of the canopy and warned the pilot on the intercom. Taking steps to shake off any possible pursuer Bathgate banked and climbed steeply, and a few seconds later Peulevé reported that it had disappeared, though the evasive manoeuvres had directed them away from Hodges and they were now in danger of becoming lost. Making contact using his VHF radio, Hodges told Bathgate that he would switch on his landing lights as a means of signalling to the wayward Lysander and after a few nervous minutes Bathgate sighted him once again, circling over the torchlights of the reception committee below, arranged in a mirrored 'L' shape.

Prior to an air operation those organizing the reception would be given a specific Morse recognition signal to flash up at the incoming aircraft (on this occasion it was 'SC'). After confirming that the code was correct and answering with the pre-arranged reply of 'RA', Bathgate hurriedly told his passengers to prepare for landing and began making his approach, steeply descending over some tall trees at the threshold of the field and landing parallel to the long upright of the L on the improvised grass runway. At 12.45 am both Lysanders were safely on the ground but were vulnerable every minute they spent waiting, and with the engines still running Peulevé and his companion quickly slid back the canopy and scrambled down the ladder while the reception committee unloaded the luggage. As soon as they were all out no fewer than six agents were waiting to board for the return flight, including one of SOE's most successful organizers, Ben Cowburn (*Germain*); John Goldsmith (*Valentin*, an agent previously attached to the CARTE circuit); and Rémy Clément (*Marc*), who worked for one of F Section's most controversial figures, Henri Déricourt.

Born in 1909, Déricourt had begun his aviation career as an aerobatic pilot before joining French postal courier *Air Bleu* in 1935. After the armistice he continued to fly civilian aircraft in and out of the unoccupied zone until 1942, when he managed to escape to England via Gibraltar, having been secretly offered the chance of a job with the airline BOAC; on arrival he enlisted with the RAF instead, and in November was transferred to 161 Squadron. Whilst at Tempsford he met André Simon and before the end of the year

SOE had taken him on for the job of Air Operations Officer, his task being to find and manage secret landing grounds for F Section's Lysander operations. Code-named *Gilbert*, he was dropped close to Orléans in January 1943, and by mid-March his small FARRIER circuit had achieved its first successful action, receiving two aircraft at a field near Poitiers. He continued to ferry agents in and out of France through the summer, with 'Milliner' being FARRIER's twelfth pick-up operation that year; however, what Peulevé and the group did not know was that Déricourt had been in collusion with the Gestapo for some time. Although the nature and circumstances of *Gilbert*'s relationship with the Germans has been the cause of much discussion, it's clear that mailbags bound for London containing circuit reports and other correspondence were intercepted with his help. Déricourt was also aware that Parisian gangsters working for the Nazi security services were secretly trailing agents from his landing grounds, in order to gain intelligence on the networks they were to join.

Within five minutes of their arrival the Lysanders had taken off again, leaving Déricourt to briefly introduce himself and request each of them to hand over their pistols as a security measure, in case they were stopped by a German patrol. He then told the group that they would be making their way along the vineyard paths using bicycles to reach the main road, where they would wait until the early morning when the curfew would be lifted. Unfortunately Beekman had never ridden a bicycle before and had to accompany Déricourt on a tandem. Peulevé was completely nonplussed, finding it impossible to believe that after all the training undergone through SOE's schools, an agent would not be able to ride a bike.

After securing their suitcases on racks they moved off, and after an uncomfortable and wearisome journey of several miles the group at last collapsed into a circle, all of them reaching for their rum flasks. As they caught their breath Déricourt began enquiring about a consignment of francs he was expecting, but unfortunately nobody had been given any money to deliver. This oversight caused him to explode with rage, 'expressing his grave doubts as to the sanity and parentage of those safely ensconced in London',[1] though the rum eventually mollified his invective. They continued to wait in the field by the road until six o'clock, when they were able to resume their journey towards the town of Angers. Along the way they had to overtake a column of German soldiers, and on first sight of the enemy Beekman was so nervous that she lost her balance, causing her to drive the tandem off the road and into a hedge. The sight of her legs in the air met with whistles and shouts from the soldiers, though an NCO came to her aid and helped her back onto the bicycle, making a point of resecuring her suitcase that had slipped off the rack; only later did she mention to the group that it had contained her wireless set.

Arriving at Angers, they sat in a bistro opposite the station drinking acorn coffee while Déricourt gave them instructions to take the seven o'clock train, making it clear that they should travel separately. He also arranged to meet Peulevé, Despaigne and Beekman again the following morning at the Café Monte Carlo off the Champs Elysées, where he would brief them on any relevant news concerning their circuits and destinations (Derringer was to make his own way out of Paris, to begin a RF circuit in the Vosges mountains in eastern France). The group having split up to board the arriving train, Peulevé clambered into a busy carriage and squeezed into the only space left in the corridor; feeling the exertions of the previous hours he sat on his suitcase and dozed off with his head on the window. On two occasions he was asked to move aside by passengers wishing to pass; only half-awake, he absent-mindedly mumbled 'sorry' in English, though thankfully it passed unnoticed and he completed the rest of the trip without incident.

Arriving at Gare Montparnasse in the afternoon, he gave his luggage to a porter to carry to the entrance, in order to bypass the 'economic control' which inspected Parisians for black market goods brought in to supplement their meagre rations in the city. Walking out of the station, Peulevé waited for the porter to appear; when he failed to do so, he went back inside to see his opened case sitting on the counter of the control and he was asked by the inspector to explain why he was carrying so many tins of stomach and kidney powders. Unfazed by the situation, he replied that in these days of rationing he had become a victim of acute dyspepsia and bladder trouble, and so always carried a good supply of remedies. Taking one of the large tins containing several hundred thousand francs, the inspector shook it, looked inside, and smelt the powder. Satisfied with his search, he checked Peulevé's papers and let him go. Having been subjected to so many spot-checks during his first mission, he showed no signs of apprehension when questioned by a policeman, and casually made his way towards the exit.

Looking for a hotel for the night, he was faced with another security consideration – although it was easiest to take a room some-

75

where close to the station, these were obvious targets for German searches in the pursuit of any Frenchman on the run. However, he was very tired, and walking across the street he entered a small hotel which appeared unremarkable, until he recognized the sound of a BBC French Service news bulletin emanating from under the counter. There were serious penalties for playing such broadcasts and Peulevé was taking a risk even standing in the hallway, let alone staying there as a resident. However, in the same moment a woman appeared and asked what he wanted.

Showing him a modestly furnished room upstairs, she returned a few minutes later asking him to fill in a *fiche* (hotel registration form), which he knew would very likely be checked by the local police later that evening. Having filled out his details according to his false identity the woman returned and, glancing at his suitcase, commented, 'One can see that you have come a long way, Monsieur. Have a good night's sleep.' It was obvious that despite SOE's best efforts the case bore signs of English provenance, and it occurred to Peulevé that it was possible that other agents might have stayed there and had perhaps even been arrested; yet the fearlessness of the hotelier playing her radio at full volume left him feeling strangely secure. Taking the precaution of placing his revolver under the pillow he soon fell asleep and despite a fitful night did not receive any German visitors. Waking early the next morning, he checked out and went to meet Déricourt as planned.

Walking through the streets of Paris in 1943 was an unnerving experience for anyone who had known the city before the war. After the invasion many affluent Parisians had left for the southern un-occupied zone, reducing the population to just one million, a third of its pre-war size. Civilian motor traffic had also disappeared from the streets owing to the scarcity of petrol (making it possible to drive the length of the city in ten minutes), being replaced by the use of bicycles and *vélo-taxis* (rickshaws), directed by German road signs that stood on every corner. Unlike those in the country who might have access to local produce, city dwellers also had to queue for everything, while increasing numbers of laws sought to constrict their ability to do the simplest things: travelling, shopping or using public services were now activities controlled by detailed regula-tions, with special restrictions being imposed on Jewish citizens. The police could also instigate *rafles* or round-ups, suddenly cordoning off an area without warning and deporting all men who could not prove their exemption from the STO.

Passing through this sombre imitation of the capital, Peulevé was quickly reacquainted with the familiar feeling of being in the midst of the enemy, walking past soldiers dressed in all varieties of uniform and rank, knowing that he was always only a hair's breadth away from arrest. Although he was well aware of a constant need to stay alert, he couldn't help feeling a certain sense of equivocation when considering the purpose of his mission:

All the training in the world would never make me the detached, semi-human, cold plumber sent to do that job. I saw Germans in the street that looked just like any British soldier, enjoying a spot of leave, taking a beer in a bistro, strolling around the streets of Paris like a lot of tourists. It had been drummed into me that every dead one was a trick to us, and as I walked passing them that morning towards the café from which I had to make my contact, I thought that it would have been so much nicer if I could have gone up to some of them and introduced myself as another foreigner enjoying the sights to be seen in the City of Lights. But even our mild British brain washing made all of them appear as monsters and with a gloating pride I walked passed them thinking that the least corporal could get instant promotion by just grabbing me and hustling me into the nearest Gestapo centre.[2]

Perhaps these ponderings had the effect of slowing down his journey, for he arrived late at the café and found it deserted. Considering Déricourt's association with the Germans, this may have been fortuitous; certainly Despaigne, who had arrived on time, had been shocked when Déricourt started to bombard him with questions about the details of his mission, though he had no intention of supplying him with any information. It may have been that he and Beekman were under German surveillance as they left the café, though it made little difference to the fate of their circuits. Despaigne successfully made contact with DETECTIVE in the Carcassonne area and would live to see France liberated, but Beekman was not so fortunate. Joining the northern MUSICIAN circuit based around St Quentin, she and her Canadian organizer Gustave Biéler (*Guy*) were arrested four months later when a local German D/F team finally closed in on the source of her wireless signal. Deported to Germany, she was executed at Dachau concentration camp in September 1944 along with three other F Section women agents,

Madeleine Damerment (*Solange*), Eliane Plewman (*Gaby*) and Noor Inayat Khan (*Madeleine*).

Using the café's telephone, Peulevé rang one of the contact numbers he had been given in London, letting it ring three times before hanging up, then ringing again. Giving the pre-arranged password, he received instructions on how to find the address and was told to arrive at seven that evening for dinner. Taking the *Métro* (one form of transport that had remained relatively unaffected by the occupation) he arrived at 2 Avenue Champaubert, just a few hundred metres south of the Eiffel Tower in the fifteenth *arrondissement*, the address of an ex-French Army major named Marc O'Neill (despite his surname, O'Neill was French by birth, his family having emigrated from Ireland in the eighteenth century). Operating under the false name of Marc Blatin and code-named *Tyrone*, O'Neill had originally been responsible for the OCM's Parisian operations and now was running a sizable SCIENTIST sub-circuit, assisted by another of de Baissac's W/T operators, an impetuous young Glaswegian engineering student named Marcel Défence (*Dédé*). More importantly for Peulevé, he was also the letter box through which he would contact O'Neill's colleague and old friend André Grandclément. However, as soon as Peulevé entered the flat it became obvious that something was seriously wrong, and in an agitated state O'Neill explained that the Gestapo had arrested Grandclément at the Café Monte Carlo on Avenue de Wagram earlier that day, just minutes before he had planned to meet him.

This was an important coup for the Germans and a great loss for SCIENTIST. The son of a famous French admiral, Grandclément had seemed destined for a military career but was forced to retire from the Army after contracting tuberculosis in 1934. Despite his weakened constitution André still managed to return to his unit and served with distinction during the German offensive at Sedan in May 1940; returning to Bordeaux after demobilization, he then set about creating a Resistance group named '*Le Groupe Ouest*', which he constructed using his job as a travelling insurance agent as cover, arranging secret meetings with hundreds of ex-officers based in the Gironde and several neighbouring departments. Agreeing to incorporate his following into the south-western division of the OCM movement in 1942, it was only a matter of time before his organization came to the attentions of SOE, and initial contact was eventually made through the organizer of the Paris BRICKLAYER circuit, France Antelme (*Renaud*), who suggested a meeting with Claude de Baissac at the beginning of the following year.

A partnership between Grandclément and de Baissac promised the supply of British resources to several thousand OCM members, and a substantial force for SCIENTIST to mobilize in the event of a possible Allied landing later that year; agreeing to work together, de Baissac began to concentrate most of his efforts on arming Grandclément's men. Contrary to London's directive to form small coordinated bands of *résistants* able to carry out sabotage actions on local targets, SCIENTIST's OCM alliance soon created a huge underground army of more than 20,000 men across south-western France, and by August 1943 it had received over a 120 supply drops, delivering 7,500 Stens, 300 Bren machine guns, 1,500 rifles and more than 18,000 pounds of explosives.

Such high levels of activity were bound to attract attention and Grandclément's name was eventually given away by a group of *résistants* arrested in mid-July. Although he was in Paris at the time, Grandclément's wife Lucette had been visiting Bordeaux and was also taken by the Gestapo; a raid on their apartment in turn led to the discovery of a photograph of her husband, along with a list of his OCM and other Resistance contacts, loosely disguised to resemble an index of André's business clients. The real nature of these names quickly led to perhaps as many as 250 arrests across Bordeaux,[3] and Grandclément's identification and subsequent arrest in Paris now left O'Neill with no option but to disappear before the Germans arrived.

This sudden change of circumstances left Peulevé with a difficult choice. His only route to the Corrèze was through the OCM network in the south-west, and continuing with the mission would mean risking contact with 'blown' (exposed) contacts that may well be under surveillance by the Germans. The alternative was to abandon his objectives and return to England, either by air, across the Channel or through Spain again. For another agent this decision might have been a simpler one – even though leaving France would be difficult, to become entangled in a collapsing circuit was asking for trouble.

Yet thoughts about this being the 'last chance to wipe the slate clean'[4] preyed heavily on Peulevé's mind – were he to turn back now, the sense of failure would be unbearable. Though he knew it ran counter to his training Peulevé felt that he must press on and began discussing alternative travel arrangements. O'Neill had had contact with Charles Corbin, a middle-aged police inspector working with SCIENTIST's new organizer Roger Landes, now using the code name *Aristide*. (Landes had arrived in October 1942 as a replacement W/T operator for Peulevé and took de Baissac's role after his return to London in August.) If Peulevé could enlist the help of Landes in Bordeaux, there might be a possibility of finding a way into the Corrèze before Grandclément's organization was completely compromised.

Taking the train for Bordeaux, he would now have to move very cautiously to avoid any traps that the Gestapo might set. Eventually reaching his destination at six the next evening, he wearily walked out of the Gare Saint-Jean and saw a young man being stopped by a German soldier, who asked him to open his suitcase. Suddenly pulling out a pistol, he shot the guard and made a run for the tram leaving a few yards in front of the station; two other soldiers started to fire at him, but he managed to board it unharmed. As the tram carried the *résistant* away from the scene it appeared that he had got away successfully, but a few minutes later the conductor found him dead, slouched in one of the seats. It turned out that his case contained a wireless set that he'd just transported from Paris; having been stopped he decided to take the German with him before swallowing his 'L' tablet to avoid capture. The guards on the tram had been changing at that moment – had he not taken his own life, he would have stood a good chance of getting away.

This commotion was enough for the Germans to round up everyone in the vicinity and question them thoroughly. Already on edge due to the sudden change in his plans, Peulevé did his best to hold his nerve as he explained that he was a purchasing agent exporting goods to Germany, and produced several documents to prove his story. Combined with his elegant attire and some fast talking, this was enough to satisfy the interrogator and with great relief he was waved on and swiftly walked away from the crowd.

One of the addresses that Peulevé had been given in London was that of the Café des Chartrons, overlooking the River Garonne on the Quai des Chartrons; run by a man called Bertrand, it served as a letter box for the SCIENTIST circuit. However, since de Baissac's departure the café had come under Gestapo surveillance and Peulevé was about to walk straight into their trap. Landes, who had been informed of Peulevé's imminent arrival, was planning to intercept him at the train station before he got to the café, which he knew to be blown. Unfortunately there was some confusion over the date of

Peulevé's arrival, which meant Landes having to keep a more or less constant lookout to save him from certain disaster. Luckily he was able to recognize his old training partner as he walked away from the station and moments later also ran into Alain Boyau (*Alain*), an OCM liaison agent who had by chance been travelling on the same train, though the latter decided to return to Paris immediately after hearing the news about Grandclément. For the second time that afternoon Peulevé had evaded capture, but it was now evident how dangerous his journey to the Corrèze was going to be.

Thankfully Landes had always been very conscious of the risks to his personal safety and only contacted those he thoroughly trusted. He called on a particularly reliable couple to hide Peulevé, taking him to a safe house run by François and Marguerite Faget, a family of black market wool merchants at 29 rue de Guynemer, in the suburb of Cauderan. Landes told him that he would be in touch once he had consulted Corbin to arrange his onward trip out of the city, but before Peulevé could leave SCIENTIST was to be dealt a significant and ultimately fatal blow.

Following his arrest, Grandclément had been escorted back to Bordeaux and placed in the hands of Hauptsturmführer Friedrich Dhose, the SD chief for the Bordelais area. He skilfully played on Grandclément's right-wing outlook, persuading him that France faced a serious communist threat now that the Russians were pushing the Wehrmacht back towards Germany. Although his allegiance was to the OCM, Grandclément had also forged links with a number of FTP groups, and it was these that Dhose concentrated on, suggesting that his work with the Resistance gave implicit support to their aspirations of a Soviet-dominated French state. He then offered a deal: were he to collaborate and provide the locations of SCIENTIST's arms caches, Dhose would agree to the release of his wife, being held at Fort du Hâ prison in Bordeaux, and many of the OCM members already under arrest. Grandclément appeared to have been taken in by the idea that he could work with the Germans and still remain a patriot, agreeing to give details on over 130 arms dumps across the south-west region.

Allowed to leave Gestapo headquarters alone on the morning of 24 September, Grandclément went to see Corbin with the intention of gaining support for the creation of new 'maquis blancs', dedicated to fighting communists rather than Germans. Although W/T operator Marcel Défence had recently returned to Bordeaux and was staying at the house (he had become besotted with Corbin's daughter Ginette since his arrival in April), Grandclément insisted on seeing the more senior Landes, and he was quickly summoned. Standing in front of his small audience with his shoulders stooped, the slight and sickly-looking Grandclément began to explain how the Germans had forced him to give up information about Landes' operations, and it soon became clear that his future plans to collaborate would be disastrous for SCIENTIST, threatening to destroy months of work; yet according to Défence he also pleaded with the British agents to return to England immediately, as the terms of his pact would not be enough to save them from the Gestapo. Landes knew that the safest option would be to stop Grandclément before he could act and had taken the rare precaution of arriving armed for this meeting. However, although he drew his pistol, *Aristide* hesitated to pull the trigger in the presence of Corbin's wife and daughter, and Grandclément walked away unscathed. It was to be a decision that he would later regret and marked the beginning of a desperate race between him and Dhose, each trying to reach SCIENTIST's arms caches before the other.

During this turmoil Landes was relieved to have another experienced SOE agent around and Peulevé's counsel was a valuable source of support in this volatile situation; yet the risks were increasing daily, and he was in great danger whenever he left the Fagets' house. Though it made sense to get out of Bordeaux as soon as possible, a route into the Corrèze would firstly require the help of one of Grandclément's OCM lieutenants, Roland Girard. At the end of 1942 Girard had been sent to build up relations with Resistance leaders in the Corrèze and establish an OCM influence in the area, employing two *agents de liaisons*, Jean Charlin and André Noël.

At the end of September, Corbin arranged for Peulevé and Landes to meet two of Jean Charlin's men, who were apparently willing to help but also had requests of their own to make. Peulevé's first impressions of them inspired little trust and it soon became obvious they were collecting substantial amounts of money from local people, loaned on the understanding that the British Government would reimburse them after the war. These loans, like the one Peulevé took from the Jewish family in Perpignan, were supposed to be acknowledged via the BBC's French broadcasts using a phrase selected by the payee; however, they had no means to radio London and so were anxious for help to legitimize their actions. Conferring with Landes, Peulevé agreed that there was no evidence that their money had been used for Resistance purposes. Nonetheless, he would need to string them along until they had led him into Brive-la-Gaillarde, the town where de Baissac's Corrèze contacts were based. Despite his misgivings, Peulevé had little choice but to follow these guides if he was to continue his mission, and took a train for Brive in the first week of October.

Chapter 8

Author

Repeatedly invaded by the English through the Middle Ages and later fought over by the Huguenots and Catholics during the vicious Wars of Religion, the Corrèze had been left economically devastated by its long history of conflict, and largely remained a neglected rural backwater even into the twentieth century. Characterized by steep, thickly-wooded hills, ancient valleys and deep gorges, its landscape was dotted with medieval fortresses, ruined chateaux and other re-minders of its bloody past, rising slowly up to the huge Millevaches Plateau in the Haute-Corrèze, a wild, sparsely-populated expanse of forests, lakes and moorland on the western edges of the Massif Central. For most *corréziens* life had changed little over the centuries – inhabiting the innumerable isolated villages and hamlets scattered across the department, they still depended upon agriculture and livestock for their survival, the region being particularly renowned for its *foie gras*, walnuts and truffles. The terrible atrocities witnessed by their ancestors had bred an inherent distrust of foreigners and outside interference, and in some ways the arrival of German forces represented yet another attack on their long-established way of life, hardening the resolve of many to fight back.

Known as the 'Smiling Gateway to the South', the respectable market town of Brive was one of the Corrèze's biggest commercial centres, and lay directly on the main routes running between Bord-eaux and Clermont-Ferrand, Limoges and Toulouse. The original siege walls that had earned it the name 'la Gaillarde' (the Gallant) were long gone, replaced by tree-lined boulevards that followed the same lines, encircling the thirteenth-century church of Saint Martin at the heart of the town. With a population of around 30,000, Brive had been the site of the first recorded act of French resistance when local activist Edmond Michelet went from door to door distributing leaflets against the occupation in the summer of 1940, but after the dissolution of the unoccupied zone the town was dominated by a garrison of several hundred Germans, and in early 1943 Michelet and many of his colleagues were arrested by Gestapo raids in Brive and the nearby prefecture of Tulle. These losses were a serious setback for the Resistance, yet there were always others willing to take their places, even though they understood that capture meant death or deportation.

One SOE report described the structure of the Resistance in the Corrèze at this time as 'very confused'.[1] This was something of an understatement. Through 1943 the region's clandestine networks had become complex and extremely fragmented, and the challenges involved in successfully coordinating them were daunting. The areas around Tulle had a history of communist support, and the FTP attracted a motley collection of Russians, Spaniards, Jews and other fugitives who had fled from the north to fight under their banner. They were well organized and regulated, but since mid-September had been carrying out numerous assassination attempts and guerrilla attacks on German targets, provoking serious reprisals amongst the local populations.

The other major resistance force, separate and increasingly hostile to the communists was the Gaullist *Armée Secrète* (AS), which was also attracting growing numbers of *réfractaires* to its maquis in the Corrèze and neighbouring Dordogne to the west. It began setting up camps in the early spring of 1943, though by mid-June the first of these at Chambon had been overrun by the GMR (*Groupes Mobiles de Réserve*, a paramilitary extension of the Vichy Police), and was soon followed by the discovery of several others across the Haute-Corrèze, leading to many arrests, deportations and executions.

In part these setbacks were due to poor security, but were also symptomatic of a greater problem: maquis were often established by local businessmen or regular military men with no knowledge of guerrilla tactics, and were run with varying amounts of jealous fervour which easily led to overconfidence and complacency. As the sole British representative in the region it was important for Peulevé to remain neutral and to convince all of these groups that cooperation with the British was worth their while. This raised a particular problem when dealing with the FTP, which was determined to remain independent of Allied strategy and follow its own political agenda, only willing to pledge that good use would be made of any arms and supplies it received. If AUTHOR was to succeed, its relationship with the communists would be crucial, and Peulevé's diplomatic skills would have to equal his capabilities as an organizer and instructor.

Arriving at Brive station, Peulevé was first introduced to Gontrand Royer (*Raffin*), an ex-armistice army colonel who had taken over from Michelet as commander for the whole of the 'R5' region (a designated military area covering the whole of the Limousin), and René Vaujour (*Hervé*), a handsome and impressive former Foreign Legion officer from Tulle who had left the 41st Infantry Regiment stationed at Brive to join the Resistance, and now held responsibility specifically for the Corrèze department. Between them they had organized small groups consisting of NCOs and men from their previous units, but much of their support still lay with the *sédéntaires*, those who remained in the local towns and villages and did not take up arms. Both recognized that Peulevé would need help to establish himself in the town, and called on a local businessman and *résistant* named Maurice Arnouil (*Pernod*), who would quickly become one of AUTHOR's most important members.

Born in Lamonzie-St-Martin near Bergerac in 1903, Arnouil had begun as an engineer with Gnome et Rhône and later worked for the Montupet factory at Ussel, where he became involved with early local Resistance groups, including Marie-Madeleine Fourcade's SIS-backed intelligence circuit ALLIANCE. Following a move to Brive in 1941 he set up his own company, 'Société d'Exploitation des Procédés Arnouil', more commonly referred to as 'Bloc-Gazo', based near the train station at 26 Avenue de la Gare. Here Arnouil manufactured *gazogenes*, charcoal-burning furnaces designed to provide an alternative means of powering cars and trucks (in these times of rationing, only the Germans, Vichy forces and doctors were likely to be seen driving petrol-driven vehicles). However, his enterprise served a more clandestine purpose when it became the preferred meeting place for the town's Resistance and a hiding place for their arms. Though his short, paunchy build did not suggest a heroic freedom fighter, Arnouil was ready to do whatever was required to help the cause, and after their first meeting he offered to provide Peulevé with a useful cover, appointing him sales director for his company. His connections with the local *mairie* also made it possible to obtain genuine papers in the name of Henri Chevalier, as well as a legitimate *permis de circulation*, which would enable him to travel freely across the region.

Using the Bloc-Gazo premises as a base, Peulevé started to construct a small body of staff to form the core of his circuit. Once again Arnouil proved invaluable, being able to suggest a number of reliable and trustworthy contacts. One of the first to be selected was a 28-year-old Corsican, Louis Charles Delsanti. Originally trained as a police inspector in Marseille before the war, an injury had led him to take the post of commissioner of Ussel in June 1942, though he was forced to resign a year later over his suspected obstruction of the STO and supplying of fake identity cards for the Resistance; having an extensive knowledge of the area and its inhabitants, he would make a very useful lieutenant. Peulevé also set to work on establishing a reception committee, which he would train in readiness to accept supply drops once suitable landing grounds had been found. For this task Arnouil recommended Paul and Georgette Lachaud, a couple who owned the Moulin du Couzoul, a mill near Daglan on the southern bank of the Dordogne. Unquestionably loyal, they were also ideally placed for such work, being far removed from the German-occupied towns and cities. In collaboration with Delsanti, the Lachauds were to head a small group that would carry out the dangerous job of waiting through the night to collect the arms and munitions dropped by RAF bombers. Their home was large enough to cache a substantial amount of *matériel* safely, and Paul Lachaud (known as 'Poulou') could use the cover of being a Bloc-Gazo customer, allowing him to visit their headquarters regularly without arousing suspicion.

During his first weeks in Brive, Peulevé also made contact with an important name he had been given in London, that of the novelist and adventurer André Malraux. Having established his literary reputation by winning the Prix Goncourt for *La Condition Humaine* in 1933, Malraux's association with resistance fighters had begun with his formation of the republican *Escuadrilla España*, an improvised air force of antiquated bombers and mercenary pilots during the Spanish Civil War. Taken prisoner in June 1940 whilst serving with a French tank regiment, he later escaped to the unoccupied zone and spent the next two years living quietly on the Côte d'Azur, refusing to endorse any of the Resistance leaders who approached him (when visited by *Libération*'s Emmanuel d'Astier de la Vigerie, Malraux declared, 'I am marching, but I march alone.')[2] Deciding to move when the Germans nullified the unoccupied zone in November 1942, he looked for a quiet retreat and chose the peaceful village of Saint-Chamant, near Argentat on the Dordogne. Remaining reluctant to ally himself openly with the Resistance, he had never-theless forged links with Arnouil through an old Spanish contact in Paris, and learnt that he had recently taken on a new employee, Henri Chevalier.

Peulevé immediately recognized Malraux's potential to mobilize support for the maquis, but he also presented certain problems: aside from his public profile, Malraux's nervous ticks and contin-ually weeping eye made him too conspicuous to undertake any clandestine work. However, he would still be a useful advisor when liaising with the various groups in the region and was already known to have established contact with the local FTP. He also sug-gested to Peulevé that one of his Spanish Anarchist comrades, Eugène 'Raymond' Maréchal, could be of use to him, particularly in the role of arms instructor. Operating under the name of Raymond Mennisier, Maréchal had previously been a gunner with Malraux's *escuadrilla*, and had nearly died from a terrible injury when his aircraft crashed near Teruel in 1936, requiring the surgeon to insert a metal plate in his forehead, giving him a grotesque appearance. Whilst he was troubled by his looks (he had to be prevented from shooting himself immediately after the accident, as he could not imagine any woman finding him attractive again), his generosity of spirit and apparent fearlessness would make him a valuable addi-tion to the new circuit.

Peulevé took to Maréchal as soon as they met, sensing that he was an ideal man to construct and lead his own personal guerrilla force. Whilst political factions were rife amongst maquis groups, a small band of men directed by Peulevé under the Spaniard's command could lead small raids on targets that Gaullist or communist groups considered too risky or unpopular. Maréchal was not apolitical, but his anarchist ideals didn't interfere with Peulevé's objectives and he had no problem in receiving orders from a British officer. He quickly hand-picked twenty compatriots to join his *Groupe Raymond*, and spent the rest of his time giving weapons training and supplying Resistance leaders with money, enabling them to buy what they needed in the way of blankets, food and clothing on the black market.

Peulevé made his first radio contact with London on 31 October, six weeks after arriving in France, transmitting from a first-floor room on Bloc-Gazo's premises using one of the three wireless sets forwarded to him by Landes, who was now planning to return to London. Although Landes had done his best to minimize the damage caused by Grandclément's actions, he had fought a losing battle since Peulevé's departure and casualties had become inevitable. One important incident involved an F Section arms instructor, Victor Hayes (*Yves*), who had been parachuted in in November 1942 to help with SCIENTIST's increasing workload, and like Défence became romantically involved in Bordeaux. Since his arrival Hayes had been staying with the family of Jean Duboué, one of de Baissac's earliest contacts, during which time he had grown very fond of his eighteen-year-old daughter Suzanne. A widower in his mid-thirties (his wife had drowned two years before), the diminutive and balding Hayes seemed an unlikely match for a girl half his age, but his feelings towards her were such that he had refused Buckmaster's order to relocate and assume command of SCIENTIST's northern sectors.

This decision to stay was a fatal one for *Yves*, as Grandclément's collaboration with the Gestapo soon gave Dhose a lead to the arms cache on Duboué's property at Lestiac, about 15 miles north-east of the city on the banks of the Garonne. Through the early hours of 14 October, Hayes and the Duboués fought off their attackers with Stens, pistols and grenades, even forcing them to call for reinforcements, but they were eventually forced to give in when Madame Duboué was wounded in the stomach – her husband and daughter were taken away for questioning while she and Hayes were placed in separate hospitals, Hayes also having been shot in the arm and leg (in his message to London, Peulevé passed on details about his transfer to the Robert Piquet military hospital in Bordeaux). Landes was understandably nervous about what information might be forced out of Hayes and planned a mission to rescue him, but he was transferred to Fresnes prison in Paris before it could be carried out. Although falling in love had affected his judgment, in the end Hayes proved that it had not weakened his nerve or his allegiance to his organizer, and refused to divulge anything of importance to Dhose before he was deported to Germany and executed. The members of the Duboué family were more fortunate to survive the war but still paid a high price for Grandclément's disclosure, Jean being sent to Buchenwald concentration camp and daughter Suzanne to Ravensbrück.

With the foundations of AUTHOR now in place, Peulevé's daily schedule became filled with a variety of different responsibilities, visiting Vaujour's isolated maquis groups to instruct them on guerrilla warfare, inspecting possible landing grounds, maintaining wireless communications with London and distributing SOE funds to other Resistance leaders. These activities became a peculiar mixture of routine and risk, and he soon developed a perpetual awareness of the dangers involved in undertaking the simplest of errands. One of the first serious threats to his life occurred on an early visit to a maquis that had been allegedly supported by the two men who had brought Peulevé from Bordeaux. Still under suspicion of spending collected funds on themselves rather than their intended cause, they had suggested that Peulevé should meet the maquis' commander who would vouch for their integrity.

Using a Chevrolet convertible given to him by Arnouil, Peulevé was directed by his companions to a steep, wooded valley. Leaving the car hidden in a turning some way from the main road, the three of them began walking towards the camp, Peulevé arming himself with a Thompson sub-machine gun (a concealed compartment had been fitted inside the car to carry it, in case of German searches). Although they appeared to know the route, Peulevé was careful to take compass readings every so often in case anything went wrong – there was always the possibility that he was being led into an ambush, and he did not wish to take any chances. However, after about 5 miles trekking through the forest they arrived at the outskirts of what appeared to be their camp.

It was similar to other maquis that Peulevé had seen since he arrived in the region, consisting of around thirty men living in tents and makeshift shelters, with a few shallow earthworks and defensive trenches around the perimeter. From his conversation with the commander, it was clear that their only arms were a few old rifles and grenades and that the men had received only the most basic of training. Even more concerning was the apparent attitude of the younger members towards security. Boredom and isolation wore down their morale very quickly and to break the monotony they would spend the weekends at the nearest village meeting local girls; this was particularly dangerous, as the Germans were known to employ prostitutes as informers. Even worse, one of these women had been recently visiting the camp for several weeks to cook for them, and had disappeared a few days previously.

When Peulevé voiced his fears over their safety the commander seemed unconcerned, replying that escape routes were in place, and with a small rearguard most of them could evade any assault – anyway, they had never been attacked before, so why expect it now? Peulevé was dismayed by this casual attitude, but could not have guessed that an attack was only hours away. As dusk approached he agreed to join them for their evening soup, but shortly afterwards the sound of strange voices on the perimeter made it obvious that they had been discovered.

Judging by their lack of stealth, it seemed that the approaching German unit had stumbled on the camp – had they crept up and surrounded it Peulevé and the group would have stood no chance. As the maquisards began firing at the startled invaders, Peulevé ran in the direction of his attackers towards a thick clump of trees on some slightly higher ground, planning to stay out of sight until the better-equipped German force had overpowered their opposition. Watching the unfolding battle from his hiding place, Peulevé was surprised to see how a few men with their antiquated arms pinned down at least a dozen German soldiers, though it was not long before they were killed or made a run for it, leaving the commander to fight alone.

Admiring the tenacity with which this Frenchman continued to defend his ground, Peulevé now felt compelled to offer some support, deciding to make his move when the Germans began their advance. As several men started to run forward to take the camp, Peulevé left his position, firing as he moved about 20 yards in front of them. To his great surprise he felled all five of his opponents 'without so much as dirtying my black marketeer's raincoat',[3] and quickly scuttled back behind the trees to await the second wave. When it failed to appear, he assumed that the remainder must have run off in pursuit of the other maquisards who were making their escape.

Taking the commander with him back to the car, Peulevé anticipated running into German reinforcements but found none, though when they later received news on the attack it turned out that the rest of the group had not been so lucky. The small force they encountered had merely shepherded the fleeing maquis towards a larger group waiting for them some distance behind the camp; half of those captured had been executed on the spot, while the rest were deported to concentration camps.

Raids like these were not uncommon through the autumn, yet they did little to discourage acts of resistance. The Prefect for the Corrèze reported that during October and November nearly 300 assassinations had been attempted by the réfractaires from local maquis. However, the cost was high and these attacks were followed by terrible reprisals, often resulting in local civilians being taken hostage and shot. Whilst some held the maquis responsible and sympathized with Vichy portrayals of them as criminals and bandits, the Germans' ruthless behaviour increasingly fuelled public support for their cause, though the approaching winter threatened many of the camps with extinction if they could not obtain substantial help from London.

Although Peulevé's brief was to coordinate resistance within a specific area, the great demand for arms and supplies meant that news of the British officer's presence spread quickly to neighbouring departments. One who was eager to make his acquaintance was Jean Vincent, also known as 'Colonel Vény', a former Foreign Legion officer who was based in the Lot and represented *Froment Action*, a paramilitary wing of the French socialist party, the SFIO (*Section Française de l'International Ouvrière*); Vény claimed to have built up substantial underground networks, but had resisted integration into the MUR and was looking for other means of acquiring support. At a meeting on Bloc-Gazo's premises, Peulevé agreed to provide both arms and training for the *Groupes Vény*, though he also made it clear that new SOE circuits would have to be formed to aid its main groups in Limoges, Marseille and the Lot. Making wireless contact with London, Peulevé received approval for the plan but was informed that no agents would be sent until early in the New Year, when his proposed landing grounds had been vetted by the RAF and the appalling weather had improved.

Peulevé had initially found it difficult to establish contact with the FTP, but was eventually able to arrange an introduction to André Bonnetot (*Vincent*), one of its regional commanders for the Dordogne; they got on well and Peulevé was able to gain his confidence by emphasizing a willingness to supply arms with no political strings attached. During a tour of the camps they also visited the regional *école des cadres* at Lespicerie, close to Montignac and the prehistoric landscape of the Vézère valley, where Spanish Civil War veterans trained classes of young maquisards in guerrilla warfare. The organization of the school was impressive, but Peulevé could see how desperate they were for weapons – the instructors even had trouble obtaining arms to show their students. Knowing that Bonnetot's men would make good use of any *matériel* they received, he pledged to deliver some of his first consignments of arms to them at landing grounds near the village of Jugeals-Nazareth, south of Brive.

Although SOE had no responsibility for the running of escape lines, Peulevé's territory lay directly on the route that Allied airmen took to reach the Pyrenees, and it became his job to find them safe houses and supply them with false identity papers – once six escapers had been received, they were collected by a white-haired schoolmistress who would take them south to Toulouse to carry on their journey across the border. With his workload increasing daily, helping fugitive airmen was an extra headache Peulevé could well do without, though he was not the only one at risk – the families who sheltered these men had far more to lose if they were discovered.

German security forces would often try to infiltrate such networks, using agents posing as airmen to collect intelligence as they were passed from one contact to the next, and as a precaution Peulevé would interrogate each man, corroborating their details with London before deciding to harbour them. On one occasion he was notified that two pilots were sheltering in the cellar of Bloc-Gazo having been picked up by Arnouil, and since the danger was much greater in the middle of town Peulevé had to move them before any check could be made on their authenticity.

Using his own car, Arnouil insisted on driving them to a safe house in one of the outlying villages and pulled up some distance from the garden gate. Peulevé made his way up to the front door but noticed that it was slightly ajar; suspicious, his right hand instinctively went into his coat pocket, where he kept a sawn-off Colt .45 revolver. Knocking on the door with the other hand, he was greeted by the face of an old woman who gave the pre-arranged password, though as he was about to offer a reply he suddenly became aware of something prodding him. Already nervous, he was shocked to see a man crouching out of sight behind a tall shrub, silently mouthing the word 'Gestapo'. Realizing that he was about to enter a trap, Peulevé kicked the door open, firing at the woman at the same time from his pocket. He withdrew his gun as the door swung open to reveal her male companion, who was killed instantly by his second shot.

The man in the bushes ran to congratulate him, explaining that this couple were imposters. Two days before he had been working in the garden when the Gestapo had arrived to arrest his wife and himself, and though his wife was taken he had been able to remain hidden behind some trees. Knowing that another airman might be delivered to them at any time, he elected to keep watch over the house and witnessed the couple that Peulevé had met arriving to take over as bogus residents; having slept rough in the barn opposite, he had eventually seen Arnouil's car coming up the road and done what he could to alert them to the danger before it was too late. Peulevé considered himself fortunate to have been warned this time, but was also humbled and inspired by this man's willingness to take such risks to prevent the capture of Allied servicemen. Examples like this continually served to remind him that resistance was not solely the work of the maquis, and that without the support of the local population they could have achieved nothing. They would also persuade him to take greater risks with his own safety.

In November, Peulevé was informed that another downed pilot was being hidden at a remote farmhouse by an elderly couple, where he would be kept until his identity was confirmed. Once his details were verified with London, Peulevé travelled to meet him and was unexpectedly honoured by the couple with a special dinner and their best wine. Later in the evening they retired to leave him to talk with the RAF airman in front of the fire, accompanied by a bottle of brandy. During their conversation Peulevé learnt that the airman was stationed close to his parents' home near Cambridge, and they soon got onto the subject of 'the availability and acquiescence of the local belles and the best pubs in which to make their charming acquaintance'.[4] However, as they chatted Peulevé suddenly noticed that although the airman invariably agreed with everything he said, he never offered any opinions of his own. Warning bells had started to ring in his mind and to test his suspicions Peulevé added a fictitious venue into their conversation. As he had predicted the pilot gave the impression of knowing this place well, mentioning several liaisons with the barmaid there.

This was enough to suggest an attempted infiltration, either by German or Vichy Intelligence. Taking a chance that he wouldn't be arrested that night, Peulevé pretended to go upstairs to bed but crept out later, walking to a café at the nearest village. The owner was known to be a friend of the Resistance and allowed Peulevé the use of his telephone to contact Maréchal, telling him to meet him there at eleven o'clock the next morning with five of his men. Maréchal turned up as arranged and Peulevé explained the situation, asking to be dropped off in the woods near the farm before they collected their suspect. Although there was a possibility that the Germans or *milice* were now waiting for them, he and his men obeyed without question, and Peulevé recalled their return that afternoon with their new prisoner:

> Our friend the pilot was surrounded by the worst looking band of brigands one could ever wish to set eyes upon. They were all dressed in an assortment of civilian and German uniforms, the latter taken off their adversaries as spoil of battle and to avoid straining our slender financial resources ... They each carried a Lee Enfield rifle over their shoulders in a manner that would have been the despair of a British Sergeant Major. Canvass belts of ammunition were draped over their other shoulders like festoons on a Christmas tree and the heavy leather belts they carried were hung with pineapple-type hand grenades. Apart from the dress and armament they were unshaven and I suspect unclean with vermin. To someone who had not come to admire, and even love, such a cut-throat-looking band ... they could only inspire fear and revulsion. To me they were a heavenly host upon which I could rely unto death, for there was not one amongst them that would not readily give his life to carry out an order.[5]

Though not immediately declaring him a spy, Peulevé interrogated the man thoroughly for two hours, though not a blemish showed in his cover. He couldn't help but admire his coolness under pressure, but still refused to believe he was genuine and openly accused him of being a German plant. Referring to London's confirmation of his identity, the pilot stuck firmly to his story, prompting Peulevé to try and force him to talk.

Maréchal proceeded with a demonstration to show what damage a small amount of plastic explosive could do, placing it around the base of a sapling before lighting the prepared Bickford fuse; a few seconds later it toppled as though severed by an axe. His men then grabbed him, ripping off his right sleeve and placing a similar charge around his shoulder. As the fuse was lit and began to burn towards his arm he fixed his eyes on Peulevé's and continued to keep silent, obviously determined not give himself up easily. Peulevé told Maréchal to remove the fuse before it reached the detonator, but knew that he still had his trump card to play, bringing up the name of the pub that he had claimed to know the previous night. Having no credible excuse for this gaffe, their suspect realized that it was pointless to continue and confessed to being a

95

German agent, describing how he had been given the identity of an RAF pilot who had died when bailing out over France, and that it was simply luck that he had come from an area Peulevé had known.

Putting his capture down to the fortunes of war, Peulevé made it clear that he had no choice but to execute him, but would offer to write to his family and summon a priest if he wished. Leaving him to write his last lines under the light of a torch, he told Maréchal to fetch the local curé, a consideration the Spaniard thought far too charitable. However, he recognized Peulevé's troubled conscience, throwing him his brandy flask as he walked off while the rest started to dig a shallow grave with their bayonets.

Waiting for Maréchal's return, Peulevé found himself in the surreal situation of making conversation with a man he was about to kill. Accepting a swig of brandy to calm his nerves, the German talked about his family, explaining that he was at Oxford before the war and that although he felt the need to fight for his country he did not necessarily agree with Hitler's policies. As the autumnal light began to fade Maréchal and a terrified old priest finally appeared, and after receiving confession the agent was asked if he wanted a blindfold; he refused, but asked that he be allowed to give the command to fire. Peulevé agreed and did his best to instil some semblance of respect into Maréchal's men as they lined up. After the execution Peulevé felt unable to stay at the scene any longer, but asked for the others to place a wooden cross at the head of the grave before they left.

His actions had prevented a serious threat to the escape line and may have saved many lives, but these thoughts did nothing to assuage Peulevé's guilt and frustration over the nature of this event:

> With a heavy heart I departed to the farm where I spent a sleepless night in thinking what an utter waste of gentle human beings our incompetent and unforseeing politicians had led us into ... Here was I, peaceful I had always thought, in the middle of such a war that I had to summarily decide on the death of what could only have been a perfectly good human being, for the simple reason that he was born in a different geographical location to myself.[6]

Though there was no doubt about the mutual loyalty felt between Peulevé and Maréchal, the gruesome postscript to this story served to highlight how different their capacities were for compassion towards their enemy. Some weeks later Peulevé asked Maréchal to take a photograph of the grave, intending to send it to the dead man's family, but Maréchal replied that it wasn't possible, as the corpse had been loaded into a crate labelled as machinery and sent to the Gestapo HQ at Avenue Foch in Paris, accompanied by a note asking them not to send any more agents through Allied escape lines, signed 'British Intelligence Service'. For the Spaniard this was a big joke, and he was surprised when his friend did not share it.

Peulevé was clearly shaken by this episode, but knew that others were hunting for him just as keenly. Although he spoke French without an accent, and often presented himself as a French delegate from the *Conseil National de la Résistance* (a unified resistance body under de Gaulle's leadership), some of the *corréziens* he met could not believe that his English looks weren't an obvious giveaway to the Germans, and inevitably a number of those arrested spoke of a British agent working in the region. The Gestapo had also begun to receive help from former OCM officer André Noël, who like Grandclément had agreed to collaborate and had installed a number of informers in the area. Acting as Grandclément's intermediary, Noël twice attempted to try and lure Peulevé into meeting with him, but Peulevé's instincts told him to refuse and he failed to appear on both occasions.[7]

Despite the Germans' increasing efforts to capture him, a more dangerous threat already sat within his own ranks: a colleague had told him that one of the surviving contacts from Bordeaux was continuing to collect funds for the Resistance under dubious means, and intended to dispose of Peulevé if he did not promise to contact London on his behalf. Considering this to be a real liability to the circuit's security, Peulevé decided that there was now no option but to eliminate him. He arranged a rendezvous outside Brive, from where they could walk to a nearby safe house and 'discuss' the matter. There was to be no one else involved.

Arriving early on the day, he drove some yards beyond the area they had agreed to meet in order to watch for any signs of a possible ambush. However, his contact arrived alone as requested and they drove to the nearby house, situated well away from the roadside and concealed by dense woods. Unlocking the door, Peulevé invited his victim to enter first:

As I followed him in, I had the knife ready and suddenly closing my left hand over his mouth, cut through his jugular vein as easy as picking a winkle out of its shell. As I lowered him to the floor, I felt that the sergeant major who had taught me to practise this neat flick of the wrist with a knife in Scotland would have been proud of my first effort ... I do not think it took him long to die but I stayed a few minutes until I could feel no pulse and laid him out straight and saintly on the floor. Driving back, I had no feeling of revulsion such as one reads about and merely felt that I had done a good job with the knife as I had been taught to do, and eliminated a pest that, at best was preying on worthy Frenchmen faithful to our cause and at the worst got rid of a potential security risk who might have got me first.[8]

Although he had narrowly avoided capture or death on numerous occasions, these events had begun to accrue in Peulevé's mind, and reminded him 'of how fate can, like a cat with a mouse, play with you for hours when every moment you think is your last, and then release you to run down your mousehole to safety and tremblingly relive those awful moments'.[9] Constant vigilance for potential dangers was a fundamental part of an SOE agent's life in the field, but the physical and mental toll of the past two months was now beginning to tell, and he described how at this time 'my nerves were such that I was scared of my own shadow.'[10] As the sole British agent within the circuit he realized that he could not continue much longer without support, though Poirier and the agents to assist Vény's groups in the Lot were not expected for several more weeks yet. Perhaps the instructor's reservations about Peulevé at Meoble Lodge had been justified: could he stand the 'prolonged strain' that AUTHOR now demanded?

To relieve some of the pressure he began looking for a full-time W/T operator to deal with his growing backlog of wireless traffic, and Arnouil suggested a 24-year-old French Air Force radio operator, Louis Bertheau, who was based at Meymac near Ussel in the Haute-Corrèze. Originally from the Loiret, Bertheau had moved to the area after demobilization with his wife Rosa, who had their first child, Michèle, in December 1941; however, although he took an office job to support his young family and tried to concentrate on his academic studies, Bertheau eventually felt compelled to offer his services to the local Resistance. Looking for a way to make use of his radio skills, he came into contact with a local *réfractaire* named Jean Melon at the end of June 1943, who knew of a Madame Dumond (otherwise known as 'Tante Jim') who ran the youth hostel at Ussel. Dumond had long-established connections with the local ALLIANCE intelligence network, and was able to place Bertheau with a local maquis, though it was only a matter of days before the camp was dissolved and Dumond was arrested. Knowing how valuable a trained wireless operator would be to another group, she managed to pass on a final message recommending him to Arnouil, who knew her from his time in Ussel in 1941.

After checking his background, Bertheau (code-named *Tilou*) was summoned to Brive for instruction on W/T procedures and began transmitting from a safe house on the outskirts of town, though this soon proved unsatisfactory and Peulevé decided to relocate him back in the Haute-Corrèze. On the morning of 27 November, Jean Melon arrived by train to assist with the move and accompanied Bertheau on a visit to Bloc-Gazo, where they met Peulevé and were told to pick up a W/T set from Le Sporting, a restaurant on Avenue Maillard by the Corrèze river. Making discreet enquiries at the counter later that day, the waitress immediately yelled for assistance, declaring, 'It's about the suitcase!' Moments later an old woman appeared, beckoning them to follow her to a back room where they were handed the heavy B1 set.

Planning to return to Meymac, they left Bertheau's flat in rue François-Villon just before four o'clock the next morning, carefully dodging the curfew patrols as they made their way through the deserted streets towards the station. Though most people had arrived the evening before and were sleeping on the train they eventually managed to find a nearly empty carriage, but after placing the wireless suitcase on the rack above their heads they heard the sound of Germans approaching and saw the beam of a torch light. Suddenly noticing the sign *Réservé à la Wehrmacht* on the window, they rushed for the door, hearing the shouts from other passengers as they were being thrown off. Melon grabbed the case and made a run for it, whilst Bertheau attempted to stall one of the soldiers by apologizing for their mistake. As he rushed down the platform Melon barged through a group of guards, but they found the terrified man so funny that they didn't think to check the contents of his luggage.

Reaching the end of the train, they left the suitcase in the mail van before squeezing into one of the packed carriages and completed the journey without any further interruptions. Once back in Meymac they began transmitting from the Moulin de Breuil, a mill owned by Melon's parents where they had been hiding Jews and *réfractaires* for some months; with Melon posted at the window on the lookout for any German patrols, Bertheau was soon in almost daily contact with London, and together they were making three regular trips a week to Bloc-Gazo, dropping off the messages received and collecting any replies waiting to be sent. Despite the obvious dangers in carrying such material, Melon chose to courier Peulevé's telegrams in the lining of his hat, a hiding place that proved good enough to avoid detection when passing through German checkpoints.

With the wireless situation solved, Peulevé could afford to get away from the circuit for a while and took a train south to see André Girard (not to be confused with *Carte* in Antibes), a retired croupier and colleague of Audouard's who had sheltered him briefly in 1942 at his villa in Cannes. Aside from offering him somewhere to stay, Girard also loaned 300,000 francs to Peulevé's circuit, in return for the usual promise of a BBC message to confirm the deal. The change of scenery and Girard's hospitality did him some good; however, he could not stay for more than a few days, mindful that there was still much to do before the end of the year.

Through the autumn the *Armée Secrète* and FTP groups had continued to grow across the Corrèze, though the MUR suffered a setback when the Gestapo set a trap for Gontrand Royer, arresting him at Limoges on 13 December. His place was taken by René Vaujour, who enlisted the help of his old comrade Captain Marius Guédin (*Georges*), another long-serving ex-army *resistant*; Guédin had a bookish appearance, but his direct approach made him an ideal field commander, despite his disagreement over Peulevé's arming of the FTP (relations between the AS and the communists would continue to deteriorate over the following months). More support also arrived with the integration of the ORA (*Organisation de Résistance de l'Armée*), which represented officers from the disbanded armistice army. Although politically opposed to de Gaulle, the ORA's R5 section agreed to work under Vaujour, and their leader Guillaume d'Ussel (*Nicolo*), the second son of the Count of Ussel, would now act as one of his lieutenants.

By Christmas, Peulevé was at last ready to notify London that the Lachauds' reception committee and several other landing grounds selected by the maquis were ready to receive supply drops. This marked the completion of the initial stages of his mission and was a significant milestone for a man who had waited so long to prove himself. Having passed unscathed through the carnage of the Grandclément affair and its repercussions, he had established the foundations of his circuit with only minimal support from Landes' SCIENTIST and was now ready to create a much more effective body of resistance across the Corrèze and Dordogne. Yet with the impending arrival of an Allied invasion time was running out and over the following months Peulevé would be increasingly forced to jeopardize his own safety in order to achieve AUTHOR's objectives.

Chapter 9

Vindication

AUTHOR's first supply drop was delivered on the night of 6/7 January to a landing ground between the villages of Vayrac, Carrenac and Floirac, situated on the Causse de Gramat, a vast, arid, limestone plateau south of the Dordogne valley. Cylindrical metal containers measuring nearly 6 feet long and weighing up to 70 kilos were parachuted from the bomb bays of aircraft filled with arms, ammunition, medical supplies and other equipment, while other more bulky items such as wireless sets would be pushed out through a hole in the fuselage in separate packages, covered in a protective material called Hairlok (a mixture of hair and latex rubber).

This reception committee received a total of fifteen containers and five packages, the contents of which had already been specified by Peulevé according to pre-defined loads prepared by SOE's packing stations. For example, an agent ordering twelve containers from 'Load A' could expect to receive: 6 Bren light-machine guns; 36 Lee-Enfield rifles; 27 Sten guns; 5 pistols; 52 assorted grenades; 150 field dressings; and approximately 10,000 extra rounds of ammunition. Other standard loads could also include explosives or anti-tank weapons, while bespoke orders could be made up depending on the requirements at the time, with any available space being crammed with cigarettes, clothing, foodstuffs or other creature comforts.

The local maquis who collected this first consignment were eager to celebrate their successful operation, but had barely begun to unpack it before they were alerted by another announcement on the BBC's *messages personnels* service,[1] which broadcast the phrase 'le petit poisson rouge sera blanchi à la chaux' (the little goldfish will be scalded), indicating that another drop would follow the next night. However, this flight would not just bring weapons and ammunition – following Peulevé's discussions with Vény in November, organ-

102

izer George Hiller (*Maxime*) and his wireless operator, Cyril Watney (*Eustache*), were to arrive to begin work on creating a new circuit in the Lot named FOOTMAN.

During their briefing in London, Buckmaster had told them that their contact would be called Henri Chevalier, but did not reveal that he was actually a British agent, or that he was already known to Watney. Notified of their imminent arrival, Peulevé made arrangements for them to stay with Vény's lieutenant in the Lot, Jean Verlhac, whose house stood on the edge of Quatre-Routes, a small village a few miles north-west of their drop zone. That evening the reception committee made their way to the area in two cars, Peulevé accompanied by Jean Verlhac in Arnouil's Chevrolet, with Verlhac's wife Marie and three other helpers following behind them, though as they approached the area the driver of the second car became so nervous that he careered into a signpost. Making the last part of their journey up the winding road on foot, they armed themselves with Stens and also took the precaution of carrying a stretcher and medical supplies, in case the parachutists injured themselves on landing.

Wounded agents were just one of a number of hazards that could hamper the work of a reception committee. Although the RAF might have given the go-ahead for a drop, the difficulties involved in locating a field in the middle of rural France at night meant that aircraft could easily become lost or fail to identify those on the ground (although drop zones were sometimes marked out by bonfires, receptions often used nothing more than hand-held torches). Bad weather could force an aircraft to turn back before reaching its objective, or mechanical trouble with the dropping mechanisms could result in failure at the last moment; depending on the weather conditions and type of aircraft making the drops, containers were also at risk of falling some distance from the landing ground, and the extra time spent looking for them increased the chances of being spotted by German patrols. Even then the containers and packages might be destroyed on impact if their parachutes did not open. In a report on dropping operations over France during the first three months of 1944, only 45 per cent of all operations were counted as successful, a figure that was considered a great improvement on previous months.

By the time Peulevé's group arrived at the rendezvous about twenty men from the Vayrac maquis were already in place with a lorry and cart to transport the cargo, and having positioned their torches across the field there was little to do but stand and wait in the freezing cold, although Delsanti caused some alarm when he accidentally let off a round from his Sten. After two hours standing around in this rocky wilderness the thick patches of fog drifting across the fields caused some to wonder if their delivery might be called off, but just before eleven-thirty they at last began to make out the distant drone of aircraft engines.

Fortunately the previous night's drop had included an S-Phone, a portable UHF radio-telephone invented by SOE to enable an agent to communicate with pilots overhead. Using a small directional transceiver worn by the user on a webbed harness, this apparatus could relay instructions to aircraft at low altitudes from a distance of several miles, and with a cloudless sky and the light of a nearly full moon it was a relatively simple business for Peulevé to guide the two bombers towards their target. Passing over the field they circled for a few minutes before making their run, Hiller and Watney safely jumping from their Halifax to join the trail of parachutes left in its wake. After landing amongst some rocks and removing his harness and overalls, Hiller was the first to be greeted by the reception party:

> Henri was waiting for us on the ground itself, a dashing figure in his golf suit with his sports overcoat and hat low over his face ... I had parted with all my paraphernalia and, with my dark grey overcoat and my briefcase in my hand, I looked a rather curious person from England, a bedraggled and hatless city gent. The maquisards, a fierce looking band of all sizes, dressed in every variety of leather and shooting jackets, pressed around to see the two Englishmen [Watney had joined him by this point] ... and to compare them with Henri, until then the only specimen in the district.[2]

Watney had been especially surprised by the reception, recognizing that the mysterious Henri Chevalier was in fact Peulevé, whom he had previously requested to work with. The seven containers and five packages that had also been dropped were hastily being dragged over dry stone walls and through hedges to the waiting lorry nearby; amidst the shouts of people giving orders, Peulevé explained that this was not one of his primary landing grounds and Hiller could see that he was anxious to get away:

> Henri was getting impatient, and having given orders for the disposal of the containers, decided to get the most compromis-

104

ing items off the field. We crowded into a large blue car; the Stens were put in the back so as not to be in anyone's way. We were packed so tight that no one could have got at their pistols, so *Michel* [Watney] and I thought.[3]

Hiller and Watney had both been startled by the nature of their reception – apart from Peulevé's flamboyant appearance, he had greeted them in English (contrary to security training), and they were now sitting on parachutes that they had expected to be buried. When asked about this, Peulevé explained that the silk was far too valuable, being a useful bribe when dealing with Resistance leaders, although some of it was also donated to the women for underwear.

As the maquisards transported the collected arms to a barn in the nearby village of St-Michel-de-Bannières the others drove back to the Verlhacs' house, though as they approached Quatre-Routes they were waved down by three Vichy policemen who had been informed about the earlier goings-on near Carennac. Eager to see the newly-arrived Englishmen they'd heard about, they peered inside the car but were soon disappointed, convinced that Watney was the only foreign parachutist and that the cool-headed Hiller was really French (probably because of his excellent grasp of the language). Although this surreal situation appeared to be disastrous for all of them, Verlhac was responsible for organizing the local dairies in the area and threatened to stop making his regular cheese deliveries if they weren't allowed to continue on. It seemed an unlikely way to intimidate the law, but to Watney's astonishment the policemen let them pass. This wasn't the only occasion where such influence was helpful and Watney later learnt that the local gendarmerie 'were generally under the thumb of Madame Verlhac, who being ... a woman of considerable character, simply saw that they got no milk if they caused any unpleasantness.'[4]

Hiller and Watney were expected to stay for several days at the house, while Peulevé and Arnouil returned to Brive. The following morning Peulevé reported to Watney that his wireless set had probably been dropped on a different landing ground (another eight containers and five packages had been collected on the same night by another reception committee near Quatre-Routes) and a replacement would have to be sent as the maquisards had commandeered whatever had fallen into their hands. Vény also made an appearance later that morning, accompanied by Colonel Henri Collignon, who planned to incorporate his Toulouse networks with Vény's in the

Lot. Greeting the two new agents, Vény seemed genuinely surprised to see that they had been sent, having expected 'perfidious Albion' to have fallen back on its promises of help. Following their introductions, Peulevé proceeded to give Hiller some background on the region and advise him on the first steps for FOOTMAN; Hiller's briefing in London had stressed that his main objective must be to consolidate Vény's groups into the *Armée Secrète* as far as possible, and within a few days he and Watney were moved out to separate safe houses where they could begin an assessment of the situation.

By the end of the first week of January, Peulevé's reception committees had gathered more than seventy containers and twenty packages, with only two of the seven aircraft sent being unable to drop their cargo. These first batches of arms were of inestimable worth in proving that SOE and AUTHOR were serious about aiding the maquis, and on a personal level demonstrated that Peulevé's word could be trusted. The arrival of explosives also gave much greater scope for sabotage work, and within just a few days an opportunity arose to strike at one of the main factories at Figeac in the Lot.

A sympathetic foreman at the Le Ratier plant, which produced 300 propellers a week for Heinkel and Focke-Wulf aircraft, had already passed detailed plans of the works to the local MUR leaders at the beginning of the year. Verlhac discussed the possibility of launching an attack on it with Peulevé, Hiller and others from the Vény group on the afternoon of 17 January, and all agreed to give it their support, with Peulevé supplying the explosives. Two days later Hiller prepared seven 3-lb plastic charges on the Verlhacs' kitchen table before handing them to a team of five of Vény's men led by André Saint-Chamant, who entered the Le Ratier premises later that night using the foreman's keys. Their raid was a complete success: the comprehensive destruction of three precision machines and two furnaces was enough to shut the factory down for the rest of the war, and it would later be considered as one of F Section's most effective sabotage actions.

A few days afterwards Peulevé received word from London that Poirier had completed his training and would be dropped with a young, promising recruit of de Baissac's, Jean Renaud-Dandicolle (*Verger*), on the night of 28/29 January. Though returning to his home country, Poirier was to continue to present himself as British officer Lieutenant Jack Peters, and would be code-named *Nestor*. Parachuting safely, they soon realized that they were a long way from their intended drop zone – due to pilot error they had in fact been dropped deep in the neighbouring Cantal department, more than a hundred kilometres south-east of their designated landing ground near Marcillac-la-Croisille. Taking a train to Brive early the next morning, Poirier planned to contact Peulevé at the Bloc-Gazo premises, the address of which he had been given in London, though he hadn't taken into account the fact that it was Saturday and the office was closed. Not wishing to take a chance by checking into a hotel, the two men found shelter in Saint-Sernin Church further down the avenue, taking in one Mass after another to avoid the cold. However, as evening approached they were eventually forced to leave, having no choice but to sleep rough on the outskirts of town.

Following a second very uncomfortable night exposed to the elements they made their way back to Bloc-Gazo on Monday morning. Peulevé was astonished to see the half-frozen Poirier walk through the door. Having attended their planned reception at Marcillac-la-Croisille, he had heard the aircraft pass overhead but had only received packages containing their personal effects, and assumed that the drop must have been aborted for some reason (Peulevé diplomatically refrained from telling Poirier that he had also taken the liberty of picking out a couple of his shirts, as he was waiting for his own to come back from the laundry). After introducing Poirier to Arnouil and the rest of the Bloc-Gazo crew, Peulevé suggested that he take a room at the Hotel Champanatier on rue Dumyrat where he was staying (the Champanatier was one of the few hotels in the area not requisitioned by the Germans, and was just around the corner from Arnouil's premises). He also gave Renaud-Dandicolle instructions for his onward journey to Paris, where he was to prepare the way for his organizer Claude de Baissac and a new SCIENTIST circuit in Normandy, the original having folded. Unable to achieve any more in the aftermath of the Grandclément affair, Landes had left for Spain with his assistant Corbin at the end of November (Défence also returned to London, taking a boat across the Channel two months later, though he would be caught and executed on a later mission).

After Arnouil had prepared his papers in the name of Jacques Perrier, a fruit machine salesman (a useful job title that enabled him to travel and carry large amounts of money without suspicion), Poirier was invited to lunch at a quiet inn near Tulle, where a meeting was planned with André Malraux and George Hiller. Poirier

107

and Hiller were already old friends – having first met during their teens whilst Hiller was attending the Lycée Janson de Sailly in Paris, they had been unexpectedly reunited just a few weeks before when both of them were hunting for the same Michelin map at Orchard Court.

During the afternoon Malraux's monologues, which ranged from the siege of Stalingrad to Lawrence of Arabia (a particular interest of his) left them exhausted, though after their meal the conversation moved on to his half-brother, Roland Malraux, who had been involved with the Resistance for some time. Having previously been private secretary to writer André Gide and Russian correspondent for *Ce Soir*, the 31-year-old Roland was a 'more relaxed, more elegant, somewhat worldly'[5] figure compared with André, and had already been responsible for introducing his younger brother Claude to an F Section agent named Philippe Liewer (*Clement*).

A journalist by trade, Liewer was a serious, methodical character who had been recruited by F Section agent George Langelaan in Nice during September 1941, though Langelaan's arrest just a few weeks after their meeting led the police to raid Liewer's house in Antibes; he spent ten uncomfortable months in Mauzac prison camp in the Dordogne before escaping over the Pyrenees, eventually making it to London in September 1942. After being trained as an organizer, Liewer (now renamed 'Geoffrey Staunton') returned to France in April 1943 to begin the SALESMAN circuit, covering Rouen and the port of Le Havre. Amongst his helpers was Claude Malraux, who soon became Liewer's second-in-command and assisted in SALESMAN's successful sabotage attacks on naval targets, factories and railway lines later that year.

In February 1944 Liewer returned to London, leaving Claude, code-named *Cicero*, in charge. Although not directly involved with Claude's work, Roland had been willing to support the circuit's operations, offering his small ninth-floor apartment on rue Lord Byron near the Arc de Triomphe as a safe house, and André felt that he could also act as a useful lieutenant for Peulevé. On a brief trip to Brive Roland agreed to the idea and promised to return as soon as he had attended to his affairs in Paris.

The arrival of Poirier as his assistant was a great relief to Peulevé, but he was aware that the quickening growth of his network was beginning to compromise its security. Even though the arrival of Hiller and Watney had shifted some of his responsibilities to a separate circuit, the increasing need to provide training and additional landing grounds for the maquis meant that he was forced to take bigger risks. The safety of Bertheau and Melon at Meymac had also become a concern, as a spotter plane had several times circled their radio post at the Moulin du Breuil.[6] During a wireless transmission to London on 20 February the aircraft became even more inquisitive and flew just a few feet above the house, prompting them to quickly move their two wireless sets (a second set had arrived in January) to the house of Madame Hohenauer, who ran the youth hostel in Meymac and was already well known to Bertheau.

Although they continued to transmit from their new location, a jealous local FTP group soon began to cause trouble, hanging a sign outside the hostel declaring it to be residence of the local *milice* chief, and in desperation Hohenauer's young daughter Suzanne was sent to consult Peulevé. He told her to return with a message that a new safe house would be found for Bertheau in Brive, and Arnouil approached the commercial director of Bloc-Gazo, Armand Lamory, for help. Lamory agreed to offer the use of his house at 171 Route du Tulle in the suburb of Lascamps on the outskirts of Brive, and Bertheau arrived there on 5 March, leaving his assistant Melon in Meymac.

Poirier moved out of his hotel room to join Bertheau, though it wasn't long before they both became uneasy with this location, as members of the network began to pay them frequent visits in full view of the neighbours. Moreover, the first-floor rooms they were occupying gave them no chance of escape if they were called on by the local Gestapo or *milice*, as the only exit was down the staircase to the front door. Poirier voiced his fears, but Peulevé felt that such risks were now essential if they were to succeed; however, it was agreed that Poirier should move back to the Hotel Champanatier while they worked on finding an alternative location for Bertheau.

Aside from the threat of denunciation, German detection of agents' wireless transmissions in occupied countries had become a sophisticated business by 1944, and local direction-finding teams were so efficient at pinpointing a signal's source that SOE advised its operators to stay on the air for no longer than five minutes. Whilst other SOE circuits greatly increased their security by transmitting from several W/T sets hidden at different safe houses, Bertheau was afforded no similar freedom of movement, despite D/F vans regularly driving past his window along the Route du Tulle. Yet to his great credit he patiently stuck to his job and was now often working through the night to maintain AUTHOR's vital communications with London.

Although Poirier's concerns about security had been acknowledged, another reported incident suggests that Peulevé may have taken even greater chances with his own safety. With his circuit's HQ at Bloc-Gazo, Peulevé spent a lot of time with Arnouil and would often lunch with him at the restaurant of the Hotel Champanatier. Unfortunately it also became a favourite haunt of local SD officer, Walter Schmald, the SS headquarters being at the nearby Hotel Terminus. Having noticed that Peulevé and his friend were regulars, Schmald introduced himself and, being bilingual, was keen to chat with them. Although on his guard, Peulevé guessed that he was more than just another thug – originally trained as a pharmacist, Schmald had become a translator for the *Abwehr* (German military intelligence) in Paris in 1941 before transferring to the SD at Limoges and later at Tulle. They apparently met on several more occasions, during which Peulevé attempted to extract whatever useful information he could about Schmald's department, though the German was altogether more interested in advice on where best to acquaint himself with the local women. London was told of this ploy to gather intelligence, but considered it far too dangerous to pursue and expressly ordered Peulevé to cease having any further contact with Schmald.

Although the situation of those living in the forests and hills of the Corrèze was still desperate, the increasing drops of supplies and money from the RAF were able to offer hope to many maquis on the verge of starvation. With the arrival of significant quantities of arms and explosives there was also much greater scope for carrying out raids on German lines of communications, and while the AS largely followed a policy of building up their strength in anticipation of D-Day, the FTP set about seriously harassing the enemy, carrying out numerous ambushes and assassinations. For Peulevé their successes during January and February signalled the turning point that he had been waiting for, and he was keen to take part in many of their actions:

> At last I could feel that I need no longer run away: on the contrary, the German troops in our area had an extremely bad time from us. They kept to the roads and we kept to the hills. Every time we spotted a German convoy we pounced on it and never let up until it was annihilated. Factories, arms dumps and

railways soared skywards after our visits. It was expensive and destructive warfare. Our losses were high. The Germans came into the woods with flame-throwers and tanks, but we were experts in making retreat when our stand against them had taken its toll ... For every one German we killed, they would kill twenty or thirty hostages, taken at random from the villages through which they passed, but we never let up on them. They were haunted night and day by us, the ghosts in the wood who swooped down on them at every opportunity. This was my revenge for the years when unequal odds and circumstances had put me in the humiliating position of a fleeing coward.

My victory was not entire: the dangers were great. These I was prepared to face. The secret satisfaction of walking through their garrisoned towns in the guise of a French black marketeer ... gave me such a sense of exultation that I knew my vindication was practically complete.

Our methods of slaughter were unorthodox and strictly disapproved of by all the conventional rules of warfare. We sabotaged their war effort; we stopped their circulation on the roads of the country they were supposedly dominating. We cut short their simple off-duty pleasures by raining lead on them when they walked out of the brothels and bars; we burnt out their vehicles and killed their drivers when they switched on the ignition to start their cars; we poisoned their wines and we threw the trains off the lines when they went back to Germany for leave.

Their reply to this treatment was the coward's way out. They took revenge on the women, children and old men ... But they could not get us out of the woods.[7]

Having formed Peulevé's small elite squad for special operations, Raymond Maréchal was eager to join in, though his exploits were described by his commander as being 'brave to the point of being extremely rash'.[8] One of these involved the use of a French Army scout car, which had been discarded in 1940 and was later reconditioned by Arnouil and hidden in some woods. Peulevé had intended to retrieve it closer to D-Day when the fighting was likely to become more open, but Maréchal soon came up with a more immediate use for it. Placing Bren guns at its front and rear and three flagpoles on the bonnet flying British, French and American flags, he would take to the moonlit streets with two of his maquisards, opening fire on any German he could find. Soon word began spreading about 'The Phantom American' and his raids, instilling such fear in the local garrison that some soldiers preferred to face a court martial rather than go on curfew patrols.

Terrorizing the occupying forces in the area also relied on less openly confrontational, but equally ruthless measures. One ploy involved using pocket torches – replacing one of the batteries with a small amount of high explosive, the switch could be used to fire a detonator, producing a device capable of removing the hand of an unsuspecting and inquisitive soldier. When they hung their great-coats up in the cafés and bars of the local towns and villages, these torches would be surreptitiously dropped into their pockets by boys who were too young to join the maquis. They were deliberately dropped into the right-hand pockets, assuming that once the soldier had donned his coat and walked off down the street, he would find the torch and curiosity would inevitably lead him to try to switch it on to see if it worked; the result would prevent him being able to fire a rifle again. Peulevé reported that these devices were very suc-cessful in lowering morale and increasing the numbers of local troops sent back to Germany, though the expected reprisals against the locals did not materialize, possibly due to the Germans' belief that the torches were dropped by Allied aircraft and had been picked up in the streets.

According to his own memoirs, Peulevé's most successful strike against the local forces came on 10 March, when the maquis he was visiting near Montignac was alerted to the presence of a German convoy by plumes of smoke a few miles away (the local farmers regularly lit pre-prepared bonfires as a signal to warn them of any imminent threat).[9] The area's steep valleys with their winding narrow roads were ideally suited to ambushes, and Peulevé had already shown the maquisards how to mine roads by digging up a strip of asphalt, laying charges in the trench and detonating them from a hiding position from behind the trees. Yet despite having used this method successfully to eliminate a patrol some days before, they had carelessly failed to reset the trap. With little time left before the convoy reached them, it was decided that thirty men should lay an ambush either side of the road – when the first armoured vehicle appeared it was likely that its crew would inspect the uncovered trench before moving forward, which offered the opportunity to take the convoy by surprise.

Sure enough the first truck stopped as expected and moments later several soldiers appeared with mine detectors to check on the disturbed area. A few seconds later the maquisards opened fire, forcing them to run for cover in the ditches; as they could not return to their vehicle, the trucks behind them were also unable to move forwards, making them easy prey for the other fighters scattered behind the pine trees on the slopes above them. A number of German and Vichy troops were cut down as they threw themselves out of their vehicles, but the remainder of the force, which Peulevé estimated at several hundred men, soon began to return fire, leading to a stalemate with neither side making any ground. With no obvious way out of the deadlock, the initiative was taken by two Russian recruits who suddenly appeared brandishing the group's new Bren guns, still covered in packing grease. Directing their fire at two of the trucks further back, they caused panic amongst those on board and gave Peulevé enough time to direct his men on the slopes to hurl down grenades on the remaining vehicles.

Within half an hour the entire convoy was reduced to a trail of burning wrecks and the resulting confusion made it easy to pick off those soldiers who had not managed to escape; any wounded were dealt with as savagely as maquisards captured by the Germans, being despatched with a shot to the back of the neck. As they sat around the fire in the evening the Russian duo were fêted as heroes for their actions and Peulevé shared in their elation, though for him the victory was another personal act of exoneration, offering more 'sweet vengeance for those miserable early days of running away'.[10]

A few days before the return of Roland Malraux, Peulevé received news from Arnouil that yet another *résistant* had arrived in Brive, whose cover had been blown in the Savoie. Having a meeting to attend in the Dordogne, he asked Poirier to interrogate this man and ascertain whether he might be of use to the circuit. Meeting in the cellar of Bloc-Gazo's premises, Poirier was shocked to find that the man in question was his father, Robert. Though willing to bring him into the organization, Poirier had to fill him in on what had happened since his departure from Cannes, and make it clear that he was now known as 'Captain Jack', using the cover of a British officer for security purposes. In addition to keeping their family connection secret, there was also the more delicate issue of whether he would have a problem receiving orders from his son. He needn't have worried and the following morning 'Commandant Robert' returned to Bloc-Gazo to agree to his terms.

Meanwhile Peulevé had been investigating a young, fiery maquis leader based in the Dordogne: René Coustellier (known as 'Soleil') was a 23-year-old *réfractaire* who had fled Avignon for the area around Belvès, one of the medieval fortified towns known as *bastides* dotted across the southern Dordogne, and had requested a rendez-vous at St Laurent-la-Vallée, a few miles away from the Lachauds' mill at Daglan. Meeting in front of the village's thirteenth-century church, Paul Lachaud introduced the piratical-looking Soleil and his bodyguards to Peulevé and Arnouil before travelling to a house at nearby Grives, where they discussed Soleil's requirements. Despite having communist connections, Coustellier obviously commanded his maquis with great individuality, possessing an uncanny ability both to inspire his followers and instil terror in the hearts of local collaborators, who he pursued relentlessly. In need of arms and especially ammunition, Peulevé was willing to offer Soleil his help and they agreed to meet in two days to work out the details, this time at the house of Abbé Merchadou, a former pilot and *résistant* who often hid arms in his little church at Sagelat. Soleil's contacts in the area could provide Peulevé with an opportunity not only to expand AUTHOR's territory, but also a means of diverting the Germans' attention on his network by setting up a secondary head-quarters in the Dordogne. In return for delivery of parachuted supplies, Soleil promised to acquaint Poirier with the region and help him select a suitable safe house in the area.

Peulevé was equally astonished to see Poirier's father when he arrived back at Bloc-Gazo, having got to know him during his time at Beaulieu-sur-Mer whilst his leg was in plaster. Seeing how exhausted he looked, Robert suggested that Peulevé go to Savoie to stay with Madame Poirier for a few days. He gratefully accepted the offer, but before he could leave sudden news arrived of a crisis developing in Rouen.

Upon returning to Paris, Roland Malraux had been warned that his brother Claude, the acting organizer of SALESMAN, had just been arrested by the Gestapo, and that his network was now rapidly unravelling – unfortunately Claude had been the victim of a set-up involving an informer posing as a potential recruit, and was caught with two suitcases full of documents on the evening of 8 March, including details of sabotage carried out by the circuit. Though only on the periphery of SALESMAN, Roland and his wife Madeleine knew they were in danger if they stayed, and immediately took another train south. Reaching Brive station, Roland got off and told

Leonard Auguste Peulevé and his wife Elizabeth.
(Peulevé collection)

Eva Peulevé, in the garden at Grove Avenue, Twickenham, 1931. *(Peulevé collection)*

Leonard Peulevé with the Royal Army Service Corps, 1915. *(Peulevé collection)*

Annette Peulevé.
(Peulevé collection)

Harry and Arthur Larking on the French Riviera, summer 1932. *(Peulevé collection)*

Harry (far left), Annette (back row, third from right), Eva (front row, middle) and her sister Katherine (third from left), at a family reunion outside 126 Alderney Street, 1936. *(Peulevé collection)*

Harry during his time with the BBC, 1937.
(Peulevé collection)

Staff Sergeant
Peulevé before
leaving for France,
early 1940.
(Peulevé collection)

Orchard Court,
where F Section's
agents were briefed
on their missions.
(Author)

Captain Hilaire Poole joins F Section, March 1942. *(National Archives)*

Maurice Buckmaster, head of SOE's French Section. *(National Archives)*

Francis Suttill – 'Prosper'. *(National Archives)*

Buckmaster's assistant, Vera Atkins. *(National Archives)*

André Girard, leader of the CARTE network. *(National Archives)*

Claude de Baissac, organizer of the SCIENTIST circuit. *(National Archives)*

Isidore Newman, CARTE's W/T operator from April 1942. *(National Archives)*

Peter Churchill, SOE's liaison officer to CARTE. *(National Archives)*

Harry poses for a family portrait just before departing for his first mission in July 1942. *(Peulevé collection)*

Jacques Poirier. *(Archives Départmentales de Corrèze, 60J 519)*

Peulevé on crutches outside the Poirier family house, Beaulieu-sur-Mer, November 1942. *(Peulevé collection)*

Denis Rake, Peulevé's companion in Jaraba. *(National Archives)*

Passport photo of Peulevé, probably taken in Gibraltar, April 1943. *(Peulevé collection)*

Violette Szabó at the time she became a secret agent. *(Carve Her Name with Pride, Pen & Sword Books)*

Cyril Watney.
(Watney family)

Brive-la-Gaillarde, 1944. The main road on the right is Avenue de la Gare, leading down to the church of Saint-Sernin. *(Archives Muncipales de Brive-la-Gaillarde)*

Colonel René Vaujour, commander of the Armée Secrète in the Corrèze. *(Centre d'études et musée Edmond-Michelet, Ville de Brive-la-Gaillarde)*

Maurice Arnouil, one of the founders of Peulevé's AUTHOR circuit. *(Centre d'études et musée Edmond-Michelet, Ville de Brive-la-Gaillarde)*

26 Avenue de la Gare, the site of Arnouil's 'Bloc Gazo' premises in Brive. *(Author)*

Louis Bertheau, AUTHOR's W/T operator from December 1943. *(Musée de la Résistance Henri Queuille, Neuvic)*

André Malraux, in the role of 'Colonel Berger', 1944. *(L'Humanite/Keystone, France; Camera Press, London)*

Peulevé's assistant Louis Delsanti, former police commissioner of Ussel. *(Musée de la Résistance Henri Queuille, Neuvic)*

Jean Melon, photographed with Bertheau's W/T sets at the Moulin du Breuil, January 1944. *(Jean Melon)*

George Hiller, FOOTMAN's organizer in the Lot. *(Judith Hiller)*

Memorial marking the field near Carennac where George Hiller and Cyril Watney parachuted to Peulevé's reception committee on 7/8 January 1944. *(Author)*

Lamory's safe house at 171, Route du Tulle. Bertheau transmitted from the upstairs room at the front of the house. *(Peulevé collection)*

Roland Malraux. *(Baron Gaillarde/Gamma, France; Camera Press, London)*

Forest Yeo-Thomas, deputy head of SOE's RF Section and known to the resistance as 'The White Rabbit'. *(National Archives)*

84 Avenue Foch, the Paris headquarters of the *Sicherheitsdienst*. *(Author)*

Aerial view of US bombing of Buchenwald concentration camp, 24 August 1944. The main camp and its rows of prison blocks (top) are largely untouched, while clouds of smoke obscure the site of the Gustloff arms factories (right). *(US National Archives)*

Block 46, the 'guinea pig' block where Peulevé, Yeo-Thomas and Hessel switched identities. This picture was secretly taken by prisoner Georges Angéli in June 1944. *(Buchenwald Archive)*

Arthur Dietzsch, Kapo of Block 46. *(US National Archives)*

Dr Erwin Ding-Schuler, the SS doctor in charge of Block 46. *(Bundesarchiv)*

Ding-Schuler's secretary Eugen Kogon, giving evidence at the Buchenwald war crimes trials in Dachau. *(US National Archives)*

Peulevé after his return to the UK, 1945. *(Peulevé collection)*

Edmond Michelet presenting Peulevé with the *Medaille de la Résistance,* Brive, June 1948. *(Peulevé collection)*

Just married: Peulevé and Marie-Louise outside the British Consulate General, Tunis, March 1952. *(Peulevé collection)*

Harry with Marie-Louise and Madeleine. *(Peulevé collection)*

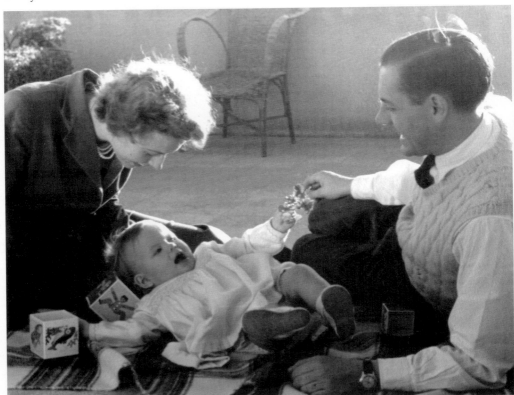

Visiting Jean-Pierre and Madeleine at Marie-Louise's parents' house in Odense. *(Peulevé collection)*

The last portrait of Harry Peulevé, taken in early 1963. *(Peulevé collection)*

Grave and plaque at
the British Cemetery,
San Jerónimo, Seville.
(Author)

Memorial plaque outside
171 Route du Tulle. *(Peulevé
collection)*

Madeleine to stay at her parents' house in Toulouse until she heard more news from him, now intending to dedicate himself entirely to Peulevé's network.

Although the collapse of SALESMAN had just begun, Peulevé had no idea that this catastrophe was about to put Violette in great danger, having now become a fully-trained SOE agent herself. Having already guessed that she might be waiting to drop into France, he had requested that London send him a female courier to deal with his ever-increasing workload on the chance that she might be assigned to him, but as he suspected that Vera Atkins already knew of his connection with Szabó he was not surprised when she didn't arrive. His pragmatic outlook did little to reduce his anxiety, however, and in his own words 'my imagination played all sorts of tricks and my heart was very often in my boots at the thought that she would be sent to some unsafe circuit and rapidly captured.'[11]

In fact some of SOE's trainers had recommended that Violette should be returned to civilian life months earlier, long before her training was complete. Her initial selection report at Winterfold in August had highlighted some promising qualities ('Plucky and persistent in her endeavours. Not easily rattled ... could probably do a useful job, possibly as a courier'),[12] but her performance on the Group A course in Scotland during September had raised some serious concerns. Although she undertook the assault courses with characteristic enthusiasm and was considered a crack shot by her Highlands instructors, there were growing doubts about her psychological stability, and it seems that her single-minded determination to avenge her husband's death was perhaps overshadowing her other qualities. The Commandant reluctantly reported:

> After a certain amount of doubt, especially at the beginning of the course, I have come to the conclusion that this student is temperamentally unsuitable for this work. I consider that owing to her <u>too</u> fatalistic outlook in life and particularly in her work, the fact that she lacks the ruse, stability and the finesse which is required and that she is too easily influenced; when operating in the field she might endanger the lives of others working with her. It is very regrettable to have to come to such a decision when dealing with a student of this type, who during the whole course has set an example to the whole party by her cheerfulness and eagerness to please.[13]

Yet with preparations mounting for D-Day demand for female couriers was high, and Buckmaster chose to ignore these recommendations, passing her on to the finishing school at Beaulieu. Unfortunately she suffered another setback when she injured her ankle on her first parachute jump at Ringway, but following a period of convalescence Violette steeled herself to retake the course, and successfully gained her wings at the end of February.

It took just a week for F Section to assign Violette as assistant to Roland's contact Philippe Liewer, the original organizer of SALESMAN, who was planning to return to Rouen later in March. Orchard Court had no idea of the disaster that had just overtaken the circuit, though fortunately the arrests of Claude Malraux, W/T operator Isidore Newman (Peulevé's companion during the CARTE fiasco) and a dozens others had just been reported to Peulevé through Roland, who had been informed by Claude's wife. A message was sent immediately via Bertheau to warn London of the situation:

FROM MACKINTOSH RED
12TH MARCH 1944
BLUFF CHECK OMITTED   TRUE CHECK OMITTED

FOLLOWING NEWS FROM ROUEN STOP XLAUDEMALRAUX
DISAPPEARED BELGIVED ARRESTED BY GESTAPO STOP RADIO
OPERATOR PIERRE ARRESTES STOP IF CLETENT STILL WITH
YOU DO NOT SEND HEM STOP DOFTOR ARRESTES STOP
EIGHTEEN TONS ARMS REMOVED BS POLIFE STOP BELEIVE
THIS DUE ARRESTATION OF A SEFTION FHEIF WHO GAVE
ASRESSES ADIEU[14]

[FOLLOWING NEWS FROM ROUEN STOP CLAUDE MALRAUX
DISAPPEARED BELIEVED ARRESTED BY GESTAPO STOP RADIO
OPERATOR PIERRE ARRESTED STOP IF CLEMENT [Liewer's
codename] STILL WITH YOU DO NOT SEND HIM STOP DOCTOR
ARRESTED STOP EIGHTEEN TONS ARMS REMOVED BY POLICE
STOP BELIEVE THIS DUE ARRESTATION OF A SECTION CHIEF
WHO GAVE ADDRESSES ADIEU]

This garbled message gives some idea of the problems faced by Buckmaster and Atkins who received such badly mutilated telegrams on a daily basis. However, it was clear enough for F Section to realize that sending Liewer and Szabó would be far too dangerous and probably saved both of them from walking straight into the midst of a blown circuit.

By the middle of March, the results of Peulevé's work were clearly evident. The Prefect for the department recorded that seventeen cantons of the Corrèze were now in the hands of the maquis, while just nine belonged of the Germans, and the police had reported no fewer than ninety Resistance operations since the end of February. He now had approximately 2,500 men under his command across the Corrèze and Dordogne, of which two-thirds were based in AS maquis camps, and his dealings with Bonnetot had also produced at least another 1,500 in the FTP. Though records are incomplete, Peulevé and Bertheau are known to have sent eighty-three messages to London and received 118, and conducted twenty-four dropping operations between January and March 1944, probably netting in the region of 400 containers, enough *matériel* to fully equip several thousand men. The rise of the maquis was of course not down to one man's efforts, but the role Peulevé played was fundamental in their ability to train, arm and mobilize their forces. It is no exaggeration to suggest that without his determination to make AUTHOR a success, resistance in the Corrèze would have remained largely an unarmed struggle.

Yet these achievements had come at a considerable cost. Despite delegating more of his responsibilities, Peulevé was being drained by the demands of his role and arranged for Poirier to share a more equal load when he returned from the Savoie – having established a safe house at Siorac-en-Périgord through Soleil, Poirier would now work on establishing himself in the eastern Dordogne, while Peulevé concentrated his efforts on the Corrèze. Yet thinking of Jacques' long separation from his family he had a sudden change of heart about his imminent trip. Despite being desperately in need of some time away, he knew that his friend had not seen his mother since leaving the Riviera in 1942 and consequently made the selfless decision to stay, insisting that Poirier go instead. Though neither of them could have known it, Peulevé's judgement was about to alter the courses of both their lives irrevocably.

Chapter 10

Retribution

On the morning of Tuesday 21 March, Peulevé said goodbye to Poirier and took his usual route down the back stairs, discreetly leaving the Champanatier by a side door and walking the short distance to Bloc-Gazo's offices. Whilst in town he was alerted to a problem concerning the supply drop planned for the next day: the dropping area, situated near a disused aerodrome, had suddenly been occupied by a German anti-aircraft battery posted there on training duties. It was imperative that London was told to cancel the operation as soon as possible and Roland Malraux, only having joined the organization a few days before, accompanied Delsanti and Peulevé to visit Bertheau at his hideout on the Route du Tulle. Travelling in Peulevé's Chevrolet across Brive in the brisk, bright afternoon, they parked on the road outside Lamory's house and made their way up the stairs to the larger of the two rooms on the first floor, taking turns to keep a lookout from the front window while the others began preparing Peulevé's telegram for London and deciphering several other messages received by Bertheau over the past few days.

Around half-past three Arnouil left his house on nearby rue Edouard Branly, walking the few hundred yards to join the group as arranged. Turning right onto the Route du Tulle, he was about to cross the road when two black Citroëns sped past him and suddenly halted 100 yards further up, directly outside Lamory's address. Arnouil quickly began retracing his steps as he saw one uniformed officer and three others in civilian clothes get out and run to the front of the house, bursting in through the unlocked door. Tearing through the lounge and up the short staircase to the first floor, they were shocked to come face to face with Peulevé and his team in the front room, standing around a wireless set screwed down on a table. Peulevé immediately tried to burn his silk codes in the stove but was dismayed to find that they would not catch light, while Bertheau, in mid-transmission, had the presence of mind to tap out 'nous sommes pris!' (we are taken) before raising his hands. Delsanti made a frantic attempt to jump out of the window, but their situation was hopeless. Having been taken completely by surprise, there was now no chance of escape.

None of them was armed (though the wardrobe in the room concealed a number of guns), and the SD officer quickly ushered them down the stairs and into the back garden, leaving one of his men to guard them whilst the rest of the house was searched. As they waited one of the Lamorys' neighbours, a *milicien* named Adrien Dufour, began shouting abuse over the fence behind them and it soon became clear that he had been responsible for tipping the Germans off. Believing Peulevé to be the head of a group of Jewish black marketeers, he had been only too aware of the frequency with which people had recently been visiting the house. In fact, many in the neighbourhood had avoided walking past number 171 since Bertheau's arrival at the beginning of March, having been suspicious of the numerous strangers who would park their cars outside at night (some had already guessed its connections with the Resistance and even begun to refer to it as 'La Maison des Anglais').[1] As Poirier had feared, a simple lack of precaution had finally led to their discovery.

Having expected to find nothing more than a few small-time criminals dealing in contraband liquor, Walter Schmald was completely confounded by the sight of these *résistants* caught in the act, though he was even more surprised to see Peulevé among them, recalling how they had become acquainted in Brive some weeks before. Schmald's glee was evident and Peulevé even congratulated him on making such an important haul, but he was furious with himself for being the one responsible for this catastrophe, having been temporarily distracted from the window during the few crucial seconds when the two cars drove up.

Once the search was completed Schmald was keen to get his prisoners as quickly as possible to Tulle and the four of them were marched to the gate with their hands on their heads. Split into pairs, Peulevé and Roland Malraux were hustled into the dickey-seat of one of the Citroëns; thankful that they had not been handcuffed, Peulevé was at least able to dispose of some of the incriminating papers he was carrying by stuffing them behind the seat, though he

119

knew that other messages and codes would have been found during the search of Bertheau's room.

They were immediately driven to the Waffen-SS barracks in Tulle, where a brief interrogation included questions relating to one of the directors of Bloc-Gazo, a Jew named Roger Lang. Peulevé said that he knew nothing of him, attempting to try and pass himself off as an escaped British POW trying to make his way to Spain with the help of the Resistance. He knew this story wasn't likely to hold up since he had had no opportunity to get his story straight with the other three, but thought that it might buy them some time.

They spent the night in Tulle, being driven the next morning to the Gestapo HQ in Limoges. Using a translator, Peulevé was first questioned by SS Obersturmführer Joachim Kleist, who began with the wireless messages found at the house. It soon became impossible to maintain his initial alibi and he was eventually forced to admit that he had been sent to work in France with the Resistance. He also declared that his mission was to arrange landing grounds for paratroops and gliders after D-Day, which appeared to satisfy his interrogator. The Gestapo officer then presented him with material showing the extent of the Germans' understanding of SOE and its networks, including pictures of *Prosper* (Francis Suttill, with whom he had trained at Wanborough Manor and Meoble Lodge) and members of his circuit based in and around Paris, maps of the areas in which they operated and details on several STS training schools in England. Peulevé was unflustered by this, knowing that it would not have been difficult to obtain information on SOE schools from other captured sources, though he could not be sure about the other evidence.

After this session Peulevé was taken to Limoges jail, where he rejoined his companions. They used the limited time they had together to work out a rudimentary cover story, largely based on the premise that Peulevé was the W/T operator, with the other three acting as nothing more than *agents de liaisons*. The next afternoon all four men were taken to the Gare Bénédictins and put on a train for Paris; during their journey one of their guards made light of Peulevé's situation, saying that he would be most likely exchanged for a captured German agent in England. However, given the circumstances of his arrest he knew that the Gestapo were likely to try and get as much information out of him as possible.

On arrival at Austerlitz station Peulevé was immediately taken to Avenue Foch, a grand, tree-lined Haussman boulevard leading from the Arc de Triomphe toward the Bois de Boulogne. Numbers 82 to 86 had become the main headquarters of the German counter-intelligence services and Peulevé was escorted through the gates of the luxurious balconied villa at 84, used by the SD for interrogating foreign agents. Having been separated from the others, he was led up the elegant marble staircase and into a room on the second floor where two men were waiting, the taller, white-haired one being Dr Josef Goetz, originally a languages teacher who now acted as a specialist within an SD sub-section dedicated to wireless counter-espionage. Goetz wasted no time in asking about the codes and messages found at the Lamory house and soon began pressing him for information on where other radio sets could be found. Having claimed to be the only wireless operator in the group, Peulevé maintained that all his equipment had been captured at the house (as he knew that two silks and two wireless sets would have been found in the first-floor room, this would seem at least plausible). Goetz seemed to be taken in by this story, although a closer examination of Peulevé's clothing would have changed his mind, as he was still carrying another silk sewn into his trousers.

Once the interrogation had ended Peulevé was removed to one of the dozen cells on the top floor of the house which had originally been used as servants' quarters; inside he found a box of clothes, which to his surprise appeared to have been issued to another SOE agent. An hour later he was called for again and as he walked past the guardroom he caught a glimpse of a man next door working on a drawing, instantly recognizing him as John Starr (*Bob*), another F Section agent whom he had known in London. Unfortunately he didn't get a chance to talk or signal to him, instead being taken into an office occupied by a forty-year-old SD auxiliary named Ernst Vogt, who worked as a translator for the Commandant, SS Sturm-bannführer Hans Kieffer. As a result of his success with previous interrogations of F Section's agents, Kieffer had allowed Vogt to conduct interviews without him being present.

Introducing himself as Ernest, his manner was relaxed, offering Peulevé cigarettes and other items clearly captured from parachute drops, suggesting tacitly that RAF supplies were falling regularly to German reception committees rather than French ones. Vogt also told him that if he cooperated and told the truth, a military tribunal and probable execution could be avoided. To emphasize that SOE was now completely compromised, he produced photographs of various agents known to Peulevé from the PROSPER network, the same ones that he had seen from the Gestapo in Limoges. Despite Peulevé pleading ignorance about these individuals Vogt doggedly continued with his approach, referring to specific details concerning the STS schools and their staffs, as well as dropping the names of several F Section officers. As with the Limoges interrogation, Peulevé was asked when he had last seen *Prosper*, though he continued to deny any knowledge of him.

The subject of Francis Suttill and the collapse of his circuit has become one of the most contentious aspects of SOE's history. Born in 1910 at Mons-en-Baroeul near Lille to a French mother and English father, Suttill became a successful London barrister in his twenties before joining the East Surrey Regiment at the outbreak of war. F Section quickly identified his sharp intellect and impressive leadership abilities during selection at Wanborough, and he dropped into France in October 1942 with the objective of building a new Paris circuit to replace the ill-fated AUTOGIRO, which had collapsed earlier that year. Under the code name of *Prosper* (possibly taken from the name of a fifth-century saint) he quickly began gathering support in the areas around Paris, assisted by female agent Andrée Borrel (*Denise*) and W/T operator, Gilbert Norman (*Archambaud*). It did not take long before Suttill was ready to begin receiving supply drops and by spring of 1943 the reach of his PROSPER circuit spread across twelve departments, being assisted by an increasing number of smaller sub-networks including JUGGLER, BUTLER, PRIVET and PUBLICAN. Henri Déricourt's FARRIER also received additional F Section agents by Lysander and Hudson to manage this rapid expansion, and Déricourt had personal contact with Suttill as well, using his wireless operators to coordinate air operations with London.

In April the SD made a significant breakthrough when they arrested Germaine and Madeleine Tambour, two sisters whose names had appeared in André Girard's CARTE dossiers, stolen from André Marsac's briefcase in November 1942. In addition to working for Girard, the Tambours had also acted as a letter box for members of PROSPER, which obviously presented a serious security threat for Suttill. He made two desperate and unsuccessful attempts to try and free them before being recalled to London in May, during which time he declared his suspicions about the loyalties of both Déricourt and Bodington. Déricourt had no part to play in Suttill's return to France on the night of 20/21 May, but the arrests of several PROSPER agents a month later led the SD to the addresses of its key members, and on the eve of Saint Prosper's feast day, 24 June, Suttill, Andrée Borrel and Gilbert Norman were all arrested and taken to Avenue Foch.

In Vogt's retelling of the story, he mentioned that Suttill had refused for a long time to divulge any details of relating to its networks, but had finally broken his silence when he was shown copies of PROSPER mail passed to the SD by Déricourt:

> When the Gestapo produced a photostat copy of a report that this agent [Suttill] sent to London giving all details of his circuit, this agent had then said to the Gestapo 'Well since you know everything I am prepared to answer any questions.' The Gestapo told him that in exchange for any information this agent could give as to the location of arms dumps or his sub-organizations, the Gestapo would guarantee the lives of everybody who was working for him providing they agreed to deliver the arms they had in their keeping to the Gestapo without resistance ... They [Vogt] told me that in many cases the presence of Prosper with them in visiting these arms dumps helped to convince the people that it was all over and that it would be better not to resist. They then told me that Prosper had concluded a pact with them, that his life and all subsequent agents arrested would be guaranteed providing these agents were willing to deliver the arms they had in their keeping. They said that this was an agreement with the chief Headquarters in Berlin. They told me that Prosper was in a camp in Germany.[2]

There is no definitive account of exactly what occurred in those last days of June, but it seems that Kieffer may have obtained the cooperation of Gilbert Norman, and that Norman could have also been brought in during Suttill's interrogation to persuade him to talk.[3] Whether or not anything was actually forced out of Suttill before his transfer to Germany will probably never be known, but either way the end result for PROSPER was unquestionably disastrous, with the number of arrests following the SD's investigations estimated at between four and fifteen hundred. The promises given by Himmler to spare the lives of PROSPER's agents subsequently proved to be worthless, and Suttill, Norman and Borrel would all later be executed in concentration camps.

In the light of this information, Peulevé decided that his best option was to admit to knowledge of *Prosper* but to fabricate another cover story. After Vogt had solemnly typed the fictitious details he gave regarding his date of birth, address and so on, he rang a bell. Soon afterwards Kieffer appeared, accompanied by Starr. Peulevé was at a loss as to what to make of his compatriot:

> When I was confronted with Starr he immediately greeted me by saying 'Hallo, old chap, how are you?' This rather surprised me and all I could say to him was – 'What is this racket?' He replied – 'It's not a racket, they have got me out of Fresnes [prison] to do drawings for them, but that is all.' The look on the Gestapo man's face showed me that he obviously knew or would know that the details I had given them concerning myself were false.[4]

Put back in his cell on the fifth floor, Peulevé returned an hour later to the same room where Vogt was waiting for him. As he had predicted, Vogt said that he had wasted his afternoon on collecting his details, as they were all false. He then showed Peulevé his personal details on a sheet of paper, which to his astonishment were all correct. Vogt made it clear that an agent was working for them in Orchard Court, who passed the real identities of all F Section's people to the SD. Peulevé did not believe that this was possible, since even someone in Orchard Court would be unlikely to know every agent's personal details, though it was conceivable that the information came from Starr or another interrogated member of the Resistance. However, he did not see how he could continue to deny this information and admitted to it being accurate.

Vogt then started to ask about his circuit. A list of the locations of parachuting grounds had been captured from Lamory's house, which he proceeded to mark out on a map, telling Peulevé they would begin to search these areas for arms dumps, but Peulevé replied that there were no caches since all the arms were dropped directly into the hands of the maquis. Vogt wasn't satisfied and still believed that there must be arms somewhere in the circuit's territory; searching for something to offer him, Peulevé had the idea of giving an address of Arnouil's at Terrasson, west of Brive (Arnouil's cover was already blown and could not be compromised any further by this admission). He claimed that this was the location of the only arms dump he had, and was to be used in the event of a special job requested by London. This story was partly true, as a local farmer in Terrasson had been put in charge of a cache of AUTHOR's arms. However, some time later the farmer had mistakenly contacted another agent believing him to be a member of

Peulevé's network – unknown to Peulevé, the neighbouring STATIONER circuit led by Maurice Southgate (*Hector*) had installed a maquis in the area, now commanded by one of his lieutenants, Jacques Dufour. Unconvinced that Peulevé and Poirier were SOE agents, Southgate had allowed Dufour's maquis to steal these arms for themselves, leaving nothing for the Germans to find. Peulevé knew that if this location was checked he could plead ignorance about the theft, and if interrogated the farmer would most likely back up his story.

Vogt's questions then switched to the whereabouts of maquis camps, but Peulevé maintained that he only met Resistance leaders at pre-determined times and places, and that his last meeting was supposed to have been at the railway station at Brive on the day of his arrest. As Vogt was getting frustrated he dredged up a couple of addresses of hotels and bars to placate him, claiming (falsely) that he had used them as meeting places in the past; this stalled him temporarily, but there was no shortage of other leads to follow up.

A number of wireless telegrams related to people who had given money to the Resistance, which Peulevé could do little to disguise and would probably result in the arrests of the donors. More worryingly, another message showed communication between Paul Lachaud and Bloc-Gazo, which aroused suspicions as to why a mill-owner would want to order so many spare parts from such a company (in fact this message was coded and referred to details of arms being held at the mill, not spare parts). Peulevé denied that Lachaud had any part in the circuit, though it was obvious that Paul and his wife Georgette were now in great danger.[5]

In one of the most recent messages London had mentioned the capture of a woman presumed to be a letter box, through which Peulevé could send on a report. Peulevé said that he had not used it, which was the truth, never having sent any mail since his arrival in September. As Vogt moved on to another telegram, both of them could hear the sound of footsteps running down the corridor towards them. A moment later the figure of Kieffer suddenly burst through the door. Staring at Peulevé, he asked, 'Who is Nestor?'

After witnessing the events at Lamory's house, Arnouil had circulated news of the arrests as quickly as possible, mindful that Poirier would be in great danger when he returned from the Savoie. He drove to the Verlhacs at Quatre-Routes, from where Jean Verlhac sent word on to Hiller and then to his wireless operator Cyril Watney, who was able to transmit a message to London from a

125

farmhouse near Saint-Céré in the Lot. On the evening of 23 March, Poirier was sitting in his mother's house at Saint-Gervais-les-Bains when she asked him to come and listen to the BBC *messages personnels*. Though muttering that he was 'off-duty' he nevertheless caught Watney's message: *Message important pour Nestor: Jean très malade, ne retournez pas*. Unfortunately the SD at 84 Avenue Foch were also keen BBC listeners, and it did not take them long to connect *Jean* with Peulevé.

Peulevé first denied any knowledge of what Kieffer was referring to, but was then given the BBC message in full, which also mentioned that *Nestor* (Poirier) should go to see *Maxime* (Hiller) or *Eustache* (Watney), another two names which the SD did not know of. Peulevé was now on the back foot and had to think quickly. He stated that *Nestor* had been parachuted to one of his grounds, but had then moved on and had no role within his circuit, though he had visited Bloc-Gazo. *Maxime* and *Eustache* he explained as being agents sent by London to help the Vény groups, though he did not give Kieffer addresses (in the case of Watney this would have been impossible anyway, as he had been careful enough to keep his location secret from almost everyone). None of the three would be arrested as the result of Peulevé's capture.

Still convinced that he knew more than he was giving away, the SD kept Peulevé for several more days at 84 Avenue Foch, during which time he was subjected to torture to divulge more information about the names in the BBC message and details about his circuit. In training, SOE's agents were told that they should try and hold out for forty-eight hours before talking, to allow sufficient time for safe houses to be cleared and arms dumps to be relocated, but Peulevé had no intention of giving up any remaining secrets. Poirier later commented briefly on his ordeal, mentioning that 'he was half-drowned on several occasions',[6] referring to a well-known and feared form of torture known as the *baignoire*, which was particularly favoured by the SD and Gestapo. The process involved submerging the victim in a cold bath to the point of drowning, at which point they would be pulled out and revived, sometimes with schnapps. The questioning would then resume; if the interrogators did not get what they wanted, the process would continue. Unsurprisingly it was not uncommon for victims to end up being held under too long and 'accidentally' drowned using this method. Another SOE agent, Forest Yeo-Thomas, who will appear later, gave his own recollections of undergoing this torture:

I was helpless. I panicked and tried to kick, but the vice-like grip was such that I could hardly move. My eyes were open, I could see shapes distorted by the water, wavering above me, my lungs were bursting, my mouth opened and I swallowed water. Now I was drowning. I put every ounce of my energy into a vain effort to kick myself out of the bath, but I was completely helpless and, swallowing water, I felt that I must burst. I was dying, this was the end, I was losing consciousness, but as I was doing so, I felt the strength going out of me and my limbs going limp. This must be the end ...[7]

Peulevé's own reference to the matter was typically modest, only mentioning that 'I am certain the miseries they put me through were nothing compared with those that other people had suffered',[8] and gave a vague reference to undergoing 'a few days of the traditional physical and mental softening-up process'.[9] However, apart from repeatedly subjecting him to the *baignoire*, the SD also resorted to other medieval practices, placing matchsticks under his fingernails and also imprisoning him in a coffin-like box, perforated with ventilation holes; left in it for several hours at a time, he had to tense his limbs repeatedly in order to try and deal with the cramp it induced. Despite these brutal efforts to get him to talk he remained silent – the only information that Peulevé did give away was connected with the information that he, Delsanti and Malraux were already carrying, plus what Bertheau had left behind in his room.

Although these methods proved fruitless, German investigations back in Brive had fared little better. On the evening of 21 March, a *résistant* named Georges Michel had cycled to Arnouil's house on rue Edouard Branly, just a short distance from Lamory's address on the Route du Tulle. Unaware that Arnouil had already fled, Michel was taken by surprise when entering the house, finding Schmald and several of his men inside – having found Arnouil's name mentioned in Bertheau's telegrams, the SD had been waiting to catch anyone coming to warn him of Peulevé's capture. Schmald planned to take Michel to the SD headquarters at Tulle for interrogation, but first wanted to return to the scene of Peulevé's arrest where he and a section from the *Légion Nord-Africaine* (an SD auxiliary force made up of North African soldiers based at Tulle) continued searching and plundering the house. Whilst being held outside Michel was unexpectedly recognized by a *milicien* who had known him before the war, who approached Schmald to release him. Repeatedly

127

vouching for his good character, Michel was eventually placed in the hands of the local chief of the *milice* who freed him shortly afterwards.

With Arnouil at large, Schmald decided to use Bloc-Gazo as a means of identifying more of his Resistance contacts and devised a strangely elaborate plot. Visiting a public notary in Brive, he transferred the shares of Arnouil and another employee, Max Fouhety, to Armand Lamory and SD informer Maurice Herbin, making them the company's senior directors. A friend of Lamory's before the war, Herbin had suddenly reappeared in Brive during February 1944, visiting Bloc-Gazo and even spending several days at Lamory's house, though there is no evidence that he was responsible for the arrest of Peulevé's group or that Lamory was also working for the Germans.[10] Schmald appeared to believe that Herbin's position would enable him to gain intelligence on those using the premises for resistance purposes. However, although he was officially recognized by the rest of the Bloc-Gazo's board on 8 April, the SD's game was obvious and none of AUTHOR's contacts were caught as a result of this action.

After realizing Peulevé had been captured, Poirier made the decision to return to the Corrèze the following day, accompanied by his father who had just arrived at the house. Careful to get off the train at Quatres-Routes station rather than risk being picked up by the Gestapo at Brive, Jacques went to visit Jean Verlhac to find out what had happened. Making contact with Hiller at Verlhac's house, it was clear that Poirier was now the target of a manhunt – although the SD had not initially known who *Nestor* was, they eventually realized that he must be 'Jacques Perrier', whose false *carte d'identité* had been found on Peulevé (Poirier had given it to him in order to exchange it for a new one via Arnouil), and dozens of posters displaying his face were now being pasted throughout Brive and the surrounding areas.

Arnouil and Poirier tried to carry on arranging supply drops for the maquis but their journeys across the Corrèze put them at great risk and they were lucky to avoid arrest when they were stopped at a German roadblock carrying messages for transmission to London. At a meeting at the Verlhacs, Hiller relayed Buckmaster's new instructions to Poirier appointing him the organizer of a new circuit named DIGGER, which was to carry on AUTHOR's work. However, this development was immediately overshadowed by the arrival of Georgette Lachaud, who arrived to tell them that Raymond Maréchal had just been killed.

Before his capture, Peulevé had arranged for Maréchal's strike force to attack a sugar factory, the plan being to steal 40 tonnes of stock destined for Germany. With Soleil's help, Maréchal took three trucks and an old ambulance through the back roads of the Dordogne and Corrèze in the early hours of 24 March, laying up near the factory around eight o'clock. At midday the raid was successfully carried out and the convoy immediately began making its way back, but soon the ambulance was lagging behind, labouring under the weight of 500 kilos of sugar and five passengers. Maréchal proposed to split away from the group and head for the *bastide* of Villefranche-du-Périgord, where he would drop his cargo at a friend's house before meeting up with Soleil the following day. Travelling over the Dordogne river towards Daglan, he could not resist calling in at the Moulin du Cuzoul to tell the Lachauds about their adventure, and his party ended up spending the night there. Waking late, they breakfasted before leaving for Villefranche at two o'clock that afternoon.

At the river crossing close to Maréchal's destination, a German column of thirty-five trucks had stopped en route to Bergerac, returning to base after an unsuccessful attempt to destroy a maquis training ground in the neighbouring Lot-et-Garonne department. Just as the soldiers were climbing back into their vehicles, Maréchal's ambulance turned a corner and ran into them, halting just a few metres from the nearest truck. Two of the group burst out of the back door towards the cover of a wood at the side of the road, shooting down three Germans as they made their escape under a hail of fire. Unfortunately those remaining were less fortunate: Maréchal was instantly cut down, being wounded in the chest and leg, and quickly taken prisoner along with his two remaining companions, driver André Fertin and another *résistant* from Alsace.

About an hour later the column stopped again outside the walls of the old English *bastide* of Beaumont, when two of the three SS men shot earlier died of their wounds. Throwing the three prisoners to the ground outside the Château de Luzier, a number of their enraged comrades began frantically kicking Fertin and Maréchal, even though both were unconscious from the beatings they had already received in the truck. A few moments later their battered bodies were riddled with bullets and left by the side of the road.

129

The Alsatian was taken for questioning at Bergerac and Périgueux, and several days later the SS carried out a raid on the Moulin du Cuzoul, on 31 March. Fortunately the Lachauds were absent and had moved any arms from the premises after Peulevé's arrest. However, the Germans were intent on exacting revenge in any way they could and burned their farm to the ground after savagely slaughtering their livestock.

Poirier decided that a split with Arnouil was necessary for the sake of DIGGER's security and moved into the Château de Siorac, the safe house owned by Soleil's friend Robert Brouillet. Known as 'Charles the Bolshevik', Brouillet was an uncompromising character but not without a sense of prudence, able to rely on his extensive network of local contacts to warn him of incoming German forces long before they reached the village. Continuing to stay in contact with London through Watney, Poirier arranged for two additional SOE agents to be dropped to a landing ground near Domme, and on 9 April Buckmaster sent him a highly capable weapons instructor, Peter Lake (*Basil*, soon to be re-christened with the more Gallic *Jean-Pierre*), accompanied by a studious-looking W/T operator, Ralph Beauclerk (*Casimir*).

With his new assistants in place, Poirier was eager to disappear for a few days and left for Paris, travelling with André Malraux who had meetings with the *Conseil National de la Résistance*. Having been prompted into taking an active role in the Resistance after the arrests of brothers Roland and Claude, Malraux went to offer his services and returned as the 'R5' district commander for the *Forces Francaises Interieurs*, a military body intended to integrate and direct resistance under de Gaulle's General Koenig (ever the self-publicist, Malraux also chose to adopt the *nom de guerre* of 'Colonel Berger' after Vincent Berger, a character from his novel *Les Noyers de l'Altenbourg*). Between April and D-Day, DIGGER and Malraux would work together to try and meet the ever-increasing demand for arms and manage the influx of young men eager to join the maquis.

Having failed to elicit any new information under torture, the SD transferred Peulevé on 3 April from Avenue Foch to Fresnes prison, on the southern outskirts of Paris. Built at the end of the nineteenth century, Fresnes was commonly used to incarcerate other SOE agents, Allied airmen, French resistance fighters and political dissidents, as well as ordinary criminals; from 1942 it also held women. Comprising three four-storey cell blocks with connecting structures at right angles, prisoners were exercised in the rows of small courtyards that lay in between. Although most of its cells were much like any other prison, Fresnes also had a number of dungeons downstairs which were used as a punishment or to break prisoners psychologically, and it was into one of these 'cellules de force' that Peulevé was first introduced. There are no first-hand details of what he experienced, though another account describes what conditions were like: 'The floor was spongy and covered with fungus. The walls were clammy with moisture. Where the bed would have been there were only two iron clamps jutting out from the wall. There was no table. There was a w.c. pan but no tap.'[11] As if this wasn't unpleasant enough, the cell was also completely dark. Aside from the news shouted out by the other prisoners, Peulevé's only human contact for the next two months was with the guard who brought his meagre soup ration.

On 8 June, he was at last dragged out and moved to one of the cells upstairs, which measured about 10 feet long and about half as wide, and was furnished with a folding iron bed, a small shelf, a toilet with a push-button tap above it and a small, high window of frosted glass. The rations were better, but still only consisted of a mug of dirty water which passed for morning coffee, and midday soup, accompanied by a small amount of bread and a piece of cheese or sausage. There was also occasional exercise in one of the small yards between the blocks, though prisoners were segregated during their time outside and all communication for those in solitary confinement was prohibited. Through his long ordeal Peulevé had done what he could to keep his mind occupied, 'either dreaming of wonderful steak dinners, or, recapitulating with the aid of a piece of plaster chipped out of the wall, the theories of Pythagoras and other Greek mathematicians on the cell floor',[12] but his thoughts inevitably turned to Violette and what role F Section might have assigned her.

Although Peulevé had warned London not to send Liewer in March, another attempt had been made to infiltrate him and Szabó by parachute in early April, to assess the state of SALESMAN after the arrests of Claude Malraux and his colleagues. As Liewer was at risk of being recognized in Rouen he remained in Paris, sending Violette (operating under the name 'Corinne Leroy' and code-named *Louise*) to try and establish contact with the remaining members of the circuit in order to see what scope there was for rebuilding it. She spent three weeks visiting the addresses she had been given, but it didn't take long to ascertain that the situation was now hopeless. Although a fair number had avoided capture and could offer *Louise* information on what had happened, it was clear that the Germans had shattered SALESMAN, with nearly a hundred of its members now either dead or in custody. Making her way to Paris, she reported to Liewer on the results of her reconnaissance before they were both safely picked up near Issoudun on 30 April.

Violette had proved herself in the field and was promoted to the rank of Ensign on her return to London, though it was only a matter of days before she was requested to accompany Liewer once more, this time to restart a new SALESMAN circuit in the Haute-Vienne, adjacent to Poirier's newly established DIGGER. Having lost none of her desire to avenge her husband's death she agreed to go, even though it meant leaving her young daughter again. They left on the night of 7/8 June, parachuting to a landing ground near Sussac, south-east of Limoges, where they were received by the local FTP. Finding a lack of organization on the ground, Liewer sent Violette to ask for Poirier's assistance in the Corrèze, taking a headstrong maquis leader, Jacques Dufour (who had previously worked for Southgate's STATIONER) with her as a guide.

Travelling by car on the morning of 10 June, they picked up a young maquisard known to Dufour on their way, Jean Bariaud, before unexpectedly running into an SS roadblock about halfway between Limoges and Brive, outside the village of Salon-la-Tour – unknown to them, the Limousin was now swarming with troops from the SS 2nd Panzer Division *Das Reich*, searching for one of their officers who had been kidnapped the previous evening. Having left their base in Montauban two days before, the SS division's sprawling columns had been constantly nuisanced by SOE-backed sabotage and hit-and-run attacks as they lumbered north to meet the Normandy invasion, but the abduction of one of its battalion commanders, SS Sturmbannführer Helmut Kämpfe, by a local FTP maquis near Moissannes, a tiny hamlet just east of Limoges, had provoked an especially furious response. Within a few hours the SS had begun casting a net across the Haute-Vienne and Corrèze to catch the perpetrators, in the middle of which lay Salon-la-Tour, about 30 miles south of where Kämpfe's abandoned car had been discovered. (Kämpfe was to eventually meet his death at the hands of the maquis, but the events surrounding his final hours were never properly established.)

Leaving their Citroën behind, the unarmed Bariaud managed to make his escape across the fields while Violette and Dufour began returning fire. Pursued by soldiers and several armoured vehicles, they slowly retreated across a cornfield towards a nearby wood, but by the time they reached it Violette was completely exhausted and told Dufour that he must carry on alone. Although Dufour was able to hide with the help of a local farmer, Violette was eventually captured; transferred immediately to Limoges prison and interrogated by the Gestapo, she showed contempt for their questions and refused to give any details of her mission. Liewer planned an ambush to free her on 16 June, but she was driven off in a prison van to Fresnes before they could act, and now Peulevé and Violette were sitting only yards away from each other in adjoining cell blocks.

Expecting that it was just a matter of time before he was executed, Peulevé was somewhat surprised when on 14 July he was led out of his cell and locked into a cubicle inside a prison van, being driven back to Avenue Foch again for further questioning. As a result of the telegram that had mentioned a letter box in Lyon, the Gestapo had arrested the woman to whom he was supposed to have given his report, though she continued to deny any involvement. Peulevé was only with Vogt for a few minutes, after which he was allowed to visit Starr again, being shown into his room upstairs. Starr was unforthcoming when he asked for news on the Allies' progress, preferring to talk about his artistic endeavours instead – Peulevé could see the results of some of it, as a few portraits of SD officers at Avenue Foch hung on the walls of his room. It was also clear that he was free to roam around the building, having given his word not to escape.

Starr had been at Avenue Foch for a year. Captured near Dijon as the head of ACROBAT circuit, he was brought to the SD headquarters during the collapse of PROSPER. Whilst under interrogation Starr had written the name of his network on a map, which had been enough to attract Kieffer's attention – Starr had been a poster artist before the war, and his skills were considered valuable enough to keep him on at Avenue Foch to copy maps and other documents. Life here was considerably more comfortable than a cell in Fresnes, but Kieffer was getting more than pictures from the arrangement and it was obvious that the presence of a compliant British officer might encourage other captured agents to consider talking.

In November 1943, Starr made an escape attempt with fellow prisoners Noor Inayat Khan (*Madeleine*), a descendant of Indian royalty who for several months had taken great risks to maintain F Section's only remaining W/T link amidst the wreckage of PROSPER, and Colonel Léon Faye, one of the heads of the French intelligence group ALLIANCE. Using a screwdriver pilfered whilst mending a vacuum cleaner, they loosened the bars of their cells and planned to break out together on the night of the 25th; Starr and Faye met as arranged but Khan had been unable to free herself, and consequently both men had to spend several hours removing the bars of her skylight before successfully pulling her up onto the roof. This delay proved fatal as a few minutes later the howl of sirens warning of an imminent air raid alerted the guards and Kieffer to their disappearance. Starr and his co-escapers managed to find their way into a neighbouring building, but by this time the surrounding area had been cordoned off and all were recaptured, Faye being wounded as he made a desperate bid to get away. Enraged by this act, Kieffer demanded that each give their word not to make any further escape attempts. Khan and Faye refused and were consequently sent to concentration camps in Germany.[13] Starr, however, agreed and Kieffer decided to keep him.

According to Alfred Newton (*Artus*), another F Section agent held at Avenue Foch the same month, Starr made no attempt to dissuade agents from cooperating with the SD: 'Star [sic] told me in English "Don't lead them up the garden it's quite useless, they know everything: this is the success of Orchard Court, you should see the lorries full of containers unloaded here in the back yard every day." '[14] However, Starr's apparently casual attitude had not been enough to sway Newton, who like Peulevé decided to keep his mouth shut, regardless of what the Germans might already know.

Peulevé was confounded by Starr's pledge to Kieffer and told him that he still should try to escape. He was even more amazed by his admission that on three occasions he had gone out to dinner with Gestapo officers and his statement that he preferred 'living in Avenue Foch to breaking stones in Germany'.[15] His assessment was that Starr was trying to outwit the Germans, but perhaps didn't realize the effect that his presence might have on other agents who might have seen him as a 'living example of the way in which they [the SD] would keep their word'[16] if they agreed to cooperate. Moreover, it could lead them to deduce that SOE was more of an open book to the enemy than it really was.

Transported across Paris back to Fresnes, Peulevé was led into the entrance hall with several other prisoners. Left unguarded next to a large crowd of visitors, he began thinking about a possible escape – as they had become so mixed up with those waiting to leave, he might be able to slip out unnoticed in their midst. When the group finally started to move along he followed, making it to the main gate where they began to form a queue – each visitor had been given a *laisser-passer*, which a guard was collecting as they filed out.

As Peulevé moved closer to the gate he saw that he would have to improvise and after handing over a scrap of paper he immediately made a run for it. By the time the guards realized what was happening he was halfway down the road, though several months as a prisoner had taken its toll on his fitness and his pursuers steadily began catching him up. In an effort to lose them he decided to try and scale a garden wall, but as he hauled himself up one of the guards took aim and hit him in the thigh. Although managing to clamber over, he found that his efforts had been in vain as the garden he had entered offered no obvious exit, and within a few moments the sentries had caught up with him. Put back in his cell he waited to receive some medical attention for his wound, but by the evening it became obvious that nobody was coming. As the bullet had lodged in his leg he knew something would have to be done and finally forced himself to remove it with the aid of a spoon, before passing out. Fortunately the wound did not become infected, though his physical condition would now make any escape impossible.

Despite this setback, Peulevé could at least still try to get word to people on the outside. Giving messages to prisoners who were being released, he wrote to the Verlhacs, his friend André Girard in Cannes and Madame Faget in Bordeaux, signing all of the letters 'Henri Chevalier'. This last one was received and SOE in London were notified through a wireless transmission from Roger Landes, who had returned to Bordeaux as head of a new circuit, ACTOR, in March. Peulevé also used the Fagets' address on a Red Cross form, in order that he could receive toilet articles and underclothes.

In the months following his arrest Peulevé's parents had continued to receive the usual reassuring letters from the War Office, stating that he was safe and in good health. However, at the end of July a telegram arrived to report that he was missing, followed by a request for Leonard and Eva to visit London to obtain further news of their son. Annette went with them and recalled what happened:

135

The young major very guardedly told us that they now knew Henri had been in a fight with the Germans, and could only have been killed. I tried to convince the officer that my brother must be alive, that he knew France and was no doubt sheltering with some villager or other. But neither my parents nor the major would accept this. His possessions and clothing were sent home. Mother was too upset to pack them away, so I went and did it, even more convinced that he would need them again.[17]

The evidence of Peulevé's death probably came from a W/T message sent by Poirier on 7 August: 'From Nestor/Peters: Sorry to inform you that learnt from unconfirmed source that *Jean* executed by Germans.'[18] The 'unconfirmed source' may well have been someone in Fresnes who assumed that Peulevé had been killed whilst escaping, or from contacts Poirier made in Paris during his trip with Malraux in April; that F Section presumed the worst is unsurprising in the absence of any other information.

On the morning of 8 August, Peulevé's cell door was opened earlier than usual. The warder told him that he was leaving that day, and after waiting months for a trial he now half-expected to go directly before a firing squad. A reluctance to depart prompted a few blows from the Sergeant, and Peulevé soon found himself joining a line of prisoners on the narrow walkway outside, many of whom he recognized from London. Whispering between themselves, it seemed that most harboured similar thoughts about their fate, predicting that the Allies' advance towards Paris would probably hasten their execution. Handcuffed in pairs, Peulevé was partnered with another young W/T operator for the MINISTER circuit, Denis Barrett, and moved outside with the others towards a bus near the main gate, where a smaller group of French women prisoners was also waiting to leave. As they queued up, Peulevé was shocked to see the face of Violette amongst them, bedraggled but still apparently in good spirits, though they only had time to acknowledge each other briefly before she and the other chained women were boarded onto a separate vehicle.

Both buses made their way to Gare de l'Est, where they were joined by other prisoners from the transit camp at Compiègne, Avenue Foch and the Gestapo HQ at Rue de Saussaies. Once assembled, Peulevé and thirty-six other men were put on a carriage and divided into two compartments with grilles over the windows, guarded by a number of *feldgendarmerie* (German military police) and an SD officer from Avenue Foch named Haensel who would supervise their journey. Each compartment was only intended to accommodate eight passengers and the overcrowding made it extremely uncomfortable in the August heat.

Command of the group was quickly assumed by Squadron Leader Forest Yeo-Thomas (*Shelley*), with Maurice Southgate (*Hector*, STATIONER's head captured in May) and Henri Frager (*Louba*, *Carte*'s chief of staff in 1942) acting as his assistants, and a young French agent, Stéphane Hessel (*Greco*), as his German interpreter. A stocky, terrier-like figure in his early forties, Yeo-Thomas was the deputy head of the Gaullist RF Section and a veteran of two important missions, helping to support the work of Jean Moulin and socialist Pierre Brossolette in unifying resistance across the occupied zone. He had returned to France for a third time in February 1944 to attempt to free Brossolette, who had been captured whilst trying to return to England earlier that month, but 'Operation Asymptote' proved to be disastrous: Brossolette decided to take his own life before divulging anything to the Germans, throwing himself from the fifth floor of 84 Avenue Foch, and Yeo-Thomas was betrayed and arrested at Passy metro station on 21 March, the same day as Peulevé. Although not the oldest member of the party Yeo-Thomas had a natural authority about him, organizing the others to make best use of the space they had and obtaining permission from the guards to visit the toilet in pairs.

After leaving Paris the train moved slowly east, travelling through the night. No food or water was provided and soon all of them were beginning to suffer dehydration in the intense heat. As they neared Châlons-sur-Marne on the afternoon of the next day they heard several aircraft approaching and a few seconds later a sudden explosion and bursts of cannon fire from RAF fighters rocked the carriage, bringing it to an immediate halt. The guards began shouting in the corridors as they attempted to set up machine guns by the side of the train, whilst the prisoners stayed locked in their compartments, unable to do anything other than pray that the aircraft didn't make another run.

In the midst of the confusion Peulevé saw that three men in his group were suffering seizures, brought on by the privations they had already endured during their captivity. However Violette, accompanied by fellow agents Denise Bloch (*Ambroise*) and Lilian Rolfe (*Nadine*) had managed to avoid the gunfire and crawled along the floor in order to bring water to the men in both compartments. In recounting the incident, Peulevé was later quoted as saying, 'I shall never forget that moment ... I felt very proud that I knew her. She looked so pretty, despite her shabby clothes and her lack of make-up – she was full of good cheer.'[19] This act by the three women also made a deep impression on Yeo-Thomas: 'Through the din, they shouted words of encouragement to us, and seemed quite unperturbed. I can only express my unbounded admiration for them and words are so inadequate that I cannot hope to say what I felt then and still feel now.'[20]

The train remained motionless for several hours after the raid, but eventually the prisoners were released from their carriage and shepherded into the back of two requisitioned trucks to continue the journey, being told that if any prisoner tried to escape, all would be shot. Yeo-Thomas took the opportunity to take note of the men assembled with him; the group included the following (aliases are shown in brackets):

	Captured	Organization	Circuit/Mission
Lieutenant Elisée Allard	April 1944	F Section	LABOURER
Captain Jean Avallard	April 1944	TR	LARVA
Flight Lieutenant Denis Barrett	July 1944	F Section	MINISTER
Captain Robert Benoist	July 1944	F Section	CLERGYMAN
Lieutenant Jean Bouguennec ('Francis Garel')	Sept 1943	F Section	BUTLER
Second Lieutenant Jacques Chaigneau	Dec 1943	TR	–
Marcel Corbusier	April 1944	TR	–
Pierre Culioli	June 1943	F Section	PROSPER
Lieutenant Angehand Defendini	Feb 1944	F Section	PRIEST
Lieutenant Julien Detal	Feb 1944	F Section	DELEGATE
Jean Evesque	?	?	?
Major Henri Frager	August 1944	F Section	DONKEYMAN
Lieutenant Emile-Henri Garry	August 1943	F Section	PHONO
René Gerard	?	?	?
Lieutenant Pierre Geelen	April 1944	F Section	LABOURER
Lieutenant Bernard Guillot	April 1944	BCRA	PERNOD
Lieutenant Stéphane Hessel	July 1944	BCRA	GRECO
Lieutenant Henri Heusch	April 1944	TR	MAYENCE
Captain Desmond Hubble	June 1944	RF Section	CITRONELLE
Captain Gerald Keun ('Kane')	June 1944	SIS	JADE-AMICOL
Lieutenant Jean Lavallée	Dec 1943	TR	KLÉBER
Lieutenant Marcel Leccia	April 1944	F Section	LABOURER
Yves Loison	?	?	?
Captain John Macalister	June 1943	F Section	ARCHDEACON
Lieutenant James Mayer	May 1944	F Section	ROVER
Captain Pierre Mulsant	July 1944	F Section	MINISTER

Captain Henri Peulevé ('Henry Poole')	March 1944	F Section	AUTHOR
Captain Frank Pickersgill	June 1943	F Section	ARCHDEACON
Lieutenant Christian Rambaud	April 1944	TR	–
Captain Charles Rechenmann	May 1944	F Section	ROVER
Lieutenant Roméo Sabourin ('Mackenzie')	March 1944	F Section	PRIEST
Second Lieutenant Jean de Séguier	Dec 1943	TR	MUNICH
Squadron Leader Maurice Southgate	May 1944	F Section	STATIONER
Captain Arthur Steele	April 1944	F Section	MONK
Captain Paul Vellaud	April 1944	TR 'Jeune'	–
Captain George Wilkinson	June 1944	F Section	HISTORIAN
Squadron Leader Forest Yeo-Thomas ('Kenneth Dodkin')[21]	March 1944	RF Section	ASYMPTOTE

Believing the officer's threat of execution to be a bluff, Peulevé still planned to escape and Barrett agreed to join him. Using a watch spring he managed to pick the locks of their handcuffs and made preparations to jump from the lorry, but at the last moment they were stopped by a number of the others, who maintained that they would endanger the lives of the group by doing so.

By the evening they reached Verdun, where they were taken from the trucks and placed in stables, the men in stalls on one side, the women on the other. Although they were forbidden from meeting, the darkness of the alley allowed Peulevé to get close enough to talk to Violette without the guards noticing. Peulevé's only reference to their reunion was quoted some time later:

We spoke of old times and we told each other our experiences in France. Bit by bit everything was unfolded – her life in Fresnes, her interviews at the Avenue Foch. But either through modesty or a sense of delicacy, since some of the tortures were too intimate in their application; or perhaps because she did not wish to live again through the pain of it, she spoke hardly at all about the tortures she had been made to suffer. She was in a cheerful mood. Her spirits were high. She was confident of victory and was resolved on escaping no matter where they took her.[22]

The next morning they wearily made their way in the summer heat towards Metz, stopping at the town's Gestapo headquarters. After several hours of waiting they were put into German trucks and driven further east, passing the forlorn sight of the Maginot line and finally arriving at a camp entrance just inside the German border at Saarbrücken; this was Neue Bremme, a *straflager* or punishment camp that mainly served as a transit point for Jews,

Resistance workers and criminals who were destined for concentration camps. Though surrounded by barbed wire and machine-gun towers, Neue Bremme had virtually no facilities, consisting mainly of wooden huts, a rudimentary kitchen and a parade ground, in the middle of which sat a large tank of green, slimy water.

For the new arrivals there was an almost palpable change of atmosphere as they passed through the gate. After the trucks had stopped the men were violently ousted amidst a cacophony of shouts and insults, while Violette and the other women were led off to another area of the compound. Aided by several NCOs, the guards beat and kicked the first few of Peulevé's group as they descended onto the square, continuing with this treatment as they were made to line up. It became immediately apparent that the SS who ran the camp did as they pleased, though Hessel wasn't expecting such a harsh reception: 'It gave us a real shock, because of course we were very naïve ... we were convinced that this was the end, that Paris would be shortly liberated, that the war was practically over.'[23]

After the line-up the men were chained by the ankle in groups of five and ordered to run round the pond. This sight initially caused laughter to spread across the whole group, as being shackled together in fives made any coordinated movement virtually impossible, though the guards swiftly put a stop to their enjoyment of the bizarre spectacle. This practice was a common initiation and known in some cases to carry on for hours, though on this occasion their overseers quickly tired of the game and the party was led off to the foetid latrine, the use of which required some ingenuity with one or two coming very close to falling in.

Having undergone their brief introduction to the camp, they were once more chained together in twos before being locked in a small hut close to the camp's kitchen. Peulevé describes it as being 12 feet square, though Yeo-Thomas and Hessel both recall it being even smaller, with one small window and narrow benches running around the sides of the walls; the only other furniture was an oil drum in the corner, to serve as a latrine. Thirty-seven men in such a small space was uncomfortable, but compounded with the stifling heat, lack of water and the stench from the oil drum the conditions were soon unbearable. An arrangement had to be worked out in order to make the most of the room they had, which ended up with about two-thirds of them sitting on the benches, eight lying on the floor and the remainder standing, leaning against the wall as best they could. They would have to endure this appalling situation through the rest of the day and a very long night before being released.

When morning eventually came the group was brought out to witness the roll-call, a pitiful spectacle and their first real glimpse of what might lie ahead for themselves. Peulevé noted what the long-term effect of this camp appeared to have on its inmates:

> Living out every moment of their lives like hunted animals, they had become like it in appearance, their features were animal, bestial. Some of them had been eminent men, leaders of European thought and art; their only thoughts now were how to scrounge more food and avoid a blow. I saw something, too, of the reactions of the SS, handpicked sadists let loose to vent all their lowest instincts on helpless prisoners. My initiation into concentration camp life was beginning.[24]

They were also acquainted with the camp's water supply, the filthy tank in the middle of the camp, where they attempted to wash despite still being handcuffed. Afterwards, they were taken to the kitchen to sample the camp's rations: a thin mangel-wurzel soup and sawdust bread, which they ate while witnessing what Peulevé referred to as 'one of the lighter forms of the SS idea of fun'.[25] Having stationed SS guards behind the doors of the huts, a whistle would call out the prisoners, who each received a blow on the back of the neck as they rushed out; two blasts on the whistle would then dismiss them back to the huts before this 'fun' would begin again.

How long they actually stayed at the camp is not clear, though Peulevé states it was four days, which is corroborated by the report of another prisoner, Guillot. When brought out from the hut for the last time, they were handed over to an SD officer accompanied by a dozen *Feldgendarmerie* guards; locked into prison vans, they were then driven to the station in Saarbrücken and loaded onto a goods train. Only three guards were assigned to watch over them and the door to the truck was left open, assuming that handcuffed prisoners would not be so stupid as to try and jump from a moving train whilst attached to another man.

Yet several in the group were still willing to try any possible means of escape. Loison had managed to unfasten his own hand-cuffs and, whilst keeping a careful eye on the guards, began to free the others. A rough plan was devised to despatch the guards when night fell, after which small groups of them would jump from the train to make their way back to France. Unfortunately some of the prisoners still believed that they were bound for a POW camp and were so intent on preventing the plan that they threatened to warn their captors. For the second time Peulevé saw his chance of freedom being foiled by people he should have been counting on, and in the end there was no choice but to abandon the idea and replace their handcuffs, waiting to see where they would be taken next.

By dusk they had passed through Ludwigschafen and Frankfurt, finally stopping at Kassel where they were transferred onto another train. This time they were given a proper third-class carriage, prompting some of the group to think that perhaps they really were going to be treated as prisoners of war. Hessel asked a German officer about their destination and received a glowing report of the conditions at Buchenwald: 'There is a fine library with books in all languages, concerts on the square every night, a cinema, theatre and even a brothel. There is a finely equipped hospital and the food is very good; you get practically the same as the civilians.'[26] On reflection Peulevé later commented, 'I don't think the Captain was trying to fool us; probably, like many other Germans who had never been inside the camp, he believed Goebbels' story that it was a sort of prisoners' paradise.'[27] However, Hessel had heard very different reports about this place – a number of his left-wing friends had been political prisoners at Buchenwald in 1937 and 1938, and only survived by buying themselves out. Remembering the grim stories they had told him, he now knew something of the brutalities they were likely to face.

Chapter 11

Buchenwald

It was late on the evening of 16 August when the train finally pulled into a side track next to a small station, surrounded by barbed wire. Once assembled on the platform, they were marched off down a straight, well-constructed road, passing a garage and several modern-looking barracks along the way. In the darkness it was difficult to make out where they were being led; however, it wasn't long before they could begin to make out machine-gun towers on the perimeter ahead, and the intimidating silhouette of the main gatehouse, with a clock above and iron gates beneath. As they approached, Peulevé could make out a sign proclaiming *Recht Oder Unrecht – Mein Vaterland* (Right or Wrong – My Country), and another, *Jedem Das Seine* (To Each His Own), wrought into the gates. Once they had passed through, there was some waiting around during which time the guards began shouting 'Mitzen ab!' knocking off the hats of those who didn't understand and stamping them in the dirt. Marching off again past lines of long wooden huts, they entered a large hall where they were handed over to several men in striped uniforms, carrying the title of *Lagerschutz* (camp police) on black armbands.

One of them spoke good English and told Peulevé that special orders had been received for them, suggesting that they might be going straight to the crematorium where the executions took place. Despite offering this news, 'which he seemed to take as being quite normal',[1] he went on to describe something of life in the camp. He explained that it was largely run by the prisoners themselves: the *Lagerältester* (Camp Elder) oversaw all the departments, which were in turn supervised by the *Kapos*; beneath them were the *Blockältesters*, who were in charge of individual barracks, and numerous other positions designated for more menial tasks. Half of the inmates were German criminals, the rest of them coming from all across Europe, many having been rounded up and transported west as the Germans had retreated out of Russia. He also warned them that there were many informers in the camp and that anything they said could easily find its way back to the SS.

They were held in the block for several hours until the early morning, by which time it had become clear that they were not to be eliminated, and instead were led into the delousing area:

> We passed through a hall where we were made to empty our pockets, the contents of which were put into little bags. We then stripped, and our clothes were put on clothes hangers and enclosed in large paper bags; we were given a metal disc as a receipt. From here we went into a long room full of white-coated barbers, each of whom had electric clippers with which he shaved us completely from head to foot. After the clippers we were doused in disinfectant which burned horribly, each given a handful of soft soap and passed into an enormous white tiled room with hundreds of sprinklers in the ceiling. The hot water was turned on and we had a good shower.[2]

The earlier warning about executions was confirmed when Hessel spoke to one of the barbers, who told him that those housed in the delousing block overnight were usually bound for the crematorium the next morning. After walking out of the showers, they were issued with striped camp uniforms along with an assortment of ill-fitting civilian clothes and wooden clogs from the quartermaster's stores.

During this degrading process a scrawny young English-speaking prisoner had approached them, compounding their fears by telling them that they were in 'one of the worst concentration camps in Germany, that the death rate was appalling, the treatment the worst'[3] and that, as communists ruled large parts of the camp's internal running, they should not admit to being officers, being indicative of an elevated social position. This man was Maurice Pertschuk, a Jewish SOE agent code-named *Eugène* and known in the camp as 'Martin Perkins'. He had landed by felucca during the spring of 1942 to organize F Section's PRUNUS circuit in the Toulouse area and was arrested a year later along with his W/T operator Marcus Bloom (*Urbain*), Peulevé's training partner at Thame Park.

Having just turned twenty-three, Pertschuk had journeyed to Buchenwald in January with three other F Section men. Alfred and Henry Newton (*Artus, Auguste*) were prime examples of SOE's willingness to recruit from all backgrounds – although born to British parents, they had spent most of their working lives as variety artists, touring the Continent under the title of The Boorn Brothers. Volunteering as despatch riders for the French Government at the outbreak of war, they headed south after the collapse in 1940 and endured months of incarceration in Spain before reaching Gibraltar and Liverpool; on arrival they found out their families had been killed during their evacuation to Britain, their ship having been torpedoed after leaving Portugal. Consumed with the overwhelming desire for revenge, the brothers were quickly passed through to F Section and accepted for training in early 1942; Gielgud was left in no doubt about their capabilities for violence, recommending that Alfred in particular might be best employed in France simply as a 'thug'. Ultimately they were sent as sabotage instructors to the Lyon area in June, but dogged by poor communications, lack of money and uneasy relations with some of their contacts, their GREEN-HEART circuit largely failed to deliver, and in April 1943 they were given away by an informer and severely tortured by the infamous 'Butcher of Lyon', Gestapo chief Klaus Barbie, before being sent to Paris.

The fourth agent, a former commando named Christopher Burney (*Charles*), had met with even less luck, being sent to join AUTOGIRO in May 1942, a circuit in Normandy which had already been penetrated by the Germans. Narrowly avoiding capture when visiting the address of his contact in Caen, he soon learned that his organizer was now in jail, but rather than fleeing to Spain he chose to try and build a new circuit under his own command. It took nearly three months for the Germans to track him down, eventually finding him asleep one morning in his hotel room. Refusing to divulge any details on his mission, Burney was subjected to eighteen months in solitary confinement at Fresnes.

Despite Pertschuk's protestations to keep quiet about their officer status, Yeo-Thomas, Hessel and a number of others declared their rank and other details to the registrar (Yeo-Thomas continued to use the pseudonym 'Kenneth Dodkin', an alias which had saved him from certain execution in Paris). Having been registered they were then each given their camp number and small triangles to sew onto their clothes; Peulevé's number was 12332. The colour of the triangles denoted the type of prisoner: Peulevé's group were red, for political prisoners, green was for common criminals, yellow for Jews, pink for homosexuals and violet for Jehovah's witnesses.

Except for German prisoners, each triangle was also marked with a letter to indicate their country of origin.

The group was then taken to Block 17, a smaller building than the rest used as a quarantine or housing 'special prisoners', and separated from the surrounding blocks by barbed wire. Entering the hut they were first confronted by the washing area and latrines, with doorways on either side; one led to the living quarters, occupied by tables and lockers; the other housed the dormitory, capable of accommodating around forty men in tiered bunks lining up either side, each containing a thin straw mattress and a small blanket.

As their first day passed within the confines of Buchenwald, Peulevé and his group were still bewildered and as yet had little understanding of its real horrors. Built by prisoners in 1937 on a slope at the base of the Ettersburg mountain, a few miles outside the town of Weimar, Buchenwald concentration camp was created to provide the Nazis with a means of confining those who either opposed them politically or were considered racially or morally inferior. The SS soon installed a number of facilities outside the main compound for the benefit of its garrison, including riding stables, a falconry and even a zoo for officers' families to visit, but accommodation for those on the other side of the wire remained very different. Though the population amounted to just a few thousand inmates at the outbreak of war, this figure had tripled by late 1943, and by August 1944 the camp was chronically overcrowded, holding more than 82,000 prisoners.

For the SS, the objective of Buchenwald was largely to ensure that there was enough human labour to run the factories, and to plunder any belongings the prisoners had surrendered when entering. Who lived and died was not considered important and the actual task of supplying manpower was delegated to the *Kapos*, who reported to the SS NCOs. Thus the prisoners effectively determined each others' fates, with those belonging to the dominant factions taking control. In the early days of the camp the criminals, or 'Greens', had been given the administrative power, which gave them the freedom to hoard all the available rations for themselves and let others starve or be worked to death. However, when an efficient and skilled labour force was needed for the newly installed Gustloff arms factory in March 1943, the communists showed themselves to be far more suitable governors. Possessing more qualified workers, a greater talent for organization and a common outlook, it was to them that the SS decided to hand over the management of the camp's depart-

146

ments, including the all-important *Arbeitstatistik* (labour records office), which allotted what kind of work each prisoner would do, holding the power of life and death over thousands of men.

The communists, as Pertschuk had warned, declared that officers were the product of the ruling classes and, like the capitalists, were to be disposed of first. Shortly after his arrival, Burney had narrowly avoided being transferred to Dora, one of Buchenwald's worst satellite camps, after being accused of being one of the biggest holders of arms shares in England. Less fortunate was Marcel Michelin from the French family of tyre manufacturers, who was nearly sixty when he was sent to Buchenwald for resistance activities. The German communists were quickly onto him and through their control of the *Arbeitstatistik* bypassed medical and other formalities, deporting him to a kommando (work party) at Ohrdruf where the mortality rate was more than 2,000 a month. He died shortly afterwards. Burney stated that, owing to these Germans' particular dislike of the French, nine out of ten were sent on transports and probable death. Although the disciplined ruthlessness of the communists was in part affected by racial prejudices, these were rife throughout the camp's factions. The Russians despised the French, German and Slav populations, the Poles hated the Russians, and there was a widespread dislike for the 'bourgeois' Czechs.

The thirty-seven new arrivals had begun to attract a lot of attention from the rest of the camp and it wasn't long before some of the emaciated onlookers approached the wire with questions, asking who they were and why had they been brought here. Some of the *Kapos* even offered them cigarettes. The group was divided in its reaction, some making a point of playing to the crowd, declaring that they were agents and important members of the Resistance, while others were more reticent; Peulevé noted that their impact on this 'enormous concentrated mass'[4] of people was such that they were almost treated like royalty. The SS were certainly determined to keep them separate, ordering that they were not to take part in the daily *appel* (roll-call) in the main square, being counted on parade outside their block instead. Neither were they expected to work, or visit the canteen with the other prisoners, since food would be brought to them. Consequently they spent most of the day loitering in their compound, but were only allowed inside the block during the evening.

After Fresnes, the group was surprised to find that their rations in Block 17 were much better and Peulevé was able to regain some of the weight he had lost over the past few months. It was clear, however, that something more had to be done if the group was to avoid becoming like their SOE colleagues and Yeo-Thomas held a meeting to see what information could be gathered on the camp's structure. Unable to leave the confines of the barbed wire, they relied on visits by Pertschuk and Burney to tell them all they knew, though the latter was able to call on Pieter Cool, a Dutch naval officer who helped obtain permission for them to move around the camp.

On first inspection the numerous watchtowers around the perimeter and numbers of guards both inside and outside the electrified fences suggested that the chances of escape were negligible. Equally depressing was their first real glimpse of how bad the conditions were elsewhere in Buchenwald, especially within the separate area known as the *Kleine Lager* or 'Little Camp'. Originally built in 1942 to quarantine new inmates, the Little Camp was struggling to accommodate the rapid influx of new prisoners – each of its seventeen blocks now held as many as 2,000 men, four times the number they were originally designed for. The overcrowding became so bad that Block 61 was set aside for the administration of lethal injections in order to reduce the numbers; however, the daily toll of dead could not be cremated quickly enough and to make more room corpses were often thrown out of the blocks and left to rot in the compound. Alfred Newton later found it 'impossible to describe the dirt, the muck, and the maddening scenes of brutality, and the bad behaviour of German political prisoners in charge of the foreigners'.[5]

Though there seemed little hope of finding a way out, Yeo-Thomas had at least been able to make contact with some of the camp's resistance elements, most notably amongst the Russians and Poles who had established efficient intelligence networks. The group was also allowed to visit the *Effektenkammer* (the depository for prisoners' effects) to collect a few of their things, some of them being afforded the small luxury of shaving using a razor from Benoist's belongings. This consideration for cleanliness, along with their daily exercise regimes outside Block 17 only served to impress upon other prisoners that these people were indeed separated from the rest, and were doing everything they could to retain some semblance of civilized life. To pass the time RF agent Desmond Hubble had also retrieved a small travel chess set which was used to hold a tournament, while cards made by the young Canadian Frank Pickersgill were used to play bridge.

Three days after the arrival of Peulevé's group, 168 Allied personnel appeared at the camp under the leadership of a New Zealander, Squadron Leader Philip Lamason. Despite their eligibility to be sent to a normal POW camp, they were accused of being *Luftgangsters* or 'terror fliers' and thus were treated like all other newcomers, being stripped of their uniforms and issued only with a shirt, trousers and jacket (but no shoes) before being installed in the appalling squalor of the Little Camp. Since there was no room in the blocks they were forced to sleep on a cobbled area outside, though Yeo-Thomas managed to enlist the help of two Russian officers and smuggled several dozen blankets through to Lamason a few days later. Yeo-Thomas had also been eager to discuss the possibility of escape to England using planes based at a nearby airfield, but the plan was based on little more than fantasy and desperation, being rejected by other resistance leaders as foolhardy and likely to result in severe reprisals for the rest of the inmates.

On 24 August, the camp was the target of an Allied bombing raid, its main objective being the factory buildings nearby. Hessel comments that for those in Block 17, the sight of American aircraft was an encouraging sign: 'We thought, stupidly enough, that it meant that the camp was known, and that the horrors of the camp were known, and that the Allies would try to do something about it.'[6] However, this initial boost to morale was soon tempered by the consequences of the attack, as those trapped in the Gustloff factories and SS-owned *Deutsche Ausrüstungs Werke* (German Equipment Works) were prevented from running away by the guards, who shot anyone who attempted to flee. The raid completely destroyed all but two of the Gustloff buildings, claiming the lives of over 300 prisoners and wounding more than four times as many; an SS barracks was also hit, being responsible for the deaths of eighty SS personnel.

The confusion may have suggested the possibility of escape, but the damage to the perimeter was negligible. Some symbolic hope arose from the aftermath of this grim day, however, as Göethe's Oak, sited near the laundry and thought to be the tree under which the writer often sat in reflection, had been felled by the attack. According to a popular myth the tree's destruction would signal the fall of Germany itself and some of the more superstitious prisoners thought that this was a sign of the beginning of the end for the Nazis. In conditions such as these, such faith could make all the difference between hope and despair.

The raid predictably made things worse for Lamason's airmen who were already considered terrorists by the SS, but they were also beginning to experience the effects of exposure from sleeping out in the open, with thirty of the group being afflicted by pneumonia and pleurisy. Their future looked bleak, though Lamason and most of his group would eventually make it out of Buchenwald with the help of Burney, who had a note smuggled out to a nearby Luftwaffe station at Nohra, informing them that Allied aircrew were being held at the camp. A senior officer arrived to demand that they be treated as POWs, and had them transferred to Stalag Luft III at Sagan on 19 October.

Eleven sick men had to be left behind, including a young Canadian, Ed Carter-Edwards. Having to endure several more weeks in the filth of the Little Camp before another visit from the Luftwaffe eventually secured his release, he remembered how respite could never be found from the horrors surrounding him:

> I feel that what was responsible for the mental breakdown of many of the people ... was the realisation that there was no avenue of escape; no future; death by disease, death by starvation or being transported to work in the areas being bombed. It looked like no matter which way you turned, death faced you. While you were there and weren't actually working, you walked around aimlessly, viewing the experiences of other human beings and the indignities they suffered. It was a landscape devoid of grass, trees, shrubs – no birds – nothing but suffering, starvation, diseased bodies all around you day and night ... Death was everywhere.[7]

Early in September, Peulevé's group was able to make contact with Alfred Balachowsky (*Serge*) through Robert Benoist, both of whom had been associated with the PROSPER circuit; Balachowsky now held a responsible position in one of the medical blocks, having been professor at the Ecole National d'Agriculture and head of the Institut Pasteur in Paris before his arrest in July 1943. He had many contacts in that part of the camp and was willing to help with an escape plan, but could not offer any immediate ideas for getting them out. Meanwhile Yeo-Thomas, Peulevé, Hessel and several of the others continued to make enquiries amongst various factions, but politics and personal affiliations stifled any progress. Hessel recalls that 'somebody had tried Manhès [Henri Manhès, previously the assistant of de Gaulle's emissary Jean Moulin] and Marcel Paul

[French trade unionist] but they had said, "We are sorry . . . we have to save our people first." '[8]

Around 1.30 pm on the afternoon of 9 September the usual *appel* was supplemented by an order for sixteen men from Block 17 to report to the main gate. The names called out on the camp's loudspeakers were Hubble, Kane, Benoist, Defendini, Allard, Mackenzie, Garel, Garry, Detal, Leccia, Steele, Pickersgill, Mayer, Macalister, Rechenmann and Geelen. No one in the remainder of the group considered anything untoward in this and it had always been Peulevé's assumption that if the SS had wanted them dead they would have killed them in France. Watching them march off, Peulevé, Yeo-Thomas, Hessel, Frager and Southgate were nevertheless alarmed by the *Blockältester*'s worried look, who muttered that this was 'a bad business', though they agreed not to discuss it with the others until they had more information. As evening approached there was still no word and suspicions slowly began to turn to fear as the fates of those taken became increasingly precarious.

The next morning a Pole from the Little Camp came to inform them that the sixteen men had reportedly been beaten, but were at least still alive. Later in the day another rumour suggested that they had been seen exercising outside, but no details were forthcoming on the reason why they were being held. However, the following morning the Pole brought more gloomy news, stating that another within his organization had seen the bodies of their comrades, and it seemed that they had been executed the previous night. Shortly afterwards Balachowsky was able to pass on confirmation of the killings: having first been beaten up, all sixteen had been hanged from meat hooks in the walls of the crematorium basement at 5.30 pm, and would have probably taken five to ten minutes to die from slow strangulation. The news was broken to the rest of the group. Some, as Hessel remembers, did not think the remainder were under threat: 'They said, "So these sixteen were condemned, then perhaps we are not, because if we are, why haven't they taken us too?" '[9] However, others saw that this was probably wishful thinking. The chances were that they would all face execution and not even be spared the mercy of a quick death.

In this grim atmosphere Peulevé accompanied Yeo-Thomas to the laboratory in Block 50, where Balachowsky hid them in order that Yeo-Thomas could write two final letters. When he had finished both men set about enciphering them, Yeo-Thomas using his 'Seahorse' code and Peulevé his old Playfair; these were then passed on to Heinz Baumeister, an associate of Balachowsky's, who later smuggled them out of the camp bound inside a book. The first message read:

> Invaluable documents concerning latest research and dis-coveries bacteriological warfare also plans secret underground dumps and factories kept here at Buchenwald stop all prepared to secure them but can succeed only providing rapid assistance arrives just before or immediately upon German capitulation as camp officials will try to destroy all valuable documents warrants every effort stop speedy arrival airborne or para-troops essential will find organised assistance within camp but I have no arms stop bearer this message trustworthy and knows everything awaits reply and instructions stop acknowledge by Iodoform [coded BBC message] du moineau au lapin stop have everything under control and hope for early victory stop vingt cinq septembre all my love Barbara Tommy stop Cheerio Dizzy Asymptote.[10]

Yeo-Thomas also sent a second, longer letter to his commanding officer, Colonel Dismore ('Dizzy'):

14 September 1944
My dear Dizzy,
These are 'famous last words' I am afraid, but one has to face death one day or another so I will not moan and get down to brass tacks.
[Yeo-Thomas goes on to describe his time since being captured and the events prior to their departure from Paris.] The journey here was an eventful one, it took 8 days. The first man I ran into when being entrained was Hessel of the BCRA and the second was Hubble. We had various adventures, all were handcuffed the whole time, 19 men in one compartment and 18 in another. We could not move being packed in like sardines. The gates of the compartments were padlocked and we had very little air, no food had been provided for. We were given 1 day's rations which had to last 5 days, luckily some had Red Cross parcels or we would have starved. The train was bombed and machine-gunned on the way and we had a very narrow shave. Our escorts ran and left us helpless, had the train caught fire we would have burned like trapped rats. We had to stop at Saar-brucken for 3 days in a punishment and reprisals camp, and

were beaten up on arrival. As usual I seemed to attract particular attention and got well and truly slapped and cuffed. We were confined for three days and nights, 37 of us in a hut 9 feet by 7 feet by 7 feet. It was Hell. We then came on to this place Buchenwald. On the way our escorts plundered and stole practically all our effects. Never believe about German honesty, they are the biggest thieves, liars, bullies and cowards I have ever met. In addition, they delight in torturing people and gloat over it. Upon arrival which took place about midnight, we were locked up in the disinfection quarters and next morning we were nearly hanged summarily, but temporarily reprieved. We were stripped, completely shorn and dressed in prison rags, losing our few remaining belongings, and 16 of us, including Hubble, were told to report to a certain place. We never saw them again and found out that they were being hung without trial on the night of 11/12 September. They have been cremated so no trace remains of them. We are now awaiting our turn. There are 170 airmen (British and American) brought down and captured in France, but they are being treated as Terror Fliers and sleeping in the open, living under appalling conditions in violation of all conventions. They ought to be treated as POW. Men die like flies here. I sent a message to you through Geneva. I hope you received it, but have no means of telling. The bearer of this letter will give you all details so I will not say more – whatever he tells you is Gospel truth. He is no romancer, and he will never be able to really do justice to the horrors perpetrated here. Dizzy, see to it that our people never let ourselves be softened to the German people, or there will be another war in 15 years' time and all our lives will have been sacrificed in vain. I leave it to you and others to see that retribution is fierce. It will never be fierce enough.[11]

A third, unenciphered message was later written asking for the recipient to transmit these messages to London and pass the reply back to the camp, emphasizing the need for haste and that 'delay may mean disaster'.[12] Yet despite this urgency, Peulevé and Yeo-Thomas did not experience the panic or anxiety that one might imagine. Yeo-Thomas recalled, 'I seemed to have lost all feeling and become a machine. I had no fear of death in any shape or form, and I felt absolutely no apprehension. Never during those days did I worry for myself; it was not a matter of courage, I just cannot explain it.'[13] Peulevé was equally untroubled by the sentence that awaited him, although Violette's welfare still continued to pre-occupy his thoughts:

> I had come a long way since 1939. Having run, I had returned. During my return I had proved that, well equipped, I could dish out more than I received. I knew that I had deserved the fate of my comrades and I was waiting patiently for the rope that would put an end to the equation. One thing I knew – I had vindicated my cowardice. But what I wished ... and prayed to know was what had happened to Violet. That question, I felt sure, could only be answered when the hangman's rope had worked its effect and I was before the Eternal Judge, who no doubt would tell me exactly what the situation was.[14]

The possibility of escape now seemed further away than ever, but Yeo-Thomas continued to talk with Balachowsky. Eventually exhausting their options, one desperate plan still remained, which would involve switching identities with patients in the *Hygiene-Institut*. This innocuous-sounding unit had been established by the Waffen-SS to develop new treatments for injuries and diseases afflicting its troops and was responsible for carrying out all manner of horrific experiments on prisoners to further its research. The *Institut* used Block 46 to accommodate these 'guinea pigs', which from August 1943 also housed the *Abteilung für Fleckfieber und Virus-forschung* (Department for Typhus and Virus Research), testing new vaccines on hundreds of subjects who had either contracted typhus in the camp or been purposely infected by the clinic's staff. It would be these cases that Yeo-Thomas and his men would try to substitute.

Though the chances of success seemed negligible, it was arranged for Yeo-Thomas to see Eugen Kogon, who worked as a secretary for SS Sturmbannführer Erwin Ding, known as Ding-Schuler, the doctor in charge of Blocks 46 and 50 (the illegitimate son of Baron von Schuler, he preferred to incorporate his father's name with that of his adopted family, Ding). Kogon was an Austrian Catholic writer who had actively protested against the Nazis before they marched into Vienna in 1938, and became one of Buchenwald's first political deportees soon afterwards; an important figure within the hospital and the camp in general, he was respected for his longevity as well as his influential position. Agreeing to help, he met with Yeo-Thomas in Block 50 to work out the details.

Their plan was to approach Ding-Schuler with a proposition, requesting his assistance in return for signed testimonies from Yeo-Thomas and several other officers, stating that he had been instrumental in saving the lives of British and French servicemen. By September 1944 the Americans had already reached the Siegfried Line on Germany's western border and Ding-Schuler knew that defeat was now only months away; if he presented this evidence to the Allies it would at least provide some protection for him and his family when the details of his experiments were exposed to the outside world. Yeo-Thomas also emphasized to Kogon that, as the senior officer of the group, his priority was to rescue as many of the twenty remaining men in Block 17 as possible and that his name would be at the bottom of the list of those to be saved.

Kogon went immediately to talk with Ding-Schuler who was just about to leave the camp for ten days, leaving Yeo-Thomas nervously waiting for news. Eventually Balachowsky returned, reporting that the meeting had gone well but that a compromise would have to be made. In short, Ding-Schuler had been conducive to the idea and there was agreement in principle to the plan. However, he would only be prepared to save three men, not twenty-one. Furthermore, Yeo-Thomas must be included with them, in order to provide the testimony of the Commanding Officer. He immediately protested but was in no position to dictate terms, as Ding-Schuler would only take what he considered to be a worthwhile risk. Either three would live, or none at all.

Another hurdle also had to be cleared, in that the brutish-looking *Kapo* of Block 46, Arthur Dietzsch, would have to cooperate for the plan to work. A German political prisoner since 1924, Dietzsch had already spent six years at Buchenwald, during which time he had gained a reputation for being ruthless in his work, treating the terrified guinea-pig prisoners with indifference or even cruelty to keep order on the ward. Through Heinz Baumeister, an orderly who worked under Dietzsch, Kogon offered him the same kind of testimony offered to Ding-Schuler, though he was careful not to inform Dietzsch of the deal Yeo-Thomas had already made. The *Kapo* gave his assurance that he could be relied upon, giving Kogon and his confederates real hope that the plot might work. Even so, the restrictions imposed by Ding-Schuler meant that Yeo-Thomas had a terrible decision to make.

It had already been stipulated that he must take one of the three places to provide testimony after the war, but which two members of the group should accompany him? Balachowsky recommended that one Briton and one Frenchman should be selected, though this criterion can hardly have helped Yeo-Thomas in his agonizing choice. Moreover, it was a decision only he could make, as to explain the plan to anyone else would only jeopardize its chances.

Why he finally selected Peulevé over the other British officers isn't clear – perhaps it was the assistance he gave when coding the letters sent through Baumeister, or just his strength of character that persuaded him. As far as the third choice was concerned, Yeo-Thomas had narrowed his options down to two men: Henri Frager, probably because of his seniority in the Resistance, and his translator Stéphane Hessel, the BCRA agent whom he had known in London. Whether Yeo-Thomas felt that the younger man was more deserving of the chance or that Frager's age was against him is open to question, but in the end he opted to take Hessel. He told Balachowsky of his decision, who would only inform the other two once the plan had been initiated.

The main reason for Yeo-Thomas to go first was to test Dietzsch's trustworthiness. Once summoned to the medical block, Dietzsch would administer an injection to produce a high fever imitating typhus, after which Yeo-Thomas would return to Block 17 and wait for the serum to do its work. He would then report the next morning to the hospital, where he would be officially pronounced a genuine typhus case and taken into Block 46 as a new 'guinea pig'. If Yeo-Thomas made it safely into the hands of Kogon's team, a message would be sent for the other two to follow; should he die after being admitted, it would be assumed that Dietzsch was treacherous and the plan would be aborted.

The first stage was successfully carried out, with Yeo-Thomas being smuggled across to see Dietzsch and receive the injection, returning to Block 17 shortly after to wait for the symptoms to appear. Urgently drawing Peulevé and Hessel aside, he explained that both of them had been chosen to accompany him, but it was imperative not to divulge anything to the rest of the group. They were also told to expect Balachowsky to deliver further instructions, which they were to obey without question. The fever began to show overnight and by the morning Yeo-Thomas had reported to the Blockältester who agreed for a Czech doctor to accompany him to the hospital. As planned, Dietzsch was present to confirm the diagnosis of typhus and had him transferred to Block 46 immediately.

Yeo-Thomas sweated and shivered under the effects of the injection for another three days before feeling satisfied enough with Dietzsch's conduct to send word to the others, via Kogon, that they could now follow. No time was wasted, and on the morning of 19 September the young German chief of Block 17 allowed Peulevé and Hessel to accompany Dietzsch to Block 46 (this move was not exceptional, since healthy prisoners were known to be picked for experiments). Passing through the barbed-wire cordon that separated the block from the rest of the camp, they were hurried into a room on the first floor where they were reunited with Yeo-Thomas, who had fully recovered from his faked illness. The room was inhabited by two English-speaking orderlies, Schalker and Gadzinski, and divided in two by a row of cupboards, one side containing four beds on which Peulevé, Yeo-Thomas and Hessel would sleep. This would now be their refuge until new identities could be taken from three patients in the ward downstairs.

To increase security Dietzsch sent away several of the block's staff to attend to other duties – the fewer people in the building, the better the chances of keeping their secret. Despite having to duck as they passed the windows, they were relatively safe in their hideout and even helped with the hospital paperwork, but this still left a lot of time in which they had to amuse themselves, playing cards, chess or an improvised game of their own called 'Silly Buggers'. They would also occasionally receive odd snippets of information from Kogon, and books and cigarettes from Dietzsch. Hessel remembers the bond that developed between the three of them: 'It really was a very solid little group, and we never had the slightest tension between ourselves.'[15]

Several days later a group of Frenchmen arrived from a labour camp in Cologne, a number of which were typhus cases. On their arrival at Block 46, Dietzsch identified a few of them that resembled Peulevé and his colleagues, and Hessel undertook the macabre task of interviewing them in order to assess their backgrounds and suitability. These enquiries identified three in particular that seemed to fit their ages and physical builds: Michel Boitel, Maurice Chouquet and Marcel Seigneur. Although it was agreed that they had found the best matches, Peulevé, Yeo-Thomas and Hessel were now placed in an even more ghoulish situation, in that their chances of survival depended on how quickly these men died. All three made it clear that they would not advocate hastening their deaths to save themselves; however, that didn't make the dilemma any easier for Dietzsch, and it occurred to Hessel that he might ignore their wishes in order to eliminate the danger to his own life.

Though the plan had succeeded so far, on 4 October the dreaded *appel* was once again followed by an order for another eleven prisoners from Block 17 to assemble at the main gate. The names called were Frager, Barrett, Mulsant, Loison, de Séguier, Vellaud, Chaigneau, Gerard, Corbusier, Wilkinson – and 'Poole', the name Peulevé had given when being registered. When he did not appear with the rest of the group he was quickly traced to the hospital and two guards arrived at Block 46 to see Dietzsch; the fear of being contaminated by the patients meant that such visits were often avoided, though on this occasion they were acting under the Commandant's orders and had no choice. Dietzsch made sure that he wasn't around to talk to them when they arrived, but when they made a second visit shortly afterwards he referred them to Ding-Schuler's order that no one was to enter the ward without his consent. Knowing what severe repercussions awaited Kogon if the plan became known to the SS, Peulevé sent a note to him in Block 50:

I should like to thank you from the bottom of my heart for everything that you are doing for us. If I must go, it will not be because you have failed to do everything possible to save me.
                   With sincerest gratitude, your H.P.[16]

Dietzsch found out that a stretcher was being sent for Peulevé, and quickly had to give him an injection to induce a high temperature and simulate the appearance of typhus – had the guards realized that he was not sick, there was a good chance that the entire plot would collapse. Within a few hours the effects of Dietzsch's medication were clearly evident as Peulevé started to become delirious, his temperature having soared to 105° by the time he was wheeled onto the ward to join the guinea pig patients. Although these symptoms were convincing enough to suggest typhus, they were also beginning to pose a genuine threat to his life and Dietzsch had to keep a close eye on his condition.

The Camp Commandant, SS Oberführer Hermann Pister, had been given clear instructions from Berlin that this man was to be executed whatever his condition, and thought that it would be easiest to shoot him on the stretcher. Ding-Schuler had been away in Weimar whilst these events were happening and was hurriedly recalled by Kogon; on reporting to Pister he attempted to buy some time, making the case that a typhus patient running such a high

158

temperature could not be removed from the block due to the dangers of contamination. This request made no impression on the Commandant, who wasn't interested how it was done so long as the order was carried out. Ding-Schuler then relented slightly, agreeing that the execution could be performed by lethal injection and even offered to perform the task himself. Refusing this option, Pister did however agree to his third suggestion, which was to give the job to SS Hauptscharführer Gerhard Schiedlausky, another doctor at the camp. Having pursued a grim career experimenting on women prisoners at Ravensbrück before his transfer to Buchenwald, Dr Schiedlausky had begun to be troubled by the actions of his past and Ding-Schuler considered it unlikely that he would carry out the execution himself.

This prediction proved to be correct and worked to his advantage as Schliedlausky delegated the job to Friedrich Wilhelm, a white-haired, elderly looking medical NCO in charge of Block 61. Having a reputation for executing prisoners without hesitation, Wilhelm was also an easier man to manipulate, being known to have a weakness for the bottle. Dietzsch was waiting with schnapps when he arrived at Block 46 and encouraged him to drink so much that by the time he came to administer the lethal injection he could barely stand; led onto the ward, Dietzsch then showed him one of the other patients and explained that this was the man to be executed. Using all his powers of persuasion, he suggested to Wilhelm that injecting this pathetic case with phenol wasn't worth the effort, as he would be dead in a few hours anyway. He also offered his assistance, suggesting that if he was still alive by the morning he would finish the job on his behalf. If Wilhelm decided to go through with the execution himself, Peulevé and his two friends would have had no choice but to give themselves up. However, being too drunk to care the Sergeant was content to leave the matter in Dietzsch's hands and later reported to Schiedlausky that the prisoner had been killed.

It's difficult to understate the risks that Kogon and his helpers were taking during this time, and, in particular, the fortitude and ingenuity demonstrated to keep the plan on course and protected from potential disclosure. All manner of daily problems had to be solved, as the disappearance of these men meant having to manipulate those in charge of the *Arbeitstatistik*, keep the orderlies and foremen in charge of prisoners' records fed with plausible cover stories, arrange for a fellow conspirator to be on hand at the crematorium and countless other dodges; Kogon was later to describe how their 'heads were always in several nooses at the same time'.[17]

Peulevé was safe for the moment, but his death from typhus would only be proved by the appearance of a corpse, which still depended on the death of his chosen double, Marcel Seigneur. The young Frenchman had battled his illness for longer than expected, though by Sunday evening it seemed that he might be weakening at last. A long and uneasy night followed, with Dietzsch unsuccessfully pleading with Yeo-Thomas and Hessel to let him quicken his death, but at 7.30 am on the morning of 9 October, Seigneur finally succumbed. The substitution was made quickly: Peulevé's number was painted onto the thigh of the corpse and the crematorium recorded his death at 8.10 am, the cause being cited as pneumonia. Peulevé was now officially Marcel Seigneur, number F-76635. By the slimmest of margins he had become the first of the three to be saved, and his gratitude was obvious in the note he sent to Kogon later that day:

Dear friends!
I can't hope to find the proper words for telling you how grateful I am to you for your magnificent achievement . . . I only hope that the day may come on which I can repay at least a small part of the debt I owe you.

Forever your
MARCEL SEIGNEUR.[18]

The ten men called to the gatehouse had already been executed on the afternoon of 5 October, Frager having been granted his request for the group to face a firing squad on the SS shooting range, rather than be hanged.[19] Avallard and Evesque, recently transferred to an outside kommando, were summoned back to Buchenwald and also shot on the 7th; Rambaud followed them five days later. Kogon could not risk visiting the men in Block 46 to update the three fugitives on the situation, but they realized that it was now just a matter of time before the names Hessel and Dodkin (Yeo-Thomas' alias) would be called for, and an execution order was expected to arrive at the end of the week. However, Chouquet, who had been 'paired' with Yeo-Thomas suddenly worsened and died on Friday the 13th, and the name of Dodkin entered the camp records as another typhus victim.

Only Hessel now remained, but the longer their deception continued, the greater the danger was of the plan being discovered.

160

Although still hoping for a positive outcome, his faith began to waiver in the early part of the following week: 'I had the feeling that the plot was so dangerous . . . if it had been found out, then it would have been bad for all of us. So I told Kogon "Look, you've done marvellously for my two friends, but as far as I'm concerned I'd rather try to escape."'[20] He passed a message to Kogon:

> Today is Wednesday and there is a strong possibility that the execution order will arrive tomorrow (unless we are 'lucky' enough to get it today). Please make all the necessary arrangements for having me assigned to an outgoing shipment tomorrow . . . Anything else you can do for me over and above this would, of course, be of the greatest value. But I fear I must simply take my chances. It would be utter folly to wait any longer.[21]

But Kogon held firm and insisted that he must wait. He was proved right to do so and with the greatest of ironies, Michel Boitel died on Stéphane Hessel's twenty-seventh birthday, Friday, 20 October. Hessel sent another note the following day:

> Your good instincts did not deceive you . . . Thanks to your care, everything has come out alright. My feelings are of a man who has been saved in the nick of time. What relief![22]

It seems impossible to imagine what life must have been like for these three men during the month they spent hidden in Block 46, though Hessel points out that their emotional states were not dominated solely by fear, but rather by a perpetual state of excitement:

> We had the strong feeling . . . that we were part of an extraordinarily dangerous plot. We were both tense and exhilarated in a way. So we had fun . . . I'm sure they would have agreed with me when I say that. We were not all the time thinking, 'Is it coming?' The only terrible moment was when Poole [Peulevé] was called . . . it was a terrible moment because we said, 'What can we do? It's too late, he won't be able to escape.' And when he finally did there was also enormous exhilaration. You must think behind it . . . at our youthfulness, at our war-mindedness . . . one felt a little heroic and at the same time terribly modest.[23]

Despite the plan having worked, they still had to leave the block with identities that would stand up to inspection. Kogon had additionally researched the lives of the three dead men and collected enough information to give as much personal history as possible – in Peulevé's case, he could pass easily enough under Seigneur's profession as an electrician, having his technical background to fall back on. Ding-Schuler had wanted at least one of them to remain at Buchenwald, in order to guarantee testimony when the Allies eventually arrived, but Kogon made it plain to him that if they stayed the risks were far greater for everyone concerned, and insisted that, having signed written statements in Ding-Schuler's favour, all three must be allowed to leave. His argument won and Kogon set about making arrangements with some senior contacts to have Yeo-Thomas, Peulevé and Hessel transferred as soon as possible.

Many of the kommandos outside Buchenwald were known for brutally working their prisoners to death either in factories, quarries or on construction projects. Even so, there was a slightly better chance of escape on the outside and each man would have to take whatever chances came his way. It had been agreed that Yeo-Thomas would be the last to leave and Kogon managed to arrange for the other two to take the next transport, fittingly scheduled for Hallowe'en. Supplied with what clothing and food could be mustered, Peulevé and Hessel bade farewell to Yeo-Thomas, all three promising to meet again after the war and do what they could to bring justice for their murdered comrades. Slipping away quietly, they were relieved to be outside Block 46 for the first time in over a month but were careful to keep their heads down to avoid being recognized. The weather was atrocious, however, and hardly anyone took notice of them as they walked through the wind and rain to the main gate, joining the other men boarding the trucks for Schönebeck.

Chapter 12

Escape

The kommando at Schönebeck, also named 'Julius' after one of its Nazi officials, was situated about 100 miles north on the banks of the River Elbe, just south-east of the city of Magdeburg. Established in March 1943, the camp's main purpose was to provide semi-skilled labour for the adjacent Junkers aircraft works, producing parts for Ju88 bombers and new Heinkel He198 jets. A selection process at Buchenwald was supposed to identify those capable of handling precision tools, but unqualified workers often swapped uniforms with engineers who took the tests in their place, cheating their way onto the next transport. The reason for the deception was simple: it was known that the administration at Schönebeck considered it unproductive to work its prisoners to death and a transfer therefore offered better chances of survival. However, whilst professional tradesmen were a useful resource, their welfare was still a relatively minor concern. The SS were paid a daily rate of four Reichsmarks by Junkers for each qualified worker, but less than a twelfth of that was spent on each man's upkeep. Likewise, the mortality rate was kept low because those too ill to work or injured by factory machinery were sent back to Buchenwald if they did not recover within three weeks.

Unusually the camp was sited in the vicinity of the town, employing electrified wire fences and seven watchtowers to separate it from the poplar-lined Barbyer Strasse, the main road running through Schönebeck's eastern side. The compound was much smaller than Buchenwald and had only a kitchen, a small *revier* (infirmary), an administrative office, a food store, a parade ground and nine timber-framed blocks for accommodating its inmates, mostly Russians, Poles and French; the SS barracks stood on the other side of the perimeter. Since June a number of Luftwaffe personnel had also been posted to strengthen the guard, some adopting the methods of the SS with great enthusiasm.

The prisoners' blocks followed the same design as at Buchenwald – a washroom and latrine by the entrance leading off to a dining area and office for the *Blockältester* and *Stubendiensts* (room orderlies), and a dormitory filled with wooden triple bunks, the mattresses being made of synthetic sack cloth and filled with straw or sawdust. Overcrowding was a problem, especially at weekends when prisoners were assembled together, and it was not unusual for two or three men to have to share a single bunk.

Peulevé and Hessel encountered no problems when entering the camp and were immediately placed with 300 French prisoners in Block 4. However, two days later Hessel was suddenly transferred to another branch of the Junkers works at Rottleberode, about 30 miles south near the town of Nordhausen. Although he was physically a good likeness of Michel Boitel, they had very different backgrounds: Boitel had been a machinist by profession, while Hessel had been a student. This seriously threatened the plausibility of his cover, as the skills of each new entrant were assessed before they were assigned to a relevant department, but he fortunately managed to convince one of the engineers to make use of his German and place him in an accountant position instead.

Peulevé had less luck with his employment, being given the job of pushing out stamped aluminium parts in the *Presswerk*, one of the three large factory halls within the camp grounds. Supervised by *Kapos* and Junkers foremen, teams of prisoners would be assigned to a day or night shift rota, alternating weekly: those on days (6.00 am to 6.00 pm) worked seventy-eight hours per week, while the night shift (6.00 pm to 6.00 am) was slightly shorter, at seventy-two hours. An *appel*, lasting anything from thirty minutes to several hours, was called before and after each shift, and also at 9.00 pm. Food, consisting of a litre of clear soup, bread, sausage or cheese and coffee was doled out in the blocks at different times according to the shift patterns. Aside from the physical demands and the tedium of this new regime, the rations compared unfavourably with Buchenwald and Peulevé started to visit a corner of the compound regularly to collect a few herbs to supplement his diet.

Although it could do no good, he found it impossible to bring himself to become a part of the German war machine: 'To starve was to me unpleasant, but to make aeroplanes that were destined to

164

make the last ditch for a lost cause against us was worse.'[1] Any problems concerning the workers' efficiency or discipline was usually reported by the *Kapos* to the guards or the *Lagerältester*; however, they were just as likely to deal with the matter personally, beating the culprits with the rubber truncheons they were issued with. Those that were brought before the Camp Elder, a communist and Francophobe named Walter Pidum, did not fare any better – his preferred form of punishment involved repeatedly jabbing at an offender's jaw with the heel of his hand until he was incapable of standing. The SS made a more public show of wrongdoers, standing them next to a low brick wall by the parade ground for hours on end with their arms outstretched or behind their heads, a practice referred to by the prisoners as *'faire le papillon'* (making the butterfly).

Despite these severe penalties many prisoners continued to resist, either by working as slowly as possible or producing defective components, and Peulevé soon followed the example of his French comrades, becoming 'the most inefficient slave labourer they had'.[2] Unfortunately the *Presswerk Kapo*, nicknamed 'the spectacled snake'[3] by the inmates, was well known as being one of the most vigilant in the camp, and at the beginning of the new year Peulevé was transferred to a *straf kommando* (punishment detail) where life was much tougher. Often with only dandelion tea to sustain them in temperatures of minus 20 degrees centigrade, the kommando would be marched 14 kilometres south-east to cross the river at Barby and dig anti-tank traps against the expected Russian forces on the eastern banks of the Elbe. The effects of this brutal regime and the bitterly cold winter quickly began to wear down his reserves and he soon started to resemble the other pathetic figures that shuffled alongside him. Peulevé was aware that he was reaching his limit:

> Under these miserable conditions, with my empty belly and no prospect of any news from Violet, I had many times felt that the chapter as far as I was concerned would have been better finished at the end of a rope. Constant beating by the SS, a freezing, misty and snowbound countryside, revolting and insufficient food, a moral plane at its lowest – my heart was, by this time, in my boots. Another few months and I could not have stood more. No hope, no relief from the disastrous monotony, and above all, no news of Violet.[4]

The thought of seeing Violette again was one of the few enduring reasons he had left to keep going, but any hopes for their reunion were about to be extinguished forever.

After spending ten days at Saarbrücken, Violette, Denise Bloch and Lilian Rolfe were transported to Ravensbrück, a concentration camp for women near Lake Fürstenberg in northern Germany. Responsible for more than 80,000 prisoners by the end of 1944, the SS worked many of them to death in numerous external sub-camps and kommandos, while those who were too ill to work were summarily hanged or killed in mobile gas chambers, or used as guinea pigs for medical experiments. Violette soon made contact with several women she had known in Fresnes, but after two weeks she, Bloch and Rolfe were transferred again, this time to Torgau, a small town on the Elbe about 80 miles south-east of Schönebeck.

The conditions here were better and like Peulevé they were put to work in an aircraft factory. Despite Denise's loss of hope and Lilian's physical weakness, Violette did her best to support the other two and managed to stay remarkably positive. As Torgau appeared to be relatively lightly guarded she also set her mind to finding a means of escape, and after a few days obtained a key for one of the doors on the perimeter. However, one of the inmates had informed the guards of Szabó's plans before she could act, and following a strike by some of the prisoners in October she and her compatriots were moved again, being sent to a derelict *straflager* at Königsberg on the River Oder. For the next three months they were put to work clearing trees and rocks for a new runway at the nearby airfield, having to contend with the effects of freezing winter temperatures and the sadistic behaviour of their guards. Violette still continued to seek a way out, but slowly the back-breaking work began to consume even her seemingly inexhaustible resolve.

By the beginning of 1945 the conditions at Königsberg had reduced all three to pitiful imitations of their former selves, still clad in the same clothes they were wearing when they had left Paris in August. Although Lilian had recently been admitted to hospital she, Denise and Violette were unexpectedly recalled to Ravensbrück on a special transport leaving early on the morning of 20 January; given the unusual privileges of soap and new clothes before their journey, they began to speculate that perhaps this was the end of their nightmare and they might now be heading for the safety of Switzerland or Sweden. Yet Violette's secret fears about the real nature of this transfer proved to be well founded, and upon arrival they were immediately isolated from the other prisoners and placed in the punishment block, being moved several days later to cells in the camp's bunker. As with the male agents at Buchenwald, the authorities in Berlin had been careful to eliminate SOE's agents before the Allies could liberate them, and decisions on the fates of these three women had already been passed on to Ravensbrück's Commandant, Fritz Sühren. According to the later testimony of the Camp Overseer, Obersturmführer Johann Schwarzhuber, Violette and her two crippled companions were led out one evening around 27 January, being taken to the crematorium yard where the orders for their executions were read out. Even the usually pitiless Sühren was impressed by their courage as, one by one, each of them was made to kneel in an alley where an SS NCO shot them in the back of the neck with a small-calibre pistol; the bodies were then cremated and their clothes burned, leaving no trace of their existence.

At his lowest ebb, Peulevé sought to channel his remaining psychological and physical reserves to focus on an escape plan, and concluded that the best opportunity lay in making a run for it when walking back to the camp. In order to free himself, he began to file away at the interior side of the bolt on his ankle shackle, covering the damage with dirt or soot to avoid his work being discovered by the guards' cursory inspections. While those in the barracks amused themselves in the evenings with songs or games, Peulevé spent whatever time he could on this painstakingly slow and laborious task, and by the end of March had weakened the shackle enough to be able to break it if necessary. All he could do now was to wait for the right moment, but knew that he would have to act soon. At the beginning of the year a large pit had been dug behind the blocks for the supposed construction of a swimming pool, but many realized that the SS were preparing to liquidate their prisoners before they could be liberated.

On the evening of 11 April, Peulevé's work party was walking back to the camp when they saw flashes on the northern horizon, accompanied by the sound of artillery fire. Rumours about the advancing American forces had been rife amongst the prisoners for months, but the previous night's air raids had been particularly heavy and it seemed that this must be the sign for which they had waited so long. In fact it was the 2nd Armored Division of the US Ninth Army; dubbed 'Hell on Wheels', it had raced nearly 60 miles that day to reach the Elbe and secure a bridgehead at Magdeburg.

Deciding that this was his chance, Peulevé stopped for a moment to grab one half of his shackle, kicking at the other side as hard as he could. It snapped apart as planned and he immediately broke from the group towards a copse about 50 feet away, managing to put some distance between himself and the guards before they could let off their first shots. Fortunately their aim was poor in the fading light of dusk and by the time he made it to the far side of the trees he knew he was safe. Already demoralized by the thought of their imminent defeat his pursuers weren't interested in chasing after a single prisoner and he watched from his hiding place as they made a casual search of the area before heading back to join their party. Although anniversaries were the last thing on his mind, it was exactly two years since he had made his escape from Jaraba in Spain.

The day had been equally eventful for those back in the camp. Anticipating the imminent arrival of American forces, the prisoners became so restless that the SS were forced to confine them to their blocks until further notice. At 1.00 pm the usual *appel* was called, but many inmates refused to line up and swarmed around the perimeter, while others took advantage of the ensuing commotion, secreting themselves underneath the floors of the blocks. Resorting to the use of dogs, truncheons and rifle butts to restore order, the Camp Commandant formed the 1,546 prisoners into three groups, which were slowly herded through the gates towards Barby. Aided by members of the local *Volkssturm* (Nazi militia, composed of men ineligible for military service) and boys from the Hitler Youth, the SS garrison attempted to control the evacuation but were powerless to stop small groups of Poles, Russians and French taking flight along the way. By the evening the situation had become completely chaotic, as retreating Wehrmacht forces clogged the bridges over the Elbe and increasing numbers of prisoners took advantage of the confusion, disappearing into the darkness. Allied aircraft bombed and strafed the procession as it made its way over Barby's railway crossing, but around 1,100 men made it to the other side, stopping near Lindau in the early hours of 12 April.

Over the coming days the remainder of the Schönebeck kommando would be pushed east through the towns of Loburg, Belzig and Beelitz before turning north, passing the outskirts of Potsdam and Berlin. The intention was to stop at Sachsenhausen concentration camp at Oranienburg, but it too had been forced to evacuate as Soviet forces were rapidly closing in on the capital. Joining more than 30,000 other camp refugees walking on towards Wittstock, this ragged group watched the roadsides become littered with the bodies of those too exhausted to carry on, many being casually shot in the back of the neck and left to rot in ditches; with provisions exhausted, those not overcome by dysentery were also reduced to foraging for food, eating grass, slugs, corn grains and whatever else they could find along the way. After enduring a march of twenty-three days and 300 miles, the 470 or so survivors of Schönebeck would be abandoned at Friedrichmoor, about 10 miles west of the Mecklenburg town of Parchim on 4 May, many of their captors changing into civilian clothing and fleeing before the arrival of the Allies.

Although Peulevé had successfully escaped, he still had to find a way to the American lines. Waiting until he was sure that the work party had moved on, he began walking across the snow-covered fields towards the illuminated skies over what he thought must be Magdeburg. As night fell the temperature began to plummet and although he continued trudging north in the darkness he appeared to be making little progress towards his objective. For the next two days and nights he stubbornly pushed himself on in the direction of the fighting, now relying purely on his determination to survive and find out what fate had befallen Violette. However, even Peulevé's strength of character would only carry him so far, and by the evening of the 13 April he realized that if he did not find food and shelter he would soon be dead.

As it began to get dark he stumbled onto a railway line, which eventually led him towards a small village. Although he desperately wanted to reach it, the Americans were subjecting it to heavy fire, forcing him to take refuge in a wood on the other side of the track. Frustrated and completely exhausted, Peulevé came across a deserted anti-aircraft post, inside which he found a pullover and trousers to wear over his striped camp uniform, and an old pair of boots to replace his sabots. When he awoke the next morning he realized that the Americans had cleared the area and were crossing the railway line, moving east; however, as Peulevé attempted to leave the wood 'some misguided bastard'[5] opened up on him with a volley of machine-gun fire, and he threw himself into a ditch to avoid being hit. Crawling back to the anti-aircraft post, he would have to wait for the remaining Americans to move out before he could enter the village.

Even though he could do little about his immediate situation, he began to feel that at least the worst was over – sooner or later he would be able to carry on and surrender himself at Magdeburg or one of the nearby towns. Unfortunately this complacency proved to be ill-founded. Later that morning he spotted two figures in dark clothing walking down the railway track in his direction and as they came nearer he realized to his horror that both were wearing SS uniforms. It was too late to run even if he had possessed enough energy to do so and for a moment it seemed that they might pass by, but his heart sank as one of them began walking straight towards him, beckoning to his partner to follow.

The officers that confronted him were middle-aged and grey-haired; nevertheless, they were both carrying holsters on their belts. Unsure what to make of the pathetic figure before them, one of them enquired, 'Good day, who are you?'[6] Playing his last card, Peulevé told them that he was a Frenchman who had volunteered for work in Germany and had changed into a camp uniform when the Americans had arrived in the area to avoid being taken as a collaborator. They appeared to buy his story and told him that they were Rexists, Belgian fascists who served under a special Waffen-SS section led by Nazi sympathizer Léon Degrelle. Having avoided suspicion as an escaper, Peulevé now had an opportunity to take the initiative. Telling them that the Americans had surrounded the wood, he suggested that they should change into civilian clothes as he had done, as they would most likely be shot if captured in SS uniforms. They agreed, and began to undress:

> My intention was to get them to remove their belts with their guns which I would then seize and march them out of the wood towards that machine-gunner who was keeping me from my Allied friends, a good meal and news of Violet. Convinced by my argument, the two men dropped their belts. I seized their arms immediately and ordered them to put their hands up. I felt like a heel, but I had to get back, so I ordered them to march out of the wood in front of me.[7]

As Peulevé prepared to leave the post with his two prisoners, he told them to empty their pockets so that he could hand in their papers to the Americans. Whilst going through their belongings he found a set of pictures taken of women in concentration camps:

> These postcards were typical of the sort of sadistic dirt that one would expect to find amongst their type of men. But, to my amazement and horror, of the twelve naked women who were

being made to jump through the snow by brawny and blowsy concentration camp SS guards, one of them was Vi.

Keeping one gun on them, I gripped one of their leather belts with my last remaining strength. The photos I had taken from the wallet had dropped in the snow. I trod on them as I lashed out at their faces with the buckle of the belt. In the middle of this fury I suddenly realised what had happened to Vi. There would be no answer when I got back. I felt like killing them both and then crawling out of the wood and being shot down by the American machine-gunner. But I couldn't stand their moaning for mercy. When the blood of one who was on his knees dripped over the snow and on to the photographs, I thought 'No, I'm not the judge', and I told them to get up with their hands above their heads and march out of the wood.[8]

It should be noted firstly that there is no evidence that Szabó was photographed for such material, though it is known that similar pictures to those described were produced and circulated; nor is there any record of this incident in any SOE report on Szabó's incarceration or death. Moreover, by Peulevé's own admission he had not eaten at all for three days (or eaten properly for over six months), was under enormous strain and had become near-obsessed with the idea of seeing Violette again. His physical and psychological state at this time must therefore raise the possibility that he saw another woman who resembled her, though we will never know for sure, as he chose to leave the picture behind in the snow.

The weary, battle-hardened soldiers of the 83rd US Infantry Division might have imagined that they had seen everything in their long struggle since landing on the beaches of Normandy nearly a year before, but even they were perplexed by the sight of Peulevé's ghostly figure emerging from the wood, ordering his two reluctant SS prisoners forward. After explaining his story, the Americans sent a telegram to the British seeking verification on some of the details that Peulevé had given as proof of his identity, such as Gielgud's interview at Room 055 and the training schools at Wanborough Manor and Meoble Lodge. The message passed through Section V (a department of MI 6 responsible for counter-intelligence) and then to SOE, who soon confirmed that he was theirs and arranged for Peulevé to be transported by air under the care of Captain Josendale of OSS (Office of Strategic Services, SOE's American counterpart) to

171

21st Army Group, where he reported to Major Sainsbury of 3 Special Force Detachment. Sainsbury's job would be to interrogate him over the next two days on his time in Buchenwald and the fates of those he had known in Block 17.

Apart from a rumour about Yeo-Thomas having been sent to a kommando at Jena and Hessel ending up in Dora, Peulevé had heard little during his time at Schönebeck, but Sainsbury informed London that he could still offer a lot of other relevant information and that his memory had not been impaired by his maltreatment; Peulevé was also able to tag on a short message to his family: 'Request inform parents ... that quote I am alive and well and returning in very short time unquote.'[9] SOE's Chief Liaison Officer Robin Brook visited Buchenwald some days later in a further effort to try and trace Yeo-Thomas' movements, but there was little to go on. Like everyone visiting the newly liberated camp he could not believe what he was witnessing, repulsed by the stench and the 'matchstick people and their waif-like ghoulish appearances'.[10]

Though Brook's enquiries were mostly fruitless, Yeo-Thomas and Hessel were also still alive and would eventually make their way to the Allied lines. Having left Buchenwald on 9 November, Yeo-Thomas had been sent to a sub-camp at Gleina and assigned to the hospital as an orderly. In mid-April he was evacuated towards Czechoslovakia, but managed to escape from the train with several other prisoners; recaptured some days afterwards he was placed in a French POW camp only to escape again, walking through a mine-field with two of his comrades to reach the American lines in early May. After an unsuccessful breakout from Rottleberode in February, Hessel had been sent to Mittelbau-Dora, an underground complex carved out of Kohnstein mountain near Nordhausen; responsible for the production of V-1 and V-2 rockets, it had an appalling death rate and was one of the worst destinations for any prisoner. On 5 April, he was evacuated and put on a train for Belsen, but escaped through a hole in the floor of the carriage and made his way to Hanover, where he was picked up by the Americans a week later.

Of the original group of thirty-seven, only three others had survived: Culioli, Southgate and Guillot (Kogon, Baumeister, Dietzsch and Balachowsky were also all liberated). Culioli and Guillot escaped while being transferred to separate kommandos, whilst Southgate evaded execution by taking jobs in the hospital and tailor's shop, before hiding in the Little Camp with Burney and the Newton brothers for several nerve-wracking days until the Americans finally arrived on 11 April. However, the SS were successful in tracking down the last remaining agent on their list – having survived more than a year in Buchenwald, Maurice Pertschuk was hanged just two weeks before the camp's liberation, on 29 March.

Concluding his interviews with Major Sainsbury, plans were made to transport Peulevé back to the UK and he landed at Croydon airport on the morning of 18 April. After being welcomed back by Buckmaster and Atkins he was driven off to one of F Section's safe houses in South Kensington; they had known what to expect on his arrival, having already undergone the shock of meeting the first four 'walking scarecrows'[11] – Burney, Southgate and the Newton brothers – who had flown back two days earlier. Peulevé sent a telegram to his parents: 'Extremely glad to be back home again and longing to see you unfortunately unable come on leave so have booked room for you both at South Kensington Hotel from tomorrow night stop.'[12]

His family, having believed him to be dead for months, were naturally anxious about their reunion and arrived at the hotel, just off Queen's Gate, as arranged. However, they could never have prepared themselves adequately to meet the shadow of the person they had remembered and were inevitably shaken, though Annette noticed that he still managed to make an effort at social pleasantries: 'His head was shaven. He was emaciated, his hands were skeletal, yet he could admire my hat.'[13] His consideration for others had not been diminished by his experiences, either. Apologizing to his parents, he said that he had already made plans for them to dine with the Newtons, who had no family to greet them.

F Section had already discussed the issue of its returning agents and it had been agreed that once they had recovered enough to talk about their experiences, interrogations should be pursued with some urgency. Information about those who had been captured was often vague and came from unreliable sources, their true fates having been purposely obscured by the Nazi policy of *Nacht und Nebel* (Night and Fog), a directive issued in December 1941 by Hitler's Chief of Staff, Field Marshal Wilhelm Keitel. This order sought to erase all trace of political prisoners, resistance fighters and other enemies of the Reich by secretly deporting them to camps in Germany, where the SS could reduce their identities to a number and ignore any international conventions or treaties regarding human rights. The chaos that ensued as tens of thousands of these 'NN' prisoners were liberated meant that gathering intelligence was essential, though based on their initial findings Buckmaster and Atkins were pessimistic, estimating that perhaps only thirty of the 118 missing F Section agents might now be found.[14]

Peulevé's first report was made on 23 April, though Atkins had warned her superiors not to expect too much, as all five men were finding it impossible to concentrate sufficiently to withstand a full interrogation; the Newton brothers gave a joint submission. Peulevé also gave an interview for the *News Chronicle*, which was published a few days later. Though SOE was unknown to the public, this Buchenwald story was released just as the first shocking footage from the camp was beginning to appear in cinemas throughout the country. The front-page article, entitled 'Most Fantastic Escape', noted 'his quiet unemotional voice, as though he were describing an ordinary everyday occurrence',[15] and included details on his time in both camps, but did not refer to the names of other agents involved. Afterwards Peulevé went to Suffolk to see his family, during which time he began to dictate some of his story to his mother.

Though his physical state was slowly improving, it was arranged for him to report to a hospital in Birmingham for psychiatric evaluation. There is unfortunately no record of its assessment, though his mother described him as 'a very broken young man'[16] at this time, and there is no doubt that his ordeals had left him psychologically battered. Not only had he endured over a year of incarceration, interrogation, torture and dehumanizing treatment of all kinds, but also now believed that Violette, who he had been determined to see again, would never return.[17] There was no question that Peulevé had finally wiped the slate clean and proved himself a man of honour, but it had cost him dearly. The effects of these experiences had taken a huge toll on him, and would continue to do so for the rest of his life.

Yeo-Thomas, who had only been in England a few weeks and was only just beginning to recover, had been swift to pass his own report on Peulevé's conduct to Buckmaster. The strong impression that he had left on Yeo-Thomas had clearly motivated this short tribute, though it is also telling of Yeo-Thomas' own character that he made the effort to submit it:

> During my captivity in Buchenwald I selected the above-named officer as my second-in-command, and found him invaluable. He displayed the greatest courage under conditions of almost incredible strain, and I have the greatest respect and admiration

for his qualities and ability. I feel that it is only my duty to place this appreciation on record.[18]

Returning to London towards the end of May, Peulevé was unexpectedly confronted with a report found by the Resistance in the Gestapo archives at Limoges. Dated 23 July 1944, it was apparently a detailed summary of his interrogation, suggesting that he gave information on a number of maquis leaders as well as Hiller, Watney, Poirier and several of AUTHOR's helpers. His response on 28 May contained nothing to contradict his previous assertion that he had remained silent. Whilst he had fed the SD some blown addresses and other unimportant details, he concluded that the rest of the data must have been collated from a mixture of other interrogated sources (which may have included Delsanti, Bertheau or Roland Malraux), and the contents of the telegrams captured with him. The Gestapo report concluded by stating that Peulevé had been shot in June 1944 in reprisals for recent Allied bombing raids, which prompted him to offered the sardonic remark, 'I have evidence to show that as far as I am concerned this is definitely incorrect.'[19] He took some more leave from the first week of June, though he returned briefly to submit a more detailed report later that month.

Since his arrival in London Peulevé had been eager to find out what had happened to his AUTHOR network and although French restrictions made it impossible for him to return to Brive, he gathered whatever information he could on those he'd left behind. Having taken command of the DIGGER circuit just weeks before D-Day, Poirier and his team had successfully harried the 2nd SS Panzer Division *Das Reich* as it made its way north from its headquarters in Montauban to meet the Allied forces in Normandy. Numerous raids by the AS maquis groups of Vaujour and Guédin delayed *Das Reich*'s journey to the front for several days, though some vicious reprisals were carried out, most notably the hanging of ninety-nine civilian hostages along the streets of Tulle[20] and the massacre at Oradour-sur-Glane near Limoges, in which more than 600 civilians were killed, including 400 women and children who were burned to death in the village church. On 14 July, a massive supply drop named 'Operation Cadillac' delivered thousands of containers to the Corrèze and Lot, and its effect on the morale of Colonel Heinrich Böhmer's Brive garrison enabled DIGGER and the maquis to force its surrender. On the evening of 15 August 1944, the terms were finally agreed and Brive-la-Gaillarde became the first town in France to be liberated by the Resistance. Though he had not been there to see it, Peulevé now knew that his efforts had not been in vain. Having kept up the pretence of being a British officer for the past six months, the now legendary 'Captain Jack' was at last able to reveal his true identity to his compatriots, and in July 1945 the services of Major Jacques Poirier were officially recognized with the award of the Distinguished Service Order.

After their arrival in January 1944, Hiller and Watney's FOOT-MAN network had quickly found the *Groupes Vény* to be virtually non-existent, finding 'no arms whatever, no organisation worth speaking of, and, worst of all, neither drive nor offensive spirit',[21] and had to painstakingly build up support from scratch. By D-Day they had managed to arm 600 men in the Lot and a similar number in neighbouring Lot-et-Garonne, though their efforts were dogged by infighting between the FTP, FFI and Vény. On 22 July, Hiller was seriously wounded when he and André Malraux unexpectedly ran into a German roadblock at Gramat, and he was flown back to England a few days later, leaving Watney in charge.

Circuits FIREMAN and GARDENER had been sent in March to help Vény's groups in Limoges and Marseille, but they also encountered similar problems. GARDENER's experienced organizer Major Robert Boiteux (*Firmin*) had been told that he would find 3,000 men in Vény's groups in Marseille and a maquis of 300 in Nice – on landing he scraped together a total of fourteen. Likewise, FIREMAN's Mauritian leader Major Percy Mayer (*Barthélemy*) and his brother Edward (*Maurice*) were dismayed to find nothing more than a 'flimsy affair'[22] on the ground, though both circuits went on to establish contact with other groups and carried out a number of successful actions in July and August.

Many of Peulevé's colleagues lived to see France liberated. André Malraux, having become 'Colonel Berger' the FFI commander, had been captured in the same incident that had left Hiller wounded, but was released in August; Poulou and Georgette Lachaud, Jean and Marie Verlhac, Jean Melon and Maurice Arnouil also survived, despite having to leave their homes after Gestapo raids. However, there were three notable casualties. After being separated from Peulevé, Roland Malraux and Louis Delsanti were moved to Compiègne before being deported to Neuengamme concentration camp; evacuated with thousands of others in the final days of the war and crammed onto the *Cap Arcona* in the Bay of Lübeck, they were amongst more than 7,000 killed after the RAF attacked it and two other ships on 3 May 1945. Louis Bertheau had also been deported to Germany, being placed in Sandbostel camp near Bremen, and died in hospital from typhus on 26 April, several days after its liberation. Adrien Dufour, the *milicien* responsible for denouncing them, was later arrested and sentenced by a Limoges court to twenty years' hard labour for his actions.[23]

Having begun the process of winding down in late 1944, SOE was now largely preoccupied with disbanding itself, though some in F Section still felt a duty to do whatever it could for its returning agents and tried to find jobs to help them return to civilian life (agents did not receive 'danger money' for their missions and although they were exempt from income tax, their rate of pay was equal to that of regular officers). As a means of retaining them on the army payroll many were sent to work for the Control Commission for Germany, responsible for the post-war administration of the country, and at the beginning of August, Peulevé was to take a low-key staff officer post with the public relations branch of the films section. Like other agents who had been reduced to nervous wrecks by their experiences, Peulevé was posted to the Commission in the hope that he could pass the time out of the way, quietly doing his job until he was released from service. But it was still too early – the veneer of normality was clearly too much to bear and by early October he was evacuated by air back to England on sick leave.

Returning to hospital where he was expected to spend several weeks, Peulevé dropped in to see Buckmaster to submit a statement for Ding-Schuler's defence, feeling that 'he undoubtedly owes his life to Dr Ding',[24] though Buckmaster suggested that this could be sorted out when he was in a less agitated frame of mind. It is again reflective of Peulevé's selflessness that even in his mental agonies he was still thinking of the welfare of others, especially when considering that Ding-Schuler's interests in saving Allied agents had been born out of personal gain rather than altruism. However, his testimony would now be useless as the trial had been abandoned – having been picked up by the Americans in April, Ding-Schuler had managed to commit suicide in his cell at Freising on 11 August.

Peulevé had already submitted information on Dietzsch, in which he had made it clear that his administering of lethal injections was only done under the orders of the SS. He went on to declare that:

He was certainly instrumental in saving my life, and showed, to my mind, considerable courage in suggesting to the SS doctor

Von Schuler [sic], that he also should co-operate. At this time, Dietzsch did not know that Schuler was willing to do so, and had he not been, Dietzsch would certainly have got himself into very hot water.[25]

Dietzsch would eventually be tried at the US war crimes trials held at Dachau in 1947; found guilty of collaboration with the camp authorities in the maltreatment of those in Block 46, he was sentenced to fifteen years imprisonment but was released early, in 1950. In total twenty-two of the thirty-one Buchenwald defendants were given the death penalty, including Hermann Pister, Buchenwald's last Commandant, and Friedrich Wilhelm, the man who had been sent to murder Peulevé in Block 46. Both were hanged in 1948.

Chapter 13

Peacetime

Leaving hospital early in 1946, Peulevé thought that he might return to the BBC after his imminent demobilization, but the plan was short-lived. At the start of the war, employees at Alexandra Palace had been told that the Corporation would top up their pay whilst serving to equal their previous salary. Unfortunately Peulevé's elevation in rank[1] since 1939 meant that he had no longer been eligible for this money and consequently was requested to refund every penny. Resenting their small-mindedness in the light of what he had suffered, he refused to comply and lost any chance of returning to his old job. However, another opportunity soon presented itself: before its dissolution F Section had managed to find him an industrial relations role with Shell at one of their oil camps in Venezuela. This good news coincided with appointments of a different kind when he was made a Chevalier of the Légion d'Honneur and was presented with the Croix de Guerre avec Palme for his clandestine work with the Resistance. Several weeks later he was also awarded the Distinguished Service Order, which he received at Buckingham Palace on 26 February.[2]

Moving to South America was in many ways a relief for Peulevé, taking him away from the problems of war-torn Europe and offering the chance to build a new life. However, he encountered a serious obstacle when Shell accommodated him at an apartment of the Bellavista country club within the huge complex at Maracaibo – hundreds of expatriate workers and their families lived within the confines of the compound, and to maintain security the company employed guards to patrol the barbed-wire perimeter. With the memories of captivity still fresh in his mind, the distress caused by having to live and work in this environment made his early days very difficult; he suffered from vivid nightmares and his family suspected that he relied on drink to assuage them.

Despite these problems he managed to hold the job down, and it took him little time to find his feet and develop a circle of friends. In the spring of 1947 Peulevé returned to England, spending some time touring around the Corrèze accompanied by Vera Atkins; a year later he returned to attend a memorial service in Brive on the anniversary of D-Day, joined by former SOE chief Colin Gubbins and maquis leaders René Vaujour and Gontrand Royer. Wreaths were laid in the Hotel de Ville in memory of the children of Brive who had died during the war and Peulevé was awarded the Medaille de la Résistance by Brive's most famous son, Edmond Michelet, who had survived Dachau concentration camp after his arrest in 1943.

The details of Peulevé's movements between 1948 and 1950 are hazy, although it is known that Shell transferred him to Bogota, Columbia in 1949, and he occasionally returned to the UK to see his family. In 1951 Peulevé's term in South America came to an end and by August he was back in London, staying at the Special Forces Club in Knightsbridge, which had been established in 1946 to support SOE's former agents and personnel. The plan was to start a new tour with Shell in Tunisia at the beginning of the following year, leaving him some time to catch up with friends on the Côte d'Azur, including Arthur Larking, who now spent much of his time at the Hotel Astoria in Menton. In early October he flew back from Nice, whiling away his time at the club and seeing Cyril Watney, who was recovering from a serious car accident. Though Cyril and Peulevé had remained firm friends, Watney's family was unfortunately less impressed by Peulevé's presence, considering their long evenings in the bar detrimental to Cyril's convalescence.

Towards the end of the month Catriona Sopper, one of Peulevé's SOE friends and a regular at the club, introduced him to Marie-Louise Jahn, a beautiful 24-year-old secretary who worked just around the corner at the Danish Consulate-General. He wasted no time in inviting her out to dinner and within a few weeks their romance became a constant source of gossip amongst their friends. They travelled to Denmark for Christmas, staying at Marie-Louise's parents' home in an affluent area of Odense, a quiet provincial town best known as the birthplace of Hans Christian Andersen. Spending much of their time wandering through the snow-covered woods nearby, Peulevé's thoughts inevitably turned to the future and the prospect of returning to work for Shell without her; now very much in love, she agreed to follow him to his new posting.

180

After a brief spell in London, Peulevé left for Tunisia on 30 January 1952, Marie-Louise joining him shortly after. The French colonial atmosphere of Tunis was a pleasant alternative to the wintry streets of post-war London, and having moved into an attractive penthouse flat on the palm-lined Avenue Carnot they made friends with many French expatriates, living comfortably on what Peulevé earned. On 29 March they married at the British Consulate-General, a low-key ceremony with only the bride's parents and a few friends in attendance; their first child, Madeleine Anna Maria, was born at the end of the year, with Christopher Burney acting as her godfather.

Having established his position with Shell, Peulevé also seemed to be adapting well to his new life as a family man, but at the beginning of 1954 he was transferred to a new post as Assistant Manager for Administration at another refinery in Suez, which housed a large number of expatriate Britons. After his time in Venezuela, Peulevé knew what to expect of life in a compound, but for his wife the transition was more difficult and she inevitably found it restrictive. Although they were suitably accommodated in their own house and often spent Sundays together on the shores of the Red Sea, Marie-Louise's daily trip with Madeleine to the stretch of greenery surrounding the Shell club could not compare with the golden beaches and city life of Tunis they had known before. Now expecting their second child, they took a welcome break in England and travelled on to Odense in July, where Marie-Louise gave birth to a boy, Jean-Pierre Leonard.

Despite his growing responsibilities, Peulevé had clearly benefited from the stabilizing influence of family life. The nightmares and frustrations from his darker days had largely disappeared, and his marriage provided him with an important source of support that had previously been absent. However, long working hours increasingly led to more time being spent socializing with colleagues, and his commitments to his wife and children soon conflicted with a need for more independence. Though there seemed to be no question mark over his fidelity, Peulevé's reluctance to settle down completely began to distance him from his young family, and it was apparent that he and Marie-Louise were slowly drifting apart.

President Nasser's expansionist policies led to increasing tensions between Egypt and Israel during the following year, and by the spring of 1956 Shell had begun to evacuate of some of its workers' families out of the country. Marie-Louise and the children returned to Denmark in May, but Peulevé decided to stay behind, and for the next couple of months almost nothing was heard from him. Concerns for his safety increased when Nasser nationalized the Suez Canal Company in July – not only did this seriously threaten British and French interests, but also increased the Egyptian Government's scrutiny of foreign nationals, and many began to suspect that they were victims of phone tapping and other police surveillance.

On 9 August one of Peulevé's colleagues, Edgar Hawke, was arrested at his local golf club on orders from the Ministry of the Interior, suspected of spying for the British Government. On hearing the news, Peulevé went to the police to enquire about what had happened but was then detained as well. No explanation was given, both men being told only that they would be deported within twenty-four hours and that they could take one suitcase each with them. One of Peulevé's Egyptian friends was able to get permission for him to collect a few more items from his home, but was unable to withdraw the balance of his bank account. The following day both men were taken to Port Said, photographed on the quay and put aboard the Panamanian tanker *Caprella*, bound for Liverpool.

Whilst Peulevé's SOE background might have been considered a security threat, the growing tensions in the region meant that many expatriate workers faced similar treatment, and the Foreign Office made a formal protest on 11 August over a number of reports by British employees of intimidation. In some respects he was comparatively fortunate to have avoided being held for any longer, though his forced exit meant that most of his money and possessions were lost. In typical fashion Peulevé concealed his emotions and kept to the facts when being interviewed by the *Daily Express* via the ship's radio, and he showed nothing of his frustrations in his telegram to Annette: 'All well expect arrive 19th looking forward see you soon love – Henry'.[3]

Giving his story to several newspaper reporters after disembarking at Liverpool docks, he travelled down to London and stayed at the Special Forces Club before flying to Denmark. Although they had only been apart for a few months, Peulevé's absence had offered Marie-Louise a welcome respite from the strains of their now loveless marriage, and she had begun plans for a teaching career with a view to bringing up Madeleine and Jean-Pierre in Odense. Not wishing to return to an empty relationship and an uncertain future, Marie-Louise told him that she wanted a divorce on the grounds of incompatibility, and Peulevé made his way alone back to Copenhagen three days later. Feeling a need to get away from his problems, he spent September and October in New York City, Toronto and Montreal visiting friends; however, the combined effects of the separation and the Suez incident had affected him deeply. A friend of Vera Atkins was shaken to see Peulevé 'in such a state of depression'[4] at the club, although he did return to Denmark briefly to see the children in the first days of the New Year.

In the early part of 1957 Peulevé found a job with the Haiti branch of Dexion, a company selling storage and shelving products, a post he faced little competition for considering the country's unstable political situation. He arrived in April and moved into a pleasant villa, but it was not enough, and the absence of family ties inevitably left more time for him to brood on the past; though some memories had faded, others, such as the lingering responsibility he felt for the deaths of Delsanti, Bertheau and Roland Malraux (Delsanti and Bertheau had both left young families behind) and the demons of Buchenwald and Schönebeck had lost none of their ability to torment. He appealed to his wife to join him, but it was clearly too late for reconciliation and Marie-Louise was adamant that she and the children would remain in Odense. He returned to Canada in June to visit friends, but stayed in Haiti for the rest of the year.

During the 1950s an increasing interest in SOE's exploits led to a number of films, books, radio and television programmes, some of which inevitably sought to romanticize the lives of its agents. Buckmaster, Christopher Burney, the Newton brothers, Peter Churchill and Yeo-Thomas all became public figures after accounts of their experiences were published, but Peulevé preferred to remain in the background – aside from a need for privacy, he harboured little desire to see his life in print, even though Buckmaster had chosen to include (largely muddled) tales of his heroism in his second book *They Fought Alone*.

During his time in Suez the writer and film producer R.J. Minney had contacted Peulevé to research material for a biography of Violette, who had become one of SOE's best-known figures following her posthumous award of the George Cross in 1946. Minney was granted an interview, though his investigations placed Peulevé in an awkward position, as Minney had been informed that Peulevé was the source of the assertion in Violette's George Cross citation that she had been 'continuously and atrociously' tortured during her time at Avenue Foch. In fact there was no clear evidence for this claim and Minney later recalled how Peulevé had been evasive on this matter, commenting in a letter to the *Sunday Times* how:

> The words 'spoke hardly at all about the tortures she had been made to suffer' [quoting Peulevé during his earlier interview with Minney] seem to imply that she had been tortured. I was conscious, while he spoke, that Captain Peulevé, who had earlier confessed to me that he had been in love with Violette, was reluctant to dwell on this; nor was I prepared to press him to do so.[5]

Rather than let such obstacles get in the way of a good story, Minney chose to present a dramatized description of Violette's time at the hands of the SD; it may not have been historically accurate, but the British public's insatiable appetite for tales of wartime heroes and heroines ensured the book's success. Published towards the end of 1956, *Carve Her Name with Pride* became a best-seller and work began on a film adaptation the following year, starring Virginia McKenna as Violette and Paul Scofield as fictional character 'Tony Fraser', merging Liewer's and Peulevé's real-life roles. Directed by Lewis Gilbert and released in 1958, it was well received, with McKenna being nominated for a BAFTA for her performance.

Uncomfortable with Minney's depiction, Peulevé corresponded with a more critical SOE biographer, Elizabeth Nicholas, who had already published a biography of Noor Inayat Khan and was researching the lives of several other female agents, confirming to her that he had not stated that Violette had been tortured. However, in 1958 the publication of Nicholas' *Death Not Be Proud*, coinciding with the release of Jean Overton Fuller's investigation of double agent Henri Déricourt entitled *Double Webs*, now raised more serious and far-reaching questions about Baker Street's operations, accusing Buckmaster and other former SOE officers of incompetence, negligence and even the cold-blooded sacrifice of their own agents for strategic gain. Supporting calls for a government response to these allegations, Conservative MP Dame Irene Ward tabled a motion in the House of Commons asking for an official examination to be launched into SOE's activities, which was eventually begun in the early 1960s, though many former agents in Britain and France felt saddened by the backbiting and squabbling that had in part provoked it. For Peulevé the whole episode served as a compelling reason to keep his distance from any further controversy, with his decision to remain overseas making it far easier to avoid any more public attention.

The election of Haiti dictator Papa Doc Duvalier prompted him to leave Dexion, finding work with a Monaco-based company called Albion, which sold tax-free motor cars to the American naval fleets that frequented the ports of the Mediterreanean. Peulevé was recruited to manage its Spanish division and was based for a time near Gibraltar, but although the surroundings were pleasant enough the job failed to hold his interest for long. Resigning in September 1959, he once more found himself at a loose end and decided to spend a week in Paris, during which time he went to see Yeo-Thomas at his flat in the rue des Eaux, overlooking the Passy metro where he had been arrested in 1944. Yeo-Thomas, whose story had been published under the title of *The White Rabbit* in 1952, had begun to suffer from blackouts and other health problems caused by his time in captivity, though he was delighted to see his friend again. He had also kept in contact with Dietzsch in Germany and Peulevé asked him to send on his best wishes.

Peulevé's exact movements during the first half of 1960 aren't known, though in July his father Leonard lost his battle with throat cancer, and he returned to the UK to make the funeral arrangements. Picking up his mother and Annette from her house in Tonbridge, it was a particularly sad affair, with only the three of them in attendance at the crematorium. Eva sold their bungalow at Peacehaven to move to a residential home in Tunbridge Wells near Annette, though she had not quite lost her restless nature and continued searching for better accommodation, always being critical of the management and other residents.

Looking for a new job, Peulevé was introduced by a friend to Handy Angle, a company in the same line as Dexion. Taking on the role of overseas manager for Latin America and the Caribbean, he began work in September 1960, travelling through Jamaica, Venezuela, Trinidad, Curaçao, Peru, British Guyana, Ecuador and Guatemala before the end of the year, living out of a suitcase and often spending no more than a few days in each country before moving on. This itinerant life carried on through 1961, though he returned to the UK to see the family briefly during April. Through the summer he toured the islands from Puerto Rico down to Trinidad, and except for two brief trips to Canada he never appeared to stop. However the combined stresses of the job and the effects of his psychological war wounds were to eventually manifest

185

themselves when Peulevé suffered a major heart attack whilst in Jamaica. After several weeks recuperating he returned to work, but took some time off in April 1962 to visit friends in France, including Arthur Larking at Menton. Arriving unannounced he received a warm welcome, though later Arthur confided to Annette that Peulevé's nightmares had recently returned with a vengeance and he was now drinking heavily in order to deal with them.

Peulevé's mother maintained that he rarely spoke about his wartime days and that her knowledge of what had really happened only came from second-hand sources; repeated attempts made by Vera Atkins and his closest friends to persuade him to talk also proved fruitless. For some, at least, the atrocities of the camps went beyond verbal description, and for Peulevé there was simply nothing to be said, no adequate means by which these intensely personal experiences could be approached. A similar reaction was witnessed by Stephen Hastings, a post-war friend of Yeo-Thomas, who had introduced him to another inmate of Buchenwald whilst on a visit to Paris. Expecting some sense of camaraderie to develop between them he was taken aback when, after exchanging some brief words to ascertain a few details, the two men turned to stare at him in silence. Hastings suddenly realized his error: 'I had conceived in my ignorance that their shared experience would develop into comradeship, that they would dive happily into reminiscence, but there was nothing whatsoever for them to say. In that instant I knew the depth of the terrible experiences they shared. They were not as other men and I was far removed from them.'[6]

After a few days with Arthur, Peulevé visited Annette and Eva in Tonbridge before flying to Copenhagen in May, seeing Marie-Louise and the children for what would be the last time. Once back in London he stayed for several days at the Special Forces Club, expecting to leave for Jamaica at the beginning of June. He was dismayed at the airport to find the flight delayed, though when he returned to the club he ran into Yeo-Thomas and his partner Barbara, who had just arrived from Paris. Yeo-Thomas' health had continued to worsen since their last meeting and he had come to London for more tests, but Peulevé suggested that the delay to his travel plans was perhaps fate bringing them together again. He accompanied both of them to the hospital and visited the next day, taking Barbara to lunch afterwards in an effort to lift her spirits.

Eventually managing to make his way to Kingston, Jamaica, Peulevé was straight back into another hectic work schedule three days later. Although the demands of his job were obviously taking their toll on his health, they did not prevent him from travelling continually over the next four months, visiting Miami, Curaçao, Jamaica, El Salvador, Nicaragua, Honduras, the Cayman Islands, Brazil and Peru before finally landing in Jamaica at the end of October. Vague plans had been made with Yeo-Thomas to spend New Year's Eve in Paris, but they came to nothing.

In January 1963, Peulevé switched to become Handy Angle's manager for Western Europe and began by spending some time in Lisbon during January before moving to Milan, staying at the Hotel Gallia which he would use as a base for several weeks. Suffering from a bout of flu, he took the time to write to his mother early the following month, mentioning that his new job was no less strenuous and that he planned 'to be in Portugal by April, but everything might change before then'.[7] Whilst in Italy he made frequent trips to factories in France and had problems with the company's Italian partners, though he was soon on the move, passing through Gibraltar, Malta and Libya before returning to Milan in March.

With more business to attend to in Spain, he drove across the southern coast of France with his young Spanish assistant, Señor Maguregui, eventually arriving in Seville after two days' non-stop travelling. They checked into the opulent Hotel Alfonso XIII on the evening of 18 March and, after a few drinks with some friends, Peulevé said he was feeling unwell and wanted to retire early. Saying goodnight to his colleague, he went upstairs to his room to type a report to send to head office the next day.

The next morning the maid knocked on the door but received no response. As there was no sign outside she entered and found Peulevé's body lying on the floor. The hotel manager called the British Consul-General, Malcolm Walker, and a local doctor, who concluded that Peulevé had probably undressed and suffered a heart attack as he was about to get into bed. A brief, quiet burial service was arranged for the late afternoon of 20 March at the British Cemetery, in the village of San Jerónimo on the outskirts of the city, and was attended by Mr Walker, two of his staff and an American Protestant chaplain from the nearby US Air Force base. Annette remembered how her brother had mentioned that, when his time came, he would like to die in Seville.

Peulevé's death at the age of just forty-seven came as a great shock to many and he was unreservedly saluted by those who had known him. Buckmaster, writing his obituary, remarked that 'His modesty

187

and charm won him innumerable friends throughout the world; he was assured of a warm welcome wherever his many journeys took him, and he will be very greatly missed in many countries, not least by his friends in London.'[8] He also wrote to the family, commenting that: 'So many people loved him, he was a very attractive man and his great fund of common sense and humour endeared him to us all.'[9] Others from F Section also paid tributes: Denis Rake wrote to his mother, remembering Peulevé's courage, generosity and charm being a 'comforting thing in the dark times when we were together'[10] when in Spain during 1943; and Vera Atkins, who had never quite lost touch with Peulevé, remembered him as someone who was 'always at the centre of things',[11] though she also acknowledged that he had never fully recovered from his time in the camps. Barbara described how she managed to keep Peulevé's death from Yeo-Thomas, for fear of the effect it might have on his failing health; however a mutual friend accidentally told him some time later and he 'wept bitterly'[12] at the news. A man equally haunted by his experiences and disillusioned with post-war life, Yeo-Thomas would die less than a year later, in February 1964.

On 30 March a memorial service was arranged in Tunbridge Wells; aside from family members and friends, it was attended by Buckmaster, George Hiller, Cyril Watney, George Whitehead (who had served with RF section), Denis Rake, a group representing the Special Forces Club and a number of Handy Angle's employees.

Today the small cemetery at San Jerónimo has largely been forgotten and rarely attracts visitors; established in the mid-nineteenth century as a burial ground for drowned British sailors, it gradually fell into disuse as the city's main San Fernando cemetery began admitting non-Catholics, and the site is currently under threat from developers wanting to build on the land. Many of the tombs and headstones are now completely hidden underneath tall grasses and overgrown bushes, while others still visible have been vandalized by trespassers. A few have survived, however, and Peulevé's resting place can still be found, tiled in white with a simple black cross and a small plaque above.

Epilogue

For many SOE agents who had returned in 1945, the experience of working for months under the constant threat of capture, deportation and death in occupied territories made a return to everyday civilian life seem empty and without meaning. In some cases this sense of dislocation profoundly affected their ability to integrate back into society; yet those who had endured the camps faced challenges of an altogether different magnitude. Yeo-Thomas, Burney, the Newtons and many of their fellow agents had been left physically and mentally crippled by their ordeals, and were gradually forced to take disability pensions and early retirement over the following years. If anything can be said of Peulevé, it is that he refused to give up in the face of such obstacles and his efforts to overcome them were as valiant as any of his wartime exploits. The determination he showed to try and lead a normal life in spite of his torments is a struggle few of us can imagine, but not even a man of his fortitude could carry such a burden indefinitely.

Eva was anxious to see her son's life recorded for posterity, but discussions with Cyril Watney and George Millar, another of Buckmaster's agents who had already written about his own experiences in France, soon petered out. A further attempt was made in 1967 when a family friend at the Special Forces Club approached popular SOE writer E.H. Cookridge, but a year later he too turned down the offer, being unable to find a publisher to support the project. After briefly moving to stay with Arthur Larking at Menton, Eva returned to England and spent her last years in a nursing home, plagued towards the end by imaginings of Harry's torture and incarceration. Her daughter Annette died in November 2007. Marie-Louise Peulevé did not remarry but remained in Denmark, where she, Madeleine and Jean-Pierre still live today.

Stéphane Hessel, the last survivor of the thirty-seven Buchenwald agents, went on to pursue a diplomatic career, serving as French representative to the UN in New York and Geneva. Now living in Paris, he remains a keen supporter of humanitarian causes and has recently published an anthology of his favourite poetry. George Hiller also rose to become a respected diplomat before his death from a serious illness in 1972. Cyril Watney lives quietly in Essex. Maurice Arnouil turned his engineering talents to manufacturing washing machines in his later years, but he died unhappy and penniless in 1967. The last remaining member of AUTHOR, Jean Melon, continued to aid the Resistance after the circuit's collapse and ended up marrying Madame Hohenauer's daughter, Suzanne; they still own the Moulin du Breuil in Meymac. Following a long career with Shell, Jacques Poirier became an active supporter of France's Resistance associations and was president of Libre Résistance, which remembers those who were part of F Section's 'Buck' networks, when he died in Paris during October 2005, at the age of eighty-three.

Much has changed in Brive-la-Gaillarde since the war, although it's still possible to spot fading hotel signs and old street names from that time. Discreet plaques mark the houses of Resistance leaders and where the first clandestine meetings were held, while a memorial stands opposite the lycée where Poirier and his comrades accepted the German garrison's surrender, though it sits uncomfortably in the middle of a car park. This might suggest that reminders of the occupation have been neglected, yet the town has not forgotten the sacrifices that were made. In 1969 a plaque was unveiled at 171, Route du Tulle (now Avenue du Président Kennedy) to commemorate the twenty-fifth anniversary of the arrest of Peulevé and his comrades in spring 1944. Today, hardly anyone stops to notice the dull black tablet as they walk along this busy highway, but every year the *mairie* still sends flowers to place underneath it on 15 August, the anniversary of Brive's liberation. For a man often too modest to recognize his own achievements, perhaps such an unassuming tribute is one Harry Peulevé would have approved of.

Appendix A

DSO Citation

This officer was parachuted into France on the 30th July 1942 as W/T operator. He was dropped at some distance from the reception committee, and, his parachute failing to open properly, he broke his leg on landing. He managed to get to hospital, and having recovered sufficiently to be able to walk, he escaped into Spain where he spent several months in gaol and returned to England in May 1943.

He volunteered to return to France and was landed by Lysander on the 17th September 1943 as organizer and W/T operator in the Corrèze department. With great zeal and energy he set to work organizing sabotage teams and maquis groups in the Corrèze and the neighbouring department of Dordogne. By his tact and diplomacy he established excellent relations with the local French Resistance leaders, and by the beginning of 1944 had several thousand men under his control. He organized the reception of arms and explosives on a large scale, and through his efforts the Resistance groups in this area became some of the most strongly armed and best organized in France.

Peulevé organized and led a number of sabotage operations against enemy communications, and took part in several guerilla engagements, notably at Montignac early in March 1944, when one of his groups was attacked by 400 Germans and Miliciens. This action, during which Peulevé showed outstanding leadership and gallantry, resulted in 51 of the enemy being killed.

Towards the end of March 1944, Peulevé was arrested by the Gestapo. The direction of his circuit was immediately taken over by his second-in-command. Peulevé had organized it on such an excellent basis that his successor was able to develop a powerful movement which achieved remarkable results on and after D-Day.

Another British officer who worked with Peulevé in the field has commented on the affection and devotion which Peulevé inspired in all his men and the ascendancy which the quality of his personality had won him. 'He never asked anyone to do something which he was not prepared to do himself; and on several occasions I saw him take part in transports at a time when they were very dangerous, in order to keep the morale of his men up. In the same way he continued to work in Brive until the end, although he knew the risks he was running, because he thought it essential for the efficiency of his circuit. At the time of his arrest he knew my name and whereabouts as well as those of several of our friends. Yet he did not give any of us away. As an organizer he had the merit, which was very great at the time, of being the first to work on an F.F.I. basis in the Corrèze, helping all groups in the area as long as they were efficient. This policy, which brought him criticisms from all sides, later enabled his successor to obtain some excellent results in the Corrèze and Dordogne. Lastly I would like to say that Peulevé is one of the finest officers I have met, combining as he did shrewdness, loyalty, courage and complete devotion to his work.'

During his twelve months imprisonment, first in France and later at Buchenwald concentration camp, Peulevé was brutally ill-treated. He made several attempts to escape, and on one occasion broke out of the Fresnes prison. He was shot in the thigh and recaptured. No medical attention was given to him and he had to remove the bullet himself with a spoon. He finally escaped on 11th April 1945 from a working party which was being forced to build defences on the River Elbe. He captured two S.S. men and took them into the American lines.

Appendix B

Croix de Guerre Citation

Officier Britannique volontaire pour une mission en territoire occupé, fut parachuté en France, dans la région de Nîmes, le 30 Juillet 1942. Son parachute ne s'etant pas ouvert complètement fut sèvèrement blessé et ne dut la vie qu'au dévouement de son organisateur et à l'aide de résistants locaux. Après s'être mis un peu au repos, revint en Angleterre en Mai 1943 et fut volontaire pour une nouvelle mission. Il fut déposé en Corrèze le 17 Septembre 1943, et en étroite liaison avec les chefs de la Résistance de ce département se mit immédiatement à l'oeuvre pour organiser son armement.

En dehors de nombreux parachutages, créa des équipes de choc qui harcelèrent sans cesse les communications ennemies. En particulier dirigea personnellement son groupe le 10 Mars 1944 lors de l'engagement de Montignac où, attaqué par 400 Allemands il leur infligea de lourdes pertes dont 51 morts. Arreté quelques jours plus tard par la Gestapo et torturé de la façon la plus odieuse, refusa de parler et fut finalement déporté en Allemagne. Son organisation pu subsister grâce à son courage. Il fut un des meilleurs artisans de la Résistance en Corrèze.

Volunteering for a mission in occupied territory, this British officer was parachuted into France near Nîmes on 30 July 1942. Due to his parachute not opening completely, he was severely injured and survived only through the dutiful care of his organizer and the help of members of the local resistance movements. Recovering as best he could, he returned to England in May 1943 and volunteered for a new mission. He was dropped in the Corrèze on 17 September 1943 and, establishing close contact with leaders of the Resistance movement in this area, he immediately set about how to provide them with arms.

Apart from many organizing many parachute drops, he created assault teams which never ceased disrupting enemy communications. In particular, on 10 March 1944, during the battle of Montignac, he personally led his Resistance group against 400 attacking Germans, causing them heavy losses including 51 dead. Arrested some days later by the Gestapo and cruelly tortured, he refused to speak and was finally deported to Germany. Thanks to his courage, his organization could continue its work. He was one of the key architects of the Resistance movement in the Corrèze. [Translated by Margaret Byskov.]

Appendix C

SOE agents in France

Note: although the following agents often used several different code names, only those mentioned in the text are given here.

	Code name	Circuit/Mission	Fate
Elisée Allard	*Henrique*	LABOURER	Captured; executed at Buchenwald concentration camp, September 1944
France Antelme	*Renaud*	BRICKLAYER	Captured; executed at Gross-Rosen concentration camp, May 1944
Maurice Arnouil	*Pernod*	AUTHOR	Survived
Claude de Baissac	*David*	SCIENTIST	Survived
Alfred Balachowsky	*Serge*	PROSPER	Captured; deported to Buchenwald concentration camp; survived
Denis Barrett	*Stéphane*	MINISTER	Captured; executed at Buchenwald concentration camp, October 1944
Francis Basin	*Olive*	URCHIN	Survived
Ralph Beauclerk	*Casimir*	DIGGER	Survived
Yolande Beekman	*Yvonne*	MUSICIAN	Captured; executed at Dachau concentration camp, September 1944
Robert Benoist	*Lionel*	CLERGYMAN	Captured; executed at Buchenwald concentration camp, September 1944
Louis Bertheau	*Petit Fils; Tilou*	AUTHOR	Captured; died from typhus at Sandbostel camp, April 1945
Gustave Biéler	*Guy*	MUSICIAN	Captured; executed at Flossenburg concentration camp, September 1944
Denise Bloch	*Ambroise*	CLERGYMAN	Captured; executed at Ravensbrück concentration camp, January 1945
Marcus Bloom	*Urbain*	PRUNUS	Captured; executed at Mauthausen concentration camp, September 1944

195

Robert Boiteux	*Firmin*	GARDENER	Survived
Andrée Borrel	*Denise*	PROSPER	Captured; executed at Natzweiler concentration camp, July 1944
Jean Bouguennec	*Max*	BUTLER	Captured; executed at Buchenwald concentration camp, September 1944
Christopher Burney	*Charles*	AUTOGIRO	Captured; deported to Buchenwald concentration camp; survived
Rémy Clément	*Marc*	FARRIER	Survived
Peter Churchill	*Raoul*	SPINDLE	Captured; deported to Sachsenhausen concentration camp; survived
Ben Cowburn	*Germain*	TINKER	Survived
Pierre Culioli	*Adolphe*	PROSPER	Captured; deported to Buchenwald concentration camp; survived
Madeleine Damerment	*Solange*	BRICKLAYER	Captured; executed at Dachau concentration camp, September 1944
Marcel Défence	*Dédé*	SCIENTIST	Captured; executed at Gross-Rosen concentration camp, June 1944
Angehand Defendini	*Jules*	PRIEST	Captured; executed at Buchenwald concentration camp, September 1944
Louis Delsanti	*Frère*	AUTHOR	Captured; drowned aboard *Cap Arcona* in the Bay of Lübeck, May 1945
Henri Déricourt	*Gilbert*	FARRIER	Survived
Henri Derringer	*Toinot*	STEEPLEJACK	Survived
Harry Despaigne	*Ulysse*	DETECTIVE	Survived
Julien Detal	*Roderigue*	DELEGATE	Captured; executed at Buchenwald concentration camp, September 1944
Jacques Dufour	*Anastasie*	SALESMAN	Survived
Henri Frager	*Louba*	DONKEYMAN	Captured; executed at Buchenwald concentration camp, October 1944
Emile-Henri Garry	*Phono*	PHONO	Captured; executed at Buchenwald concentration camp, September 1944
Pierre Geelen	*Serge*	LABOURER	Captured; executed at Buchenwald concentration camp, September 1944
John Goldsmith	*Valentin*	ATTORNEY	Survived
André Grandclément	*Bernard*	SCIENTIST	Captured by the Gestapo; executed near Belin, July 1944
Victor Hayes	*Yves*	SCIENTIST	Captured; executed at Gross-Rosen concentration camp, August 1944
George Hiller	*Maxime*	FOOTMAN	Survived

Desmond Hubble	*Denys*	CITRONELLE	Captured; executed at Buchenwald concentration camp, September 1944
Noor Inayat Khan	*Madeleine*	PHONO	Captured; executed at Dachau concentration camp, September 1944
Peter Lake	*Basil*	DIGGER	Survived
Roger Landes	*Aristide*	SCIENTIST; ACTOR	Survived
Marcel Leccia	*Badouin*	LABOURER	Captured; executed at Buchenwald concentration camp, September 1944
Louis Lee Graham	*Felix*	REPORTER	Captured; deported to Fort Zinna, Torgau; survived
Robert Leroy	*Louis*	SCIENTIST	Survived
Philippe Liewer	*Clement*	SALESMAN	Survived
John Macalister	*Valentin*	ARCHDEACON	Captured; executed at Buchenwald concentration camp, September 1944
Claude Malraux	*Cicero*	SALESMAN	Captured; executed at Gross-Rosen concentration camp, April 1944
Roland Malraux	*Fils*	AUTHOR	Captured; drowned aboard *Cap Arcona* in the Bay of Lübeck, May 1945
Edward Mayer	*Maurice*	FIREMAN	Survived
James Mayer	*Frank*	ROVER	Captured; executed at Buchenwald concentration camp, September 1944
Percy Mayer	*Barthélemy*	FIREMAN	Survived
Jean Melon	–	AUTHOR	Survived
Pierre Mulsant	*Guerin*	MINISTER	Captured; executed at Buchenwald concentration camp, October 1944
Isidore Newman	*Julien*	SALESMAN	Captured; executed at Mauthausen concentration camp, September 1944
Alfred Newton	*Artus*	GREENHEART	Captured; deported to Buchenwald concentration camp; survived
Henry Newton	*Auguste*	GREENHEART	Captured; deported to Buchenwald concentration camp; survived
Gilbert Norman	*Archambaud*	PROSPER	Captured; executed at Mauthausen concentration camp, September 1944
Maurice Pertschuk	*Eugène*	PRUNUS	Captured; executed at Buchenwald concentration camp, March 1945
Henri Peulevé	*Hilaire; Jean; Edmond; Paul*	AUTHOR	Captured; deported to Buchenwald concentration camp; survived

Frank Pickersgill	*Bertrand*	ARCHDEACON	Captured; executed at Buchenwald concentration camp, September 1944
Eliane Plewman	*Gaby*	MONK	Captured; executed at Dachau concentration camp, September 1944
Jacques Poirier	*Nestor*	AUTHOR/ DIGGER	Survived
Adolphe Rabinovitch	*Arnaud*	SPINDLE	Captured; executed at Gross-Rosen concentration camp, March 1944
Denis Rake	*Justin*	FREELANCE	Survived
Charles Rechenmann	*Julien*	ROVER	Captured; executed at Buchenwald concentration camp, September 1944
Jean Renaud-Dandicolle	*Verger*	SCIENTIST	Killed in action, Normandy, July 1944
Lilian Rolfe	*Nadine*	HISTORIAN	Captured; executed at Ravensbrück concentration camp, January 1945
Roméo Sabourin	*Léonard*	PRIEST	Captured; executed at Buchenwald concentration camp, September 1944
Maurice Southgate	*Hector*	STATIONER	Captured; deported to Buchenwald concentration camp; survived
John Starr	*Bob*	ACROBAT	Captured; deported to Mauthausen concentration camp; survived
Arthur Steele	*Laurent*	MONK	Captured; executed at Buchenwald concentration camp, September 1944
Francis Suttill	*Prosper*	PROSPER	Captured; executed at Sachsenhausen concentration camp, March 1945
Violette Szabó	*Louise*	SALESMAN	Captured; executed at Ravensbrück concentration camp, January 1945
Cyril Watney	*Eustache*	FOOTMAN	Survived
George Wilkinson	*Etienne*	HISTORIAN	Captured; executed at Buchenwald concentration camp, October 1944
Forest Yeo-Thomas	*Shelley*	ASYMPTOTE	Captured; deported to Buchenwald concentration camp; survived

Glossary

AA – Anti-Aircraft.

Agent de liaison – An agent acting as a courier within a resistance network.

Arbeitstatistik – Office responsible for delegating work to prisoners.

Armistice Army – The French army of 100,000 men allowed under the terms of the German occupation.

Armée Secrète (AS) – The military wing of the Mouvements Unis de la Résistance.

Auxiliary Territorial Service (ATS) – A non-combatant military support service staffed by women.

BCRA – Bureau Central des Renseignements et d'Action, de Gaulle's Free French intelligence and resistance organization.

BEF – British Expeditionary Force.

Blockältester – Block Elder.

CD – SOE's Executive Director.

CNR – Conseil National de Résistance, a national council of resistance instigated by Jean Moulin in 1943.

Combat – A major resistance movement in the unoccupied zone.

Control Commission for Germany – Responsible for the post-war administration of Germany.

D/F – Direction-finding.

DF Section – SOE department responsible for organizing escape routes out of France.

DGSS – Direction Générale des Services Spéciales, the unified French secret service formed in November 1943.

Effektenkammer – Storehouse for prisoners' belongings.

Electra House – A department of the Foreign Office in charge of propaganda. After breaking away from SOE in 1941 it became known as the Political Warfare Executive (PWE).

EU/P Section – SOE department to coordinate Polish resistance in France.

F Section – SOE department responsible for operations in France.

FANY – First Aid Nursing Yeomanry, a female civilian auxiliary service.

Feldgendarmerie – German military police.

FFI – Forces Françaises Interieurs, a French military organization commanded by General Koenig.

Franc-Tireur – French left-wing resistance group.

Front National – French communist resistance movement.

FTP – Franc-Tireurs et Partisans, the military wing of the Front National.

Gestapo – Geheime Staatspolizei, the SS secret security police.

GHQ – General Headquarters.

GL – Gun Laying.

GMR – Groupes Mobiles de la Réserve, mobile assault brigades attached to the Vichy police.

Guardia Civil – Spanish national paramilitary police force.

Hauptscharführer – Company Sergeant Major.*

Hauptsturmführer – Captain.*

Lagerältester – Camp Elder.

Letter box – Use of an agent or secret location to pass on messages within a resistance network.

Libération-Nord – Resistance movement in the occupied zone.

Libération-Sud – Left-wing resistance group in southern France.

LNA – Légion Nord-Africaine – an auxiliary police force consisting of Moroccans, Tunisians and Algerians, recruited by French gangster and SD collaborator Henri Lafont.

LDV – Land Defence Volunteers – a civil defence force (later renamed the Home Guard).

LOP – Letter One-Time Pad.

Luftwaffe – German Air Force.

Maquis – French resistance guerrilla groups.

Milice – Vichy paramilitary organization.

MI 5 – British internal security service.

MI 6 – British secret service, also known as the Secret Intelligence Service (SIS).

MI 9 – Responsible for aiding escape and evasion across occupied Europe.

MI R – A department of the War Office set up to research guerrilla warfare.

MUR – Mouvements Unis de la Résistance, a united Gaullist resistance movement formed from Combat, Libération-Sud and Franc-Tireur.

NAAFI – Navy, Army and Air Force Institutes, a trading and recreational organization serving the British Armed Forces.

NN – Nacht und Nebel (Night and Fog), a Nazi directive to deport political prisoners secretly to Germany.

NCO – Non-Commissioned Officer.

Oberführer – Approximately equivalent to the rank of Brigadier.*

Obersturmführer – Lieutenant.*

OCM – Organisation Civile et Militaire, a resistance movement mainly composed of civil servants and army officers.

OCTU – Officer Cadet Training Unit.

ORA – Organisation de la Résistance de l'Armée, a resistance movement formed from officers of the French armistice army.

Playfair – A substitution cipher used by SOE and SIS agents.

POW – Prisoner of War.

PWE – See Electra House.

R5 – A designated military region covering Limoges and the Limousin.

RAF – Royal Air Force.

RAOC – Royal Army Ordnance Corps.

Relève – The exchange of French prisoners of war for civilian labour in Germany during 1942–3.

REME – Royal Electrical and Mechanical Engineers.

RF – Section SOE's Free French section.

Section D – A department of SIS responsible for research into sabotage and subversion in occupied Europe.

SFIO – Section Française de l'International Ouvrière, the French socialist party.

Sicherheitsdienst – SD, the SS counter-intelligence service.

SIS – Secret Intelligence Service.

SOE – Special Operations Executive.

SS – Schutzstaffel, the Nazi organization in charge of policing and state security.

STO – Service du Travail Obligatoire, the compulsory labour scheme to provide Germany with French workers from February 1943.

STS – Special Training School.

Stubendienst – Room/barrack orderly.

Sturmbannführer – Major.*

TR – Travaux Ruraux, an undercover French military counter-intelligence service working against the Nazis.

UHF – Ultra High Frequency.

Untersturmführer – Second Lieutenant.*

VHF – Very High Frequency.

Vichy – The French government under occupation, led by Maréchal Pétain.

Volkssturm – Nazi militia.

Waffen-SS – The military arm of the SS.

W/T – Wireless telegraphy.

Wehrmacht – German armed forces.

Zone non-occupé – The southern 'free' zone of France under Vichy rule.

Zone occupé – The northern half of France occupied by the Germans.

*Ranks given are equivalents in the British Army.

Notes and References

Abbreviations
HPM: Henri Peulevé memoirs.
IWM: Imperial War Museum.
TNA: The National Archives, Kew.

Chapter 1: Origins
1. In 1898 Leonard and another engineer, Charles Brown, patented designs for automating the manufacture of cartridge cases, which were successfully adopted during the First World War.

Chapter 2: Frustrations
1. HPM.
2. Montgomery, B.L., *The Memoirs of Field Marshal The Viscount Montgomery of Alamein, K.G.*, Collins, 1958, p. 49.
3. Quoted in Blaxland, Gregory, *Destination Dunkirk*, William Kimber, 1973, p. 42.
4. Erwin Rommel, 'Blitzkrieg: German Breakthrough in the Meuse, 15 May 1940', in *The Faber Book of Reportage*, Faber & Faber, 1987, p. 529.
5. Danchev, A. and Trotman, D. (eds), *War Diaries 1939–1945: Field Marshal Lord Alanbrooke*, Weidenfeld & Nicolson, 2001, p. 67.
6. HPM.
7. Quoted in Blaxland, *Destination Dunkirk*, p. 147.
8. HPM.
9. Ibid.
10. Ibid.
11. Quoted in Hawes, S. and White, R., *Resistance in Europe: 1939–1945*, Allen Lane, 1975, p. 30.

Chapter 3: The Racket
1. Quoted in Mackenzie, W.J.M., *The Secret History of SOE: The Special Operations Executive 1940–1945*, St Ermin's Press, 2000, Appendix A, p. 753.
2. Beevor, J.G., *SOE: Recollections and Reflections 1940–1945*, The Bodley Head, 1981, p. 14.
3. Howarth, Patrick, *Undercover: Men and Women of the Special Operations Executive*, Phoenix Press, 2000, p. 186.

4. Maurice Buckmaster Personal File, HS 9/232/8, TNA.
5. Ibid.
6. Marks, Leo, *Between Silk and Cyanide*, HarperCollins, 2000, p. 75.
7. Bourne-Patterson, R.A., *The British Circuits in France 1940–1944*, p. ii, in HS 8/1002, TNA.
8. Buckmaster, M., *They Fought Alone*, Odhams Press, 1958, p. 127.
9. Vera Atkins interview (1987), IWM Sound Archive.
10. Ibid.
11. Vera Atkins interview (undated), IWM Sound Archive.
12. Roger Landes interview (1985), IWM Sound Archive.
13. Quoted in Masson, Madeleine, *Christine*, Virago, 2005, pp. 155–6.
14. Hawes, S. and White, R., *Resistance in Europe: 1939–1945*, p. 30.
15. Rigden, D., *SOE Syllabus – Lessons in Ungentlemanly Warfare, World War II*, Public Record Office, 2001, p. 361.
16. Ibid., pp. 361–2.
17. Peulevé Personal File, HS 9/1178/6, TNA.
18. Ibid.
19. Ibid.
20. Louis Lee Graham Personal File, HS 9/607/1, TNA.
21. Peulevé Personal File, TNA.
22. Ibid.

Chapter 4: Scientist

1. Claude de Baissac Personal File, HS 9/76, TNA.
2. Ibid.
3. Gildea, R., *Marianne in Chains: In search of the German Occupation 1940–1944*, Macmillan, 2002, p. 28.
4. HPM.
5. Ibid.
6. Ibid.
7. Peulevé later learned that the man responsible for organizing their reception had no prior experience of this kind of work, no transport and was unsure of which field had been selected. Consequently he and his assistants heard the aircraft circling but were unable to signal to it.
8. HPM.
9. Ibid.
10. Ibid.
11. Memo in Claude de Baissac Personal File, HS 9/75, TNA.
12. HPM.
13. Ibid.
14. Peulevé complained in his report that he had been given no contacts in the event of contingencies, though this was later rebuked by Buckmaster.
15. Leslie, Peter, *The Liberation of the Riviera*, J.M. Dent & Sons, London, 1981, p. 92.

Chapter 5: Carte

1. Foot, M.R.D., *SOE in France: An Account of the Work of the British Special Operations Executive in France 1940–44* (rev. ed.), Whitehall History Publishing/ Frank Cass Publishers, 2004, p. 184.

2. 'Carte Organisation' report from D/R to D/CD, 27 Aug 1942, in HS 6/381, TNA.
3. Bodington report, 12 September 1942, in HS 6/382, TNA.
4. Report in Isidore Newman Personal File, HS 9/1096/2, TNA.
5. Ibid.
6. Buckmaster's evaluation in André Girard Personal File, HS 9/273/2, TNA.
7. Churchill, Peter, *Duel of Wits*, Hodder & Stoughton, 1953, p. 113.
8. F Section Diary, October to December 1942, HS 7/245, TNA, p. 206.
9. Churchill, *Duel of Wits*, p. 124.
10. Memo, 6 May 1943, in HS 6/381, TNA.
11. HPM.
12. Peulevé interrogation report, 11 May 1943, Peulevé Personal File, TNA.
13. Langelaan, George, *Knights of the Floating Silk*, Hutchinson, 1959, p. 183.
14. Poirier, J. (trans. John Brownjohn), *The Giraffe Has a Long Neck*, Leo Cooper, 1995, p. 40.
15. interrogation of Rake, 19 May 1943, in Rake Personal File, HS 9/1648, TNA. In a report by LAC Bromwell, an RAF prisoner and friend of Rake's in Jaraba, Le Chêne was singled out as 'a thorough rogue' who disclosed numerous details about his propaganda work, but also noted that Peulevé was 'very discreet, and tried to make the others stop talking'. (HS 6/969, TNA).
16. Quoted in Cross, J.A., *Sir Samuel Hoare: A Political Biography*, Jonathan Cape, 1977, p. 333.
17. Rake, D., *Rake's Progress*, Leslie Frewin, 1968, p. 190.
18. Ibid., p. 196.
19. Buckmaster, *They Fought Alone*, p. 124.

Chapter 6: Violette

1. Rake, D., *Rake's Progress*, p. 52.
2. 'Special Operations Executive Directive for 1943', Chiefs of Staff memorandum of 20 March 1943, in Stafford, David, *Britain and European Resistance*, Macmillan, 1980, p. 255.
3. Peulevé Personal File, TNA.
4. HPM.
5. Ibid.

Chapter 7: Grandclément

1. HPM.
2. Ibid.
3. In a later report, André Grandclément estimated the number of arrests made in Bordeaux to have been fewer, between 100 and 150 (Grandclément Personal File, HS 9/608/8, TNA).
4. HPM.

Chapter 8: Author

1. Bourne-Patterson, *The British Circuits in France 1940–1944*, p. 90.
2. Quoted in Lacouture, J., *André Malraux*, André Deutsch, 1975, p. 298.
3. HPM.

4. Ibid.
5. Ibid.
6. Ibid.
7. Landes would later direct the execution of Grandclément and his wife near Berlin on 28 July 1944. André Noël was also killed by FFI forces a month later.
8. HPM.
9. Ibid.
10. Ibid.

Chapter 9: Vindication

1. SOE's use of *messages personnels* began in 1941. A feature of the BBC French Service, these broadcasts were originally used to transmit messages from family or friends separated by the war, but were soon recognized by F Section as an ideal vehicle for simple clandestine communications, as the programme could be received by any household radio in France. Initially, a circuit would send a request for a supply drop or other assistance; if agreed to, Baker Street would then send back a short coded phrase to listen for on the BBC. The broadcast of this message would signal that the operation was about to go ahead.
2. Diary of George Hiller, courtesy of Judith Hiller.
3. Ibid.
4. Cyril Watney interview, 1988, IWM sound archive.
5. Cate, C., *André Malraux: A Biography*, Hutchinson, 1995, p. 311.
6. Having been informed by their headquarters in Paris that an unidentified transmitter was operating in the area, the local direction-finding team had brought in a reconnaissance aircraft, as the terrain in the area was impossible to cover by road.
7. HPM.
8. Ibid.
9. Despite the action on 10 March being referred to in his later SOE reports, no French sources can be found to substantiate it, though it may have been connected to an attack on a column of GMR and SD forces which passed through the area in early March.
10 HPM.
11. Ibid.
12. Violette Szabó Personal File, HS 9/1435, TNA.
13. Ibid.
14. Claude Malraux Personal File, HS 9/980/7, TNA.

Chapter 10: Retribution

1. Denise Freygefrond, 'La Maison des Anglais', in *Histoire & Histoires de Malemort*, Association des Amis de Malemort, Maugein, 2004, p. 19.
2. Peulevé report, 23 April 1945, in Personal File, TNA.
3. Correspondence with Francis Suttill; see also Foot, *SOE in France*, pp. 282–3.
4. Peulevé report, 23 April 1945, in Personal File, TNA.
5. Georgette Lachaud had in fact been arrested shortly after Peulevé's capture while delivering details concerning parachute drops, but fortunately swallowed the map she was carrying before being searched and was released several hours later.

6. Poirier, *The Giraffe Has a Long Neck*, p. 86.
7. Seaman, M., *Bravest of the Brave*, Michael O'Mara Books, 1997, p. 140.
8. HPM.
9. Ibid.
10. Peulevé had become suspicious of Herbin's increasing interest in Bloc-Gazo and told Lamory to keep him away from the premises, but saw him again at Lamory's house only a few days before the arrests. However, as Schmald raided the house with only a small force it's unlikely that Herbin had reported any signs of Resistance activity.
11. Marshall, B., *The White Rabbit*, Evans Brothers, 1956, p. 155.
12. HPM.
13. Noor Inayat Khan was executed at Dachau concentration camp in September 1944, and posthumously awarded the George Cross in 1949. Léon Faye died in Sonnenburg camp in January 1945.
14. Report by Alfred and Henry Newton, Part II, 26 April 1945, in HS 6/437, TNA.
15. 'living in Avenue Foch ...': Peulevé report, 23 April 1945, in his Personal File, TNA.
16. Peulevé report, 23 April 1945, in his Personal File, TNA. Starr was later deported to Mauthausen concentration camp but survived the war. He was cleared of allegations of treachery on his return to the UK, but still continued to feel embittered by suspicions that his cooperation with Kieffer equalled collaboration.
17. HPM.
18. Note in Peulevé Personal File, TNA.
19. Minney, R.J., *Carve Her Name With Pride*, Pen & Sword, Barnsley, 2006, p. 168.
20. Seaman, *Bravest of the Brave*, p. 162.
21. Adapted from Seaman, M., *Bravest of the Brave*, pp. 164–5. In 1940 French military intelligence had secretly begun counter-espionage activities against the Nazis using regional 'TR' networks, which were based at bogus municipal offices of 'rural works' (*Travaux Ruraux*) in Paris, Lyon, Toulouse, Limoges, Clermont-Ferrand and Marseille. In 1943 Captain Vellaud was also entrusted with the job of creating a supporting network known as TR 'jeune' (junior). The BCRA (Bureau Central des Renseignements et d'Action) was the Free French secret service established by André Dewavrin (known as Colonel 'Passy') under the direction of de Gaulle in London. From 1941 it worked closely with SOE's RF Section, sending French nationals to conduct intelligence and sabotage work. TR and the BCRA were officially merged to form the DGSS (Direction Générale des Services Spéciales) in November 1943, but rivalries between them made integration slow and each continued to work independently well into the following year.
22. Minney, R.J., *Carve Her Name with Pride*, Pen & Sword, Barnsley, 2006, pp. 168–9.
23. Stéphane Hessel interview, June 2006.
24. HPM.
25. Ibid.
26. Ibid.
27. Ibid.

Chapter 11: Buchenwald

1. HPM.
2. Ibid.
3. Seaman, *Bravest of the Brave*, p.170.
4. HPM.
5. Report by Alfred and Henry Newton, Part III, 26 April 1945, in HS 6/437, TNA.
6. Hessel interview, June 2006.
7. Quoted in Strachan, T. (ed.), *In the Clutch of Circumstance: Reminiscences of Members of the Canadian Prisoners of War Association*, Cappis Press, 1985, p. 235.
8. Hessel interview, June 2006.
9. Ibid.
10. Yeo-Thomas Personal File, HS 9/1458, TNA.
11. Ibid.
12. Ibid. These messages were passed on to a colleague of Baumeister's in Dortmund but were never transmitted, and were only handed over to the Americans when they arrived in April 1945.
13. Seaman, *Bravest of the Brave*, p. 182.
14. HPM.
15. Hessel interview, June 2006.
16. Kogon, E., *The Theory and Practice of Hell*, Secker & Warburg, 1950, p. 195.
17. Ibid., p. 194.
18. Ibid., p.195.
19. Although their names was apparently not called, camp records suggest that Heusch and Lavallée were also summoned and executed with Frager's group.
20. Hessel interview, June 2006.
21. Kogon, *The Theory and Practice of Hell*, p. 197.
22. Ibid.
23. Hessel interview, June 2006.

Chapter 12: Escape

1. HPM.
2. Ibid.
3. Lorin, M., *Schönebeck, un Kommando de Buchenwald: du Sabotage des Avions Nazis a l'Épouvante d'une Marche de la* Mort, quatrième édition, Amicale des Anciens Déportés de Schönebeck – Mülhausen – Buchenwald, 2000, p. 16.
4. HPM.
5. Ibid.
6. Ibid.
7. Ibid.
8. Ibid.
9. Yeo-Thomas papers, IWM.
10. Robin Brook interview, 1987, IWM Sound Archive.
11. Buckmaster, *They Fought Alone*, p. 188.
12. Peulevé family papers.
13. Annette Weston memoirs, Peulevé family papers.
14. 'SOE Agents Repatriated from German Concentration Camps: Minutes of a meeting held at 64 Baker Street, on Thursday, 19 April 1945, at 1100 hours', in HS 6/438, TNA. Following Atkins' extensive investigations into F Section's

missing agents, 104 casualties were eventually identified, just under a quarter of the total sent to France.

15. *News Chronicle*, 26 April 1945, p. 1.
16. Letter to Airey Neave, 16 April 1964, Peulevé family papers.
17. Following demands from Szabó's family for news on Violette's whereabouts, Vera Atkins travelled to Germany to trace the fates of Violette, Denise and Lilian, but it was not until receiving Schwarzhuber's testimony in March 1946 that she was able to confirm their deaths.
18. Note in Peulevé Personal File, TNA.
19. 'Report by Major Peulevé', in HS 6/437, TNA.
20. The atrocities at Tulle were overseen by Walter Schmald, the SD officer who had been responsible for Peulevé's arrest. Schmald was later captured by an AS maquis and executed in August 1944.
21. Report in George Hiller Personal File, HS 9/710/6, TNA.
22. Report in PE Mayer Personal File, HS 9/1011/7, TNA.
23. In a recommendation for the King's Medal for Service in 1946, Peulevé praised Arnouil's work in making the AUTHOR network a success: 'He was the father of the circuit, without whom neither myself nor my successor would have been able to contact those who later became its leaders. He was directly responsible for the success of resistance in the Corrèze and, in addition, without hesitation conveyed more than 14 escaped allied airmen to Toulouse in his own car and 4 Russians from Nancy to the Maquis. He permitted wireless transmissions from his house, hid arms in his office, organised reception committees and subsequent transport of parachuted material. A very brave and devoted helper.' (Arnouil Personal File, HS 9/54/8, TNA). Bertheau was posthumously mentioned in despatches in June 1946 for his work as AUTHOR's wireless operator and a plaque was erected to his memory in Meymac in 1990. In 2001 a memorial was also unveiled at the police station in Ussel to honour Louis Delsanti.
24. Peulevé Personal File, TNA.
25. Ibid.

Chapter 13: Peacetime

1. Peulevé's promotion to Major had been approved in March 1944 but had not come into effect due to his capture. He assumed the rank on his return to the UK.
2. Peulevé was also awarded the Military Cross, but there appears to be no official record of it, making it impossible to be sure when he might have received it and for what action. The ribbon is still in his family's possession.
3. Peulevé family papers.
4. Vera Atkins archive, IWM.
5. 'Last Days of Violette', *Sunday Times*, 28 March 1965, p. 24.
6. Hastings, S., *The Drums of Memory*, Leo Cooper, 2001, pp. 165–6.
7. Letter, 7 February 1963, Peulevé family papers.
8. *The Times*, 25 March 1963, p. 12.
9. Peulevé family papers.
10. Ibid.
11. Ibid.
12. Ibid.

Documentary Sources

National Archives, Kew: SOE Personal Files

HS 9/54/8 Maurice Arnouil
HS 9/59/2 Vera Atkins
HS 9/75, 9/76 Claude de Baissac
HS 9/100/2 Francis Basin
HS 9/138/3 Louis Bertheau
HS 9/165/8 Denise Bloch
HS 9/166/7 Marcus Bloom
HS 9/171/1 Nicholas Bodington
HS 9/232/8 Maurice Buckmaster
HS 9/1622/8 Fergus Chalmers-Wright
HS 9/314, 9/315 Peter Churchill
HS 9/352/3 Charles Corbin
HS 9/379/8 Pierre Culioli
HS 9/412/1 Marcel Défence
HS 9/416/3 Louis Delsanti
HS 9/421–5 Henri Déricourt
HS 9/420/8 Henri Derringer
HS 9/427/9 Harry Despaigne
HS 9/536/1 Henri Frager
HS 9/581/2 Lewis Gielgud
HS 9/273/2 André Girard (Carte)
HS 9/608/8 André Grandclément
HS 9/630/10 Jacques Vaillant de Guélis
HS 9/681/3 Victor Hayes
HS 9/710/6 George Hiller
HS 9/607/1 Louis Lee Graham
HS 9/923/4 Philippe Liewer
HS 9/980/7 Claude Malraux
HS 9/1011/7 Percy Mayer
HS 9/1089/4 Jacqueline Nearne
HS 9/1096/2 Isidore Newman
HS 9/1096/8 Alfred Newton
HS 9/1097/1 Henry Newton
HS 9/1172/7 Maurice Pertschuk

HS 9/1178/6 Henri Peulevé
HS 9/1196/9 Jacques Poirier
HS 9/1648 Denis Rake
HS 9/391/7 Jean Renaud-Dandicolle
HS 9/1335/4 Robert Searle
HS 9/1395/3 Maurice Southgate
HS 9/1430/6 Francis Suttill
HS 9/1435 Violette Szabó
HS 9/1458 FFE Yeo-Thomas

Other National Archives Files

ADM 199/720 KMF, MKF and various convoy reports.

138 Squadron Files: AIR 20/8301; AIR 20/8302; AIR 20/8451; AIR 20/8452; AIR 20/8458; AIR 20/8459; AIR 20/8478.

161 Squadron Files: AIR 20/8346; AIR 20/8460; AIR 20/8461; AIR 20/8474; AIR 20/8293; AIR 20/8296; AIR 27/956; AIR 27/1068.

HS 6/381 CARTE mission: André Girard; unofficial group formed in 1940, working for interim military dictatorship to replace Vichy Government.

HS 6/382 CARTE mission: André Girard.

HS 6/436 Security files: ACTOR/WEAVER enquiries.

HS 6/437; 6/438 Security files: repatriated prisoners of war; interrogations; war crimes; missing personnel; concentration camp lists.

HS 6/439 Security files: SPU 24 (Paris) vetting; interrogations of returned agents.

HS 6/574–583 Circuit and mission reports and interrogations.

HS 7/33 Section I: signals; appendices A and B.

HS 7/46 E section 1940–45; radio communications division; false document section; supplies organization.

HS 7/121 Personnel dropped by F section; expenditure in field; list of addresses.

HS 7/125 French resistance; railway sabotage.

HS 7/244 France F section Diary Jul-Sep. 1942 (pp. 1–144).

HS 7/245 France F section Diary Oct-Dec 1942 (pp. 145–315).

HS 8/143 Reports and returns: operational reviews and analyses.

HS 8/370 Industrial sabotage training (STS 17).

HS 8/435 SOE training section 1940–1945.

HS 8/1002 British circuits in France by Major Bourne-Patterson.

HS 6/969 Body lines out of Spain.

HS 16 Playfair and Wireless Operators Codes Nominal Card Index.

Imperial War Museum: Document and Sound Archives

Documents (Private papers)

Vera Atkins
Colonel M.J. Buckmaster
H.G.R. Newton MBE
Major H.L.T. Peulevé
Captain Cyril Watney
Mrs C. Wrench
Wing Commander F.F.E. Yeo-Thomas GC MC

Sound Archive
Interview / Year / IWM Ref.
Vera Atkins 1987 9551
Vera Atkins undated 12302
Robert René Boiteux 1988 9851
Robin Brook 1987 9697
Maurice Buckmaster 1983 8680
Maurice Buckmaster 1986 9452
Fergus Chalmers-Wright 1984 8188
Harry Despaigne 1987 9925
Stéphane Hessel 1989 10731
Roger Landes 1985 8641
Jacques Poirier 1988 23250
Jacques Poirier 1999 10446
Cyril Watney 1988 10123

Additional Archive Sources

Amicale Anciens des Services Spéciaux de la Défense Nationale, Paris
Archives Départementales de Corrèze, Tulle
Archivo Histórico Comarcal del Alto Ampurdán, Figueres
BBC Archives
Buchenwald Archives, Weimar
Musée Edmond-Michelet, Brive-la-Gaillarde
Musée de la Résistance Azuréenne, Nice

Bibliography

Beau, Georges and Gaubusseau, Léopold, *R.5: Les SS en Limousin, Périgord, Quercy*, Presses de la Cité, Paris, 1969.

Beevor, J.G., *SOE: Recollections and Reflections 1940–1945*, The Bodley Head, London, 1981.

Blaxland, Gregory, *Destination Dunkirk*, William Kimber, London, 1973.

Buckmaster, Maurice, *Specially Employed*, Batchworth Press, London, 1952.

——, *They Fought Alone*, Odhams Press, London, 1958.

Burgess, Colin, *Destination: Buchenwald*, Kangaroo Press, Kenthurst, New South Wales, 1995.

Burney, Christopher, *The Dungeon Democracy*, William Heinemann, London, 1945.

——, *Solitary Confinement*, Macmillan, London, 1984.

Burrin, Phillipe (trans. Janet Lloyd), *Living with Defeat: France under the German Occupation 1940–1944*, Arnold, London, 1996.

Cate, Curtis, *André Malraux: A Biography*, Hutchinson, London, 1995.

Churchill, Peter, *Duel of Wits*, Hodder and Stoughton, London, 1953.

——, *Of Their Own Choice*, Hodder and Stoughton, London, 1952.

Cookridge, E.H., *Inside SOE*, Arthur Barker, London, 1966.

Coustellier, René, *Le Groupe Soleil dans la Résistance*, Fanlac, Périgueux, 1998.

Cross, J.A., *Sir Samuel Hoare: A Political Biography*, Jonathan Cape, London, 1977.

Cunningham, Cyril, *Beaulieu: The Finishing School for Secret Agents*, Leo Cooper, London, 1998.

Danchev, Alex and Trotman, Daniel (eds), *War Diaries 1939–1945: Field Marshal Lord Alanbrooke*, Weidenfeld & Nicolson, 2001.

David, François, *Résister, Passion d'Espérance: De l'occupation nazie à la libération de Brive et de la Corrèze 11 novembre 1942 – 15 aout 1944*, Éditions les 3 épis, Brive, 2005.

Duclos, Jacques (ed.), *Maquis de Corrèze*, Éditions Sociales, Paris, 1975.

Dunn, Kate, *Do Not Adjust Your Set: The Early Days of Live Television*, John Murray Publishers, London, 2003.

Ehrlich, Blake, *The French Resistance 1940–1945*, Chapman and Hall, London, 1966.

Eperon, Arthur, *Dordogne & Corrèze*, Pan, London, 1991.

Faucon, Martial, *Francs-Tireurs et Partisans Français en Dordogne*, revised edition, La Lauze, Périgueux, 2006.

Foot, M.R.D., *Resistance*, Eyre Methuen, London, 1976.

——, *Six Faces of Courage*, Leo Cooper, London, 2003.

——, *SOE in France: An Account of the Work of the British Special Operations Executive in France 1940–44*, revised edition, WHP/Frank Cass, London, 2004.

—— *SOE: The Special Operations Executive 1940–6*, Pimlico, London, 1999.

Foot, M.R.D. and Langley, J.M., *MI9: Escape and Evasion 1939–45*, Book Club Associates, London 1979.

Forty, George, *The British Army Handbook 1939–45*, Sutton Publishing, Stroud, 1998.

Fraser, David, *And We Shall Shock Them: The British Army in the Second World War*, Hodder and Stoughton, London, 1983.

Garnett, David, *The Secret History of PWE*, St Ermin's Press, London, 2002.

Geffert, Hans-Joachim, *Baudenkmale im Kreis Schönebeck*, Herausgeber Kreismuseum Schönebeck, 1988.

Gildea, Robert, *Marianne in Chains: In Search of the German Occupation 1940–1944*, Macmillan, London, 2002.

Goldsmith, John, *Accidental Agent*, Leo Cooper, London, 1971.

Grandclément, Daniel, *L'Énigme Grandclément*, Éditions Balland, Paris, 2003.

Hackett, David A. (ed.), *The Buchenwald Report*, Westview Press, Boulder, Colorado, 1995.

Hastings, Max, *Armageddon: The Battle for Germany 1944–45*, Macmillan, 2004.

——, *Das Reich: Resistance and the March of the Second SS Panzer Division Through France, June 1944*, Michael Joseph, London, 1981.

Hastings, Stephen, *The Drums of Memory*, Leo Cooper, London, 2001.

Hawes, Stephen and White, Ralph, *Resistance in Europe: 1939–1945*, Allen Lane, London, 1975.

Helm, Sarah, *A Life in Secrets: The Story of Vera Atkins and the Lost Agents of SOE*, Little, Brown, London, 2005.

Hessel, Stéphane, *Danse Avec le Siècle*, Seuil, Paris, 1997.

Hoare, Samuel, *Ambassador on a Special Mission*, Collins, London, 1946.

Howarth, Patrick, *Undercover: Men and Women of the Special Operations Executive*, Phoenix Press, London, 2000.

Hutchison, Sir James, *That Drug Danger*, Standard Press, Montrose, 1977.

Jackson, Julian, *France: The Dark Years 1940–1944*, OUP, Oxford, 2003.

——, *The Fall of France: The Nazi Invasion of 1940*, OUP, Oxford, 2003.

Jones, Liane, *A Quiet Courage*, Bantam Press, London, 1990.

Kartheuser, Bruno, *Les Pendaisons de Tulle: 9 Juin 1944*, Edition Krautgarten Orte, Neundorf, 2004.

Kedward, H.R., *In Search of the Maquis*, Clarendon Press, Oxford, 1994.

——, *La Vie en Bleu: France and the French since 1900*, Allen Lane, London, 2005.

——, *Occupied France: Collaboration and Resistance 1940–44*, Blackwell, Oxford, 1985.

King, Stella, *Jacqueline: Pioneer Heroine of the Resistance*, Arms and Armour, London, 1989.

Knight, Frida, *The French Resistance, 1940–1944*, Lawrence and Wishart, London, 1975.

Kogon, Eugen, *The Theory and Practice of Hell*, Secker & Warburg, London, 1950.

Kramer, Rita, *Flames in the Field*, Michael Joseph, London, 1995.

Lacouture, Jean, *André Malraux*, André Deutsch, London, 1975.

Langelaan, George, *Knights of the Floating Silk*, Hutchinson, 1959.

Le Moigne, Louis and Barbanceys, Marcel, *Sédentaires, Réfractaires et Maquisards: L'Armée Secrète en Haute-Corrèze 1942–1944*, Association des Amicales des Maquis A.S. de Haute-Corrèze, 1979.

Leslie, Peter, *The Liberation of the Riviera: The Resistance to the Nazis in the South of France & the Story of its Heroic Leader, Ange-Marie Miniconi*, J.M. Dent & Sons, London, 1981.

Lorain, Pierre (trans. Michael Kahn), *Secret Warfare: The Arms and Techniques of the Resistance*, Orbis Publishing, London, 1983.

Lorin, Marcel, *Schönebeck, un Kommando de Buchenwald: du Sabotage des Avions Nazis a l'Épouvante d'une Marche de la Mort*, quatrième édition, Amicale des Anciens Deportes de Schönebeck – Mulhausen – Buchenwald, 2000.

Lormier, Dominique, *L'Affaire Grandclément*, Éditions Sud-Ouest, Bordeaux, 1991.

——, *Le Livre d'Or de la Résistance dans la Sud-Ouest*, Éditions Sud-Ouest, Bordeaux, 1991.

Mackenzie, W.J.M., *The Secret History of SOE: The Special Operations Executive 1940–1945*, St Ermin's Press, London, 2000.

Marks, Leo, *Between Silk and Cyanide*, HarperCollins, London, 2000.

Marshall, Bruce, *The White Rabbit*, Evans Brothers, London, 1956.

Masson, Madeleine, *Christine*, Virago, London, 2005.

Michel, Henri, *Histoire de la Résistance*, Presses Universitaires de France, Paris, 1958.

—— (trans. Richard Barry), *Shadow War*, André Deutsch, London, 1972.

Millar, George, *The Bruneval Raid*, Cassell, London, 2002.

Minney, R.J., *Carve Her Name With Pride*, Pen & Sword, Barnsley, 2006.

Montgomery, B.L., *The Memoirs of Field Marshal The Viscount Montgomery of Alamein, K.G.*, Collins, 1958.

Nicolson, David D., *Aristide: Warlord of the Resistance*, Leo Cooper, London, 1994.

Ottaway, Susan, *Violette Szabo: The Life That I Have*, Pen and Sword, Barnsley, 2002.

Ousby, Ian, *Occupation: The Ordeal of France 1940–44*, John Murray Publishers, London, 1997.

Overton Fuller, Jean, *Déricourt: The Chequered Spy*, Michael Russell Publishing, Salisbury, 1989.

——, *The German Penetration of SOE: France, 1941–1944*, William Kimber, London, 1975.

——, *The Starr Affair*, George Mann, Maidstone, 1973.

Paillole, Paul (trans. Robert L. Miller), *Fighting the Nazis: French Intelligence and Counterintelligence 1935–1945*, Enigma Books, New York, 2003.

Parker, Theodore W. and Thompson, William J., *Conquer: The Story of Ninth Army, 1944–1945*, Infantry Journal Press, Washington D.C., 1947.

Penaud, Guy, *André Malraux et la Résistance*, Pierre Fanlac, Périgueux, 1986.

——, *Chroniques Secrètes de la Résistance*, Éditions Sud-Ouest, Bordeaux, 1993.

——, *Histoire de la Résistance en Périgord*, Pierre Fanlac, Périgueux, 1985.

Picard, Raymond and Chaussade, Jean, *Ombres et Espérances en Quercy: Armée Secrète Vény dans leurs secteurs du Lot 1940–1945*, Privat, Toulouse, 1980.

Poirier, Jacques (trans. John Brownjohn), *The Giraffe Has A Long Neck*, Leo Cooper, London, 1995.

Rake, Denis, *Rake's Progress*, Leslie Frewin, London, 1968.

Rigden, Denis (introduction), *SOE Syllabus – Lessons in Ungentlemanly Warfare, World War II*, Public Record Office, Richmond, 2001.

Salomon, Ernst von (trans. James Kirkup), *The Captive: The Story of an Unknown Political Prisoner*, Weidenfeld & Nicolson, London, 1961.

Schoenbrun, David, *Maquis, Soldiers of the Night: The Story of the French Resistance*, Robert Hale, London, 1990.

Seaman, Mark, *Bravest of the Brave*, Michael O'Mara Books, London, 1997.

Stafford, David, *Britain and European Resistance: A Survey of the Special Operations Executive, with Documents*, Macmillan, London, 1980.

——, *Secret Agent: The True Story of the Special Operations Executive*, BBC Books, London, 2000.

Strachan, Tony (ed.), *In the Clutch of Circumstance: Reminiscences of Members of the Canadian Prisoners of War Association*, Cappis Press, Victoria, British Columbia, 1985.

Thomas, Jack, *No Banners*, W.H. Allen, London, 1955.

Todd, Olivier (trans. Joseph West), *Malraux: A Life*, Alfred A. Knopf, New York, 2005.

Trouillé, Pierre, *Journal d'un préfet pendant l'occupation Corrèze 1944*, Éditions J'ai Lu, Paris, 1968.

Verity, Hugh, *We Landed by Moonlight*, Airdata Publications, Wilmslow, 1995.

Vickers, Philip, Das Reich: *2nd SS Panzer Division* Das Reich – Drive to Normandy, *June 1944*, Leo Cooper, London, 2000.

West, Nigel, *Secret War: The Story of SOE, Britain's Wartime Sabotage Organisation*, Hodder and Stoughton, London, 1992.

Wilkinson, Peter and Astley, Joan Bright, *Gubbins and SOE*, Leo Cooper, London, 1993.

Wilmot, Chester, *The Struggle for Europe*, Collins, London, 1952.

Index